THE ECONOMY OF
UNITED GERMANY

ALSO BY W. R. SMYSER

GERMAN-AMERICAN RELATIONS

REFUGEES: Extended Exile

RESTIVE PARTNERS

THE ECONOMY OF UNITED GERMANY

COLOSSUS AT THE CROSSROADS

W. R. Smyser

St. Martin's Press
New York

330.943
S667e

All rights reserved. For information, write:
Scholarly and Reference Division,
St. Martin's Press, Inc., 175 Fifth Avenue,
New York, N.Y. 10010

First published in the United States of America in 1992

Printed in the United States of America

ISBN 0-312-04788-6

Library of Congress Cataloging-in-Publication Data

Smyser, W. R., 1931-
 The economy of a United Germany : colossus at the crossroads / W.R.
Smyser.
  p.   cm.
 Includes index.
 ISBN 0-312-04788-6
 1. Germany—Economic conditions—1990- 2. Germany—Economic
policy—1990- 3. Germany—Foreign economic relations. I. Title.
HC286.8.S69 1992
330.943'0879—dc20   91-35709
                                                                 CIP

ACF-8340

92-10062

CONTENTS

PREFACE

When the East Berliners came pouring through the Wall on November 9, 1989, when Germany was united in 1990, and when the Soviet Union was reshaped in 1991, the established order of the world shifted.

That world order shifted in economic terms just as surely as it shifted in political terms, and just as surely Germany emerged as the big long-term winner.

With Germany united, the German economy is whole and free again. It is free to be the production center of Europe. It is free to face East as well as West as it had for centuries, to be a bridge and no longer a barrier across the continent.

Simultaneously, the century-long primacy of geopolitics, which Germany helped initiate, may well have shifted lastingly toward a primacy of geoeconomics, or at least to a balance of the two.

Economic influence has again become a decisive factor shaping attitudes and events. Military force, especially nuclear military force, remains the *ultima ratio* of global affairs, but people again regard prosperity rather than security as their most immediate need.

With that change, the relations between states are based more on what Germany has, not on what it lacks. German economic power can increase German influence in all directions, perhaps especially toward Eastern Europe and toward whatever may ultimately replace the Soviet Union.

These are not theoretical speculations, but realities. The German economy and German economic doctrine shape the daily lives of Americans and others in ways we and they do not always perceive, and they shape it more than ever now that Germany is united.

Germany has frequently been among the world's largest exporters. Global interest rates are often determined and always influenced by Frankfurt decisions. The German D-Mark is the currency of choice throughout much of Eurasia and may well become even more important. Global trade agreements are subject to Germany's veto.

From the German standpoint, however, and in immediate terms, unity is not only a blessing but also a burden. It adds to the weight of the decisions that Germany must make. And those decisions all compound themselves into very fundamental choices about the way in which the German, the European, and the global economy are to be organized.

The Germans now need to decide how best to merge two separate and different economies, both of which are German. They need to help integrate Western Europe without jeopardizing the open global trading system, and they need to decide how best to help the nations that lie to the German East, however those nations may ultimately organize themselves. They must determine how best to bring their own economy into the next industrial revolution even as they do all this. Most important, they need to decide how the economic world as a whole is to function.

The answers to these questions cannot be quickly given. German economic performance, successful as it is, contains countless contradictions. It is dynamic but conservative. It is free but coordinated. It is modern but traditional. Germany's three best-known economic policymakers all retired because of failures in the economy. Germans never see opportunities without seeing hazards as well.

As if to confirm the depth of the dilemmas brought on by German unity and by the many problems that Germany now faces, the president of the Bundesbank resigned one year after German unification and the new one has only a two-year term to accomplish whatever he may regard as important.

German unity makes a book on the German economy more timely than ever, but also complicates the task of writing it. The economic and political costs of unity are immense. They will need to be paid over many years. Most of East Germany's economy will have to be overhauled and much will have to be scrapped. The policies pursued there for 40 years must end, but they have left an imprint that will be costly in many ways. And one must avoid steps that might mortgage the future of united Germany.

The full German economy will emerge in an expanded and altered form, and the way in which it is expanded and altered is one of the questions that must be posed.

Germany faces the problems of success, not those of failure, but that does not make them easier to solve. In some ways, it may even make it more difficult.

The subtitle of this book, "Colossus at the Crossroads," reflects this dilemma. The Germans now carry real weight. But they cannot follow the same policies as before, either at home, in Europe, or in the world. The rapid changes over that whole world do not make it easier to select the right policies, especially for a nation that has stressed stability and incrementalism above all.

All the questions are linked, and the answer to any single one of them may determine answers to the others. And they must all be evaluated against the background of a global economy that may well have reached the end of its long boom.

I chose to write this book because the German economy remains relatively unknown and little understood even as it is becoming a stronger force in the world. Discussion quickly falls into well-honed simplifications. English and American bookstores contain countless books about the economies of Japan, the Asian Tigers, or the European Community, but they have little on German economics.

There may be a reason for this. Global economic influence, unlike military power, accumulates quietly. It often grows more out of a country's domestic than out of its international economic policy. It may accumulate by indirection more than by direction, not because a nation wishes to be influential but merely because it wishes to be prosperous.

Germany's immense economic influence has indeed accumulated quietly. But now it is here. It is not quiet any longer. One must look at it to see which way it will turn.

My approach is that of a political economist. A nation's economy expresses in concrete form the ceaseless interactions between that nation's politics and resources, human and material. It reflects a nation's attitudes, habits, expectations, and fears. Macroeconomics, microeconomics, statistics, and models help to analyze an economy. Ultimately, however, that economy can only be understood as part of a totality, which must in turn include history, politics, and even philosophy.

John Maynard Keynes wrote that we are all the slaves of defunct economists. We are also, however, the slaves of different perceptions and of different needs. Even if the world economy increasingly becomes a single entity, national attitudes and policies will remain distinct. Our experiences do not mingle even as our markets may. Each nation will act differently in the same situation.

Germans, even more than others, will act on the basis of their particular point of view, based as much on non-economic as on economic considerations. The object of this book is to examine that point of view.

The Germans have chosen to call united Germany by the official name of the former West Germany, the Federal Republic of Germany. To avoid confusion, I will mainly use the term "West Germany" for the Federal Republic before unification. When I use the formal title, the context should clarify the area under consideration. After unification, the former West Germany is often described as "Western Germany" and the former East Germany as "Eastern Germany." I have followed that practice for convenience and consistency.

Although the German economy is united, West Germany will be the dominant economy and its practices will prevail. I have, therefore, based the chapters about Germany's economic practices and doctrines, as well as on its global role, mainly on West Germany, but I have included information on appropriate elements of the former East German economy. I have also written one chapter specifically about the prospects and the complications of unification, although the process and the effects of unification permeate every chapter as they permeate the German economy itself.

I apologize in advance for some duplication that may exist between several chapters because of my attempt to keep each internally coherent. I have held it to a minimum but could not avoid it completely.

I am indebted to Fritz Stern for the report in Chapter 11 on Raymond Aron's comments in postwar Berlin.

The manuscript was produced while I was working independently. It reflects my own views, not those of any organizations with which I may have been or may be associated before, during, or after its completion.

One

Basic Statistics of the United German Economy

Forty-five years after the collapse of the Nazi *Reich* in ruin, rubble, and disgrace, West Germany had both the world's largest number of billionaires per capita and one of the world's most generous social insurance programs. The German recovery in the West could be said to be complete. West Germany ranked among the top global exporters, and its inflation rate was among the lowest in the world.

The West German achievement was impressive indeed. West German industry had gained worldwide admiration for the quality of its products. German machine tools, automobiles, and producer electronics set the standards for their industries. West German workers were models of seriousness and competence. The German central bank, the Bundesbank, was widely regarded as a potential model for a European central bank. The *Deutsche Mark*, or the D-mark, was second in rank only to the U.S. dollar as a reserve currency and as a global instrument of exchange.

Whereas some peoples have remained poor even as their countries have become rich, most West Germans were well off indeed. They had one of the highest living standards in the world, with widespread if often understated evidence of well-being despite the pockets of poverty in the migrant and illegal alien quarters of the large cities. West Germans were financially secure, living in solid and attractive homes often free of debt, driving cars that were built to last, having large bank accounts and significant savings. Many owned property abroad. They could expect comfortable pensions when they retired, and they could expect those pensions to have real value because inflation would not be permitted to erode them.

The West German formula for success was unique. It was a distinctive mix of drive and caution, of competition and self-restraint, of a market economy functioning within a framework established by theory, custom, and widely accepted if unwritten rules. West Germany had its own system, a particular blend of initiative, coordination, and regulation.

Now Germany is united. Building on the base provided by West Germany, and after East Germany's return to its traditional well-being, united Germany should become a new economic great power. It can lay an even more legitimate claim than West Germany did to being the world's third-largest economic center. It will have the third-largest measurable gross national product. It may, after the complications of unification are overcome, return to being the world's largest exporter. It can, if it chooses, dominate whatever economic and monetary organizations may emerge across Europe. Even if it chooses restraint, it will speak with a more influential and more respected voice, and probably with a more confident one.

Germans have long tried to find the route to respect, to influence, and even to power in the world at large. Some Germans tried to find that route by diplomacy. They succeeded, but only in part. Some tried force. They failed. Now, those likely to succeed are those that tried it by economics. United Germany is now their vehicle, as West Germany was before.

THE ELEMENTS OF THE GERMAN ECONOMY AND POPULATION

The German economy is essentially a processing economy, with a high foreign trade component.[1]

West Germany's Gross National Product (GNP) in 1989, before the effects of unification came to be felt, was DM 2,260 billion. The following were the main sector components of GNP, as shown by 1984 and 1989 statistics:

Sector	Per cent of GNP	
	1984	1989
Agriculture, Forestry, Fishing:	2.0	1.6
Industry:	40.5	39.7
Commerce and Transport:	15.3	14.2
Other Services:	26.2	27.7
State, Private Households, etc.:	13.3	12.7

Employment distribution statistics show in more detail where West German production was concentrated:

West German Distribution of Employment by Sector, 1989

Sector	Per cent of employment, 1989
Agriculture, Forestry, Fishing:	1.0
Energy and Water:	2.1
Manufacturing:	38.6
of which:	
Chemicals, Refining:	2.9
Iron and Steel:	2.9
Engineering and Vehicle Building:	12.0
Electrical Engineering, Optics:	8.2
Wood, Paper, Printing:	3.6
Textiles and Clothing:	2.5
Food:	3.2
Construction:	6.3
Trade:	13.7
Transport & Communications:	4.8
Banking & Insurance:	4.1

One cannot now attempt to compare the West and East German economies, for the statistics are almost irreconcilable. After economic unification in 1990, figures about East German production became meaningless. They had always been questionable, in part because of widespread statistical juggling and in part because it was difficult to determine what production could or could not be justified economically. Efforts to relate them meaningfully to Western statistics met with little success. East German GNP was usually estimated at 12 to 14 per cent of West Germany's, but the economically justifiable portion of that GNP was much lower. Because of the statistical confusion, the West German economic authorities rarely attempted to publish all-German statistics in late 1990 and early 1991, and it would be useless to attempt to compare any East German statistics with the broad figures given above on West Germany.

Despite those statistical problems, figures on labor distribution suggest that the sector composition of the East German economy before its collapse was very much like that of West Germany:[2]

Distribution of Persons Employed

Economic Sector	West Germany	East Germany
Industry/Crafts	33.6 %	40.5 %
Construction	6.6 %	6.6 %
Agriculture/Forestry	4.9 %	10.8 %
Trade and Transport	18.6 %	16.2 %
"State" (Western)	16.0 %	
"Nonproductive" (Eastern)		21.4 %

A study conducted by a West German economic institute confirmed that the basic nature of the East and West German economies matched closely even after 45 years of separation. What is less certain, of course, is how much of East German industrial production will survive unification. Most probably, there will be a decline in the proportion of industrial production and an increase in services. Some production and labor has already moved to West Germany and will remain there. But the changes brought about by unification, whatever they may be, should not be large enough to make the basic united German economy very different from that of the former West and East German economies.[3]

The exception to the relatively close match between the East and West German economies was in agriculture, in which East Germany had twice the percentage of persons employed as West Germany. Even allowing for the inefficiency of East German agricultural production and for the cutbacks that will probably be mandated by European Community regulations, it appears probable that the agricultural sector will occupy a relatively stronger position in a united Germany than it has occupied in the Federal Republic. Two Eastern German states have historically been important agricultural producers. This may become politically as well as economically significant.

Both West and East Germany had strong export sectors. Exports in the years immediately before unification accounted for about 30 per cent of West German GNP, the highest ratio of any major state. West Germany was the world's largest single exporter in 1988 and was a strong second to the United States in 1989. In 1990, united Germany——West and East Germany together——was the largest exporter. To help finance its trade surplus, West Germany had been a consistent exporter of capital.

West Germany's trade and current account surplus was the following in the years before unification:[4]

Year	Export Surplus	Current Account Surplus
	(Million DM)	
1985	73,353	48,327
1986	112,619	85,793
1987	117,735	82,097
1988	128,045	88,336
1989	134,694	104,057
1990	110,000 (e)	72,000 (e)

The export surplus for 1990 declined, despite high German exports, because Germany was also importing at a higher pace to meet the needs generated by unification. The surplus will decline further during the early 1990s, for the same reason, and may even become a deficit. It should, however, again rise once unification is complete. It is worth noting that during 1990, despite an economic collapse in East Germany, the former East German states contributed DM 12 million to the trade surplus mainly through earlier agreed exports to Eastern Europe.

The major and growing share of West German trade was with the European Community, which in 1989 took 55 per cent of West German exports and provided 51 per cent of its imports. Non-EC countries in Europe accounted for about 25 per cent of West German trade, and the United States for about 7 to 8 per cent. Japan in the late 1980s took about 2.5 per cent of West German exports and provided about 6.5 per cent of its imports.

Several industries, mainly machine tools, engineering, ship building, chemicals, and metals dominated the West German export sector, and East German exports followed a generally similar pattern. But East German exports, in almost a mirror image, went in the opposite direction to West Germany's, with over 50 per cent going to the Soviet Union, another 25 per cent to Eastern Europe, and the remainder to the West or elsewhere.

The West German economy grew steadily from the 1950s to the present, but at a declining pace and with some exceptions. It did not grow as fast as Japan's or as those of some other Asian nations but more consistently than those of the United States or of most other European states. Although the rate of growth generally declined during those 30 years, it began to rise strongly again in 1989. There were only three years, 1967, 1975, and 1982, during which the West German GNP declined. The East German economy also grew consistently, at least by its own statistics, and also at a generally declining pace, with increasing indications during the 1980s that earlier resource misallocations were creating massive inefficiencies and jeopardizing growth.

Unification produced a dramatic rise in West German growth during 1990 and early 1991, but no direct comparisons could be made because unification had altered the dimensions of the market and of the factors of production. The East German economy virtually collapsed after unification (see Chapter 7 for details).

Neither East nor West Germany had steady population growth, and united Germany cannot be expected to have it. Thus, most West German economic growth, especially during the 1980s, resulted from productivity gains as the population remained relatively constant. From 1960 to 1990, the following elements of the West German economy changed as follows:[5]

Element	Change, 1960-1990 (per cent)	
GNP:	plus	150
Labor force:	plus	8
Time worked:	minus	18
Productivity:	plus	180

The above results were achieved by a West German population estimated at the end of 1989 to number 62 million, of whom more than 4 million, or almost 7 per cent, were foreigners.

West Germany's population had risen rapidly from 1945 to 1972 because of immigration, refugees, and a postwar baby boom. But the last West German census, in 1987, showed that the German portion of the population had actually declined by 1.3 million from 1970 to 1987, and that it was only the arrival of 1.7 million foreigners that had given West Germany a slight population increase during those 17 years.[6]

The German population distribution represents a genuine problem for German economic planners. In Western Germany, the percentage of persons under 20 declines every year, and that of persons over 65 increases. The bulk of the Western German population is between 30 and 50, helping to generate a production boom as they reach their years of peak efficiency. But that bulk is expected to reach pensionable age by the year 2010, and three decades later the population pyramid is expected to be almost perfectly inverted and the population of Western Germany is expected to have declined to 45 million——although the decline may be slowed by immigration from Eastern Germany and elsewhere. Fewer than half the population will then be of what is now defined as working age (20 to 60).

The population situation in East Germany has been somewhat less troubling, but the percentage of children in the total population has also been declining. East German population projections show a population decline into the next century, but not as dramatic as West Germany's. Unification may provoke a baby boom, at least for a few years.

The West German work force numbered about 28 million in 1990. Fewer than 2 million were registered as unemployed during 1990, with about 100,000 listed as part-time workers. Western Germany in 1990 hosted 1.6 million foreign workers, of which the largest numbers (in declining order) were Turks, Yugoslavs, Italians, Greeks, Austrians, Spaniards, and Portuguese.[7]

The former German Democratic Republic (GDR) had a population of 16.7 million in 1988, a decline of about 1.6 million after the building of the Wall in 1961, and a total work force in 1988 of 8.9 million.[8] Like West Germany, the GDR had foreign workers, about 190,000, with about 60,000 being Vietnamese and about 50,000 Poles. Smaller groups were from Mozambique, the Soviet Union, Hungary, and Cuba.[9] Most of the foreign workers, especially from the third world, left Germany after unification in 1990, but many East European workers remained and more will probably come over time.

Because of the aging population, among other things, there has been a consistent rise in social expenditures in both West and East Germany. In West Germany, the total rose from DM 205.1 billion in 1971 to a record DM 703 billion in 1990, almost a third of the West German GNP. The rate of growth slowed during the 1980s but there was never a decline. In the GDR, the total official social budget also rose consistently and at a somewhat higher rate, from 26.3 billion East marks to 110.7 billion in 1988. The combination of the two figures, with claims for Eastern Germans now being converted to D-Marks under formerly West German regulations, means that united Germany can expect to have social expenditures at about one third of GNP for some time, especially to compensate the large percentage of unemployed and early retirees in Eastern Germany. The percentage may grow even further over the long run as the population ages further, with some informal estimates indicating that by the middle of the twenty-first century one German worker will need to earn enough to pay the pensions of two retirees.

GEOGRAPHIC DISTRIBUTION

Almost every area of Western Germany has some industry, but the main industrial areas are:

- The Ruhr district in North Rhine-Westphalia, the traditional center of German coal, steel, and heavy industry.
- The concentrations of industry around several large cities, such as Hanover, Munich, Frankfurt, or Stuttgart.
- The chemical production areas that stretch mainly along the Rhine River in Baden-Württemberg and further north.
- The automobile manufacturing centers, increasingly concentrated in southern Germany in Bavaria and Baden-Württemberg.

In Eastern Germany, the main manufacturing areas are in Saxony, Saxony-Anhalt, and Thuringia, principally concentrated in the Leipzig, Dresden, Halle, and Chemnitz regions. Before World War II, Saxony was the technology center of Central Europe. The Elbe River, like the Rhine, attracts chemical and other industry along its shores.

The division of labor is much more clearly delimited along geographic lines in Eastern than in Western Germany. In Eastern Germany, the districts north of Berlin had industrial employment below 25 per cent, those around Berlin had industrial employment between 25 and 35 per cent, and those south of Berlin had over 35 per cent employment in industry.[10] No such geographical delineation for sector employment existed in Western Germany.

The future of Berlin remains a question mark. The city and its surroundings once constituted one of the most important industrial centers of Germany and Europe, as well as a transportation and communications hub. Even now, the city remains a major manufacturing center although it has been in relative decline because of its isolation. Manufacturing is reviving there, but the city will probably never recover its relative standing as an industrial site except perhaps in light industry. It is more likely to become a center for services and for East-West trade and communications, especially as it increasingly shares and takes over the functions of Germany's capital.

Principal wine production is along the Rhine and Moselle rivers in the Rhineland-Palatinate, but other important wine districts are in Hesse and Baden-Württemberg. Beer comes mainly (but not exclusively) from Bavaria.

GERMAN INDUSTRIAL TRADITION

One reason to believe that the Eastern and Western portions of the united Germany will again knit together into one large manufacturing economy is that such an economy has been part of the German tradition for centuries. Germany has even specialized in certain industries for most of the twentieth century.

A survey of the 200 largest industrial enterprises of Germany, Great Britain, and the United States between 1913 and 1973 showed Germany almost always with the largest number of corporations in four particular industries: chemicals, primary metals, general machinery, and electrical machinery.

The survey also showed consistently high German participation in other producer industries, but relatively low participation in nondurable consumer goods.[11]

Certain other aspects of German performance in the nineteenth century reveal a similar consistency:[12]

- German industry was strong in skilled technicians and managers, and often found its senior managers among engineers.
- German workers were well trained and highly motivated.
- German strengths were in production quality, enterprise organization, and export sales.
- Over one half of German exports were in industrial and electrical machinery, transportation equipment, metals, and chemicals.

The apparently unshakable consistency of German economic performance in these areas as in certain management and labor traditions remains especially striking as German industry had to recover from a number of devastating blows during the twentieth century. So does the fact that the overwhelming majority of major German companies were founded before World War I. After each of the wars that it lost, as after the Great Depression, Germany recovered strongly to regain its traditional place in the international division of labor.

The other element of the German tradition that has remained constant is its international character. Germany was the world's largest exporter in 1913, as it was to be again recently. Germany, Eastern and Western, represents the most trade-oriented of all major economies. The one third of West German GNP that went into exports far exceeded the 13-14 per cent exported by Japan and the 9-10 per cent exported by the United States. Germany, united or divided, depends on external markets. Germans can become prosperous, but they can never become complacent.

NOTES TO CHAPTER ONE

1. The statistics given in the following section are drawn from The Economist Intelligence Unit, *West Germany: Country Profile, 1990-91* (London: *The Economist*, 1990), pp. 14-33. I have ended the West German domestic statistical record with 1989 for the most part because that year represents a more accurate basis for comparison with the former East German economy and also because the West German economy in 1990 was no longer a separate economy. Chapter 2 contains more recent statistics as appropriate.

2. Sachverständigenrat zur Begutachtung der gesamtwirtschaftlichen Entwicklung (hereinafter cited as Sachverständigenrat), *Auf dem Wege zur wirtschaftlichen Einheit Deutschlands* (Stuttgart: Metzler-Pöschel, 1991), p. 241 (hereinafter cited as *1990/91 Report*); German Democratic Republic, *Statistical Pocketbook of the German Democratic Republic, 1989* (Berlin (East): Staatsverlag der Deutschen Demokratischen Republik, 1989), p. 35 (hereinafter cited as GDR, *Statistical Pocketbook, 1989*). The figures used here are not directly comparable with each other or with some other West German statistics, but the broad comparison remains valid. The figures do not reach 100 per cent on either side because of minor categories. The "state" and "nonproductive" categories cover broadly similar types of activity.

3. Ifo-Institut für Wirtschaftsforschung, "Zusammenfassung der Strukturberichterstattung 1990," cited in FRG, *Aktuelle Beiträge*, October 9, 1990, p. 32.

4. Statistics from 1985 to 1989 are based on Sachverständigenrat, *1990/91 Report*, p. 404; 1990 trade surplus figure is preliminary and is based on Presse- und Informationsamt der Bundesregierung, *Aktuelle Beiträge zur Wirtschafts- und Finanzpolitik*, Nr. 6, 1991, Feb. 11, 1991, p. 5 (hereinafter cited as FRG, *Aktuelle Beiträge*); 1990 current account surplus is based on Bundesministerium für Wirtschaft, *Jahreswirtschaftsbericht 1990* (Bonn: Bundesministerium für Wirtschaft, 1991), p. 20.

5. Ifo-Institut, *Spiegel der Wirtschaft, 1990/91* (Munich: Ifo-Institut, 1990), passim. The Ifo-Institut's figures for 1990 are estimates made in May of that year, and they proved to be somewhat below the final figures, which reflected German monetary union on July 1, 1990, and which were affected by German unification.

6. Population statistics given here are based on Bundesminister für Arbeit und Sozialordnung, *Sozialbericht 1990* (Bonn: Bundesminister für Arbeit und Sozialordnung, 1990), pp. 128-131; Deutsche Bank, "Demographic Factors and Economic Momentum," *Deutsche Bank Bulletin*, October, 1988, pp. 1-10; Deutsches Institut für Wirtschaftsforschung, "Zur langfristigen Entwicklung der Bevölkerung in der Bundesrepublik Deutschland," *Wochenbericht 32/88*, August 11, 1988, pp. 397-408; GDR, *Statistical Pocketbook, 1989*, pp. 13-14, 145-150.

7. For West German population and work force statistics, see *Spiegel der Wirtschaft*, pp. B1-B9.

8. GDR, *Statistical Pocketbook, 1989*, pp. 18, 35.

9. Presse- und Informationsdienst der Bundesregierung, *Sozialpolitische Umschau*, October 22, 1990 (hereinafter cited as FRG, *Sozialpolitische Umschau*).

10. GDR, *Statistical Pocketbook, 1989*, p. 24.

11. Alfred D. Chandler, Jr., *Scale and Scope* (Cambridge, Mass.: Harvard University Press, 1990), pp. 21-23.

12. *Ibid.*, pp. 398-400, 408, 410, 435, and 497.

Two

Growth, *Die Wende,* and the 1990s

History is sometimes written as a list of key dates, of pivotal turning points from which future directions emerged so clearly that the events that took place on those dates could be said to have created new situations and often substantially determined what was to follow.

Such a technique can help in any review of German political history since World War II, for certain key dates do set the main lines of German development. The first date was May 5, 1945, the *Stunde Null*, the Zero Hour, when the Third Reich fell and every German had to start his or her life anew. Another key date was June 23, 1949, the founding of the Federal Republic of Germany. Another was June 17, 1953, when Soviet tanks suppressed the popular uprising in East Germany. Others were the dates of physical division and reunion: August 13, 1961, when the Wall began going up; November 9, 1989, when the Wall began coming down; and October 3, 1990, when East and West Germany were united.

To those dates, however, another must be added, a date of German economic history but that also had immense political and societal significance: June 20, 1948. That date marked the day on which the Western Allies and the postwar German administrative authorities carried out price, currency, and regulatory reform, retiring the worthless *Reichsmark* and substituting the *Deutsche Mark*, the D-Mark, which was to become the currency of the Western occupation zones.

It is perhaps appropriate that postwar West Germany should have had a currency before it had a government. For the currency helped to frame the history and the achievements of the country. It even gave it a sense of identity within and outside its borders. It provided the foundation for the country's growth, stability, and prosperity, as well as for a considerable measure of its international standing.

For those who know Prussian and German history largely as a record of wars won and lost, of peoples shunted and borders shifted back and forth, of serried marchers, mass demonstrations, and hysterical oratory, it is perhaps worth reflecting that the most stable and successful state in German history was figuratively built not by the sword but by the plowshare, not in the din of battle but in the rustle of paper and the clink of coin. And that, when unity finally came, it came not only because the East Germans wanted freedom but also because they wanted to share in the prosperity founded on that date in 1948.

THE BEGINNINGS

The first several years after World War II, the years after the *Stunde Null*, were years of bitter penury for the Germans. Their land, their homes, and their property lay in ruins. Millions were forced to flee with nothing but the clothes on their backs. Tens of millions had not enough to eat or to wear. Inflation raged under the surface of the economy and of the society. Nobody wanted German currency and nobody would work or sell to obtain it. Anything of value was hoarded until it could be successfully traded, not sold. Products were not offered for the worthless *Reichsmark* but for the goods of the occupation and the occupiers. Parker pens, nylon stockings, and Camel cigarettes represented the currency of the realm, the accepted if not the legal tender of the time.

Regulations that had been left over from the Nazi era as well as the new occupation rules placed sharp limits on production. Output was to be carefully planned and monitored, and resources were to be centrally allocated. Occupation projections showed that the average German would be able to purchase a plate every five years, a pair of shoes every 12 years, and a suit every 50 years.[1]

With currency reform, that was to change. Every German, man, woman, or child, received 40 D-Marks with which to start a new life, as well as a modest conversion rate on their savings. The new currency had the support and backing of the occupation authorities as well as a carefully managed volume in circulation. Goods came out of hiding, people went to work for wages, and the foundations of the modern German state were laid. The currency reform, whose purpose it was to provide a respected store of value and widely accepted legal tender, succeeded brilliantly.

The currency reform was not carried out in isolation. It was accompanied by another measure that was at least equally important, the abolition of most of the rules, regulations, and rations that had been left over from the Nazi past or established by the occupation. That action was taken in conjunction with currency reform by Ludwig Erhard, whom the Americans had first installed as the economic administrator for their occupation zone and who was later accorded similar authority over the British-American "Bizonia." He acted on the basis of new rules planned and promulgated by the German authorities under his direction without fully advising the Allies. By July 1948, to the dismay of the Allies and their economic experts, Erhard had ended virtually all price regulations as well as countless other decrees.

The Allies accepted Erhard's action, without enthusiasm and with grave doubts about its prospects. But Erhard did find support from U.S. occupation commander General Lucius D. Clay, and could not have succeeded without it. Clay was impressed by Erhard's determination to establish a free economy.[2]

The abolition of controls was the important German contribution to their new economy, and specifically Erhard's. Although a number of regulations remained in place, some of them for years, Erhard's action changed basic attitudes. The question Erhard posed was not why a regulation should be abolished, but why it should be kept. That approach was to become one of the cornerstones of the *Soziale Marktwirtschaft*, the social market economy that brought forth the German economic revival.[3]

Prosperity and stability did not, however, come quickly or easily. During the first six months after currency reform, the cost of living rose by almost 15 per cent. Only tax reduction and continuous deregulation prevented prices from rising faster. Wages did not immediately rise to match prices, despite several strikes including one massive general strike, and by late 1949 and 1950 prices were falling.[4] A more serious problem for several years was unemployment. In early 1950, almost 2 million persons in West Germany were out of work as the unemployment rate hit 12 per cent.

The economic reforms and the new West German system received powerful support from investment funds under the Marshall Plan, from the stimulus to German industry provided by the diversion of other Western resources for Korean War production, and from the German readiness to work hard for low wages until productivity had risen. But the essential components of success were the revival of confidence brought on by Erhard's reforms and by the new currency.

Challenges to Erhard did arise, not only because of the problems involved in launching the new economic system but also because his laissez-faire philosophy did not reflect the thinking of all Germans. The Social Democratic Party (SPD) and the trade unions firmly opposed Erhard's policy. They favored a greater state role. Even members of the two parties that supported

Erhard, the combination of the Christian Democratic Union (CDU) and the Christian Social Union (CSU), questioned whether a free economy could bring prosperity out of the chaos of the postwar years. Konrad Adenauer, the CDU leader and West Germany's Chancellor after 1949, often had his own differences with Erhard, but supported his minister because there were at first no practicable alternatives to Erhard's policies. The disagreements among Germans regarding economic philosophy ran so deep that the German Basic Law in 1949 did not include any specific provisions regarding the type of economic system that Germany was to have.

Erhard and Adenauer were relentlessly attacked even after Adenauer's victory in the 1949 election. It was only by the end of 1950 and early 1951, over two years after the currency reform, that the social market economy was regarded as having proven itself and that it became the foundation for the "economic miracle." The fact that there were no national elections between 1949 and 1953 helped to give time for the reforms to work, and Adenauer— -with Erhard prominent and confident at his side—was returned in triumph in 1953 and 1957.

THE ECONOMIC MIRACLE AND BEYOND

The German boom that began in 1950 was truly memorable. The growth rate of industrial production was 25 per cent in 1950 and 18.1 per cent in 1951. Growth continued at a high rate for most of the decade of the 1950s, despite several slowdowns. By 1960, industrial production had risen to two and a half times the level of 1950 and far beyond any that the Nazis had reached during the 1930s in all of Germany. Gross National Product (GNP) rose by two thirds during the same decade. The number of persons employed rose from 13.8 million in 1950 to 19.8 million in 1960, and the unemployment rate fell from 10.3 per cent to 1.2 per cent.

By 1958, the D-Mark had become fully convertible, although Germany kept its exchange rate as low as possible to help promote West German exports. West German currency reserves had risen from DM 1.1 billion to DM 5.5 billion during the decade, and by 1961 they were twice as large as the United Kingdom's. In the spring of that year, over the objections of Adenauer and of a good part of German heavy industry, Erhard conducted the first postwar revaluation of the D-Mark, from DM 4.20 to DM 4 to the dollar, in order to reduce the risk of inflation. Fritz Berg, the president of the German Bundesverband der Deutschen Industrie (BDI), warned that the revaluation would destroy German industry, but the effect was barely noticeable.

Labor also came to benefit in due course from the boom. Although wage demands and pay increases had been modest at first, wages and salaries rose over 80 per cent between 1949 and 1955, catching up with growth.[5] West German social programs were given a considerable boost in 1957, just before the election, when the government decided to initiate a number of new programs and to expand others. The funds used for these programs were from reserves that had been accumulated between 1952 and 1956 in expectation of German rearmament. The funds had been kept in an account popularly known as the *Julius-Turm*, after the Berlin tower where the German government had kept gold that France had paid in reparations after the Franco-Prussian War. The committee that allocated the funds was known as the *Kuchen-Ausschuss*, or "Cake Committee."[6] After the DM 7 billion had been dispensed, the government had to maintain the same level of expenditures even without the *Julius-Turm* reserves, and social security payments as well as premiums began a steady rise.

In 1957, West Germany gained a new central bank, the Deutsche Bundesbank, which succeeded the Bank Deutscher Länder and was given much more authority over monetary policy. That year also saw the establishment of the Bundeskartellamt, the Federal Cartel Office designed to prevent the return of German monopolies and oligopolies. Six years later, in 1963, the Bundestag at Erhard's urging established the Sachverständigenrat zur Begutachtung der gesamtwirtschaftlichen Entwicklung, the Council of Economic Experts, to provide objective evaluations on which to base German economic policy.

The West German economy did not grow as fast or as consistently during the 1960s, in part because such a torrid pace could not be sustained, in part because the supply of fresh labor from East Germany was cut off by the Berlin Wall, and in part because the Bundesbank became disturbed about potential overheating and moved several times to slow the pace of growth. International conditions also deteriorated. In 1966, the West German GNP growth rate fell to 2.0 per cent and the cost of living rose by 3.5 per cent. Such statistics might have pleased others, but did not satisfy a West German electorate which had become accustomed to faster growth at lower inflation.

Ludwig Erhard, who had succeeded Adenauer as Chancellor, was voted out of office in December 1966 largely—although not entirely—because of the economic problems of the Federal Republic. He was to be replaced by a grand coalition of the CDU/CSU and the SPD under Chancellor Georg Kiesinger.

Under the pressure of the slowdown, the new West German grand coalition government abandoned Erhard's broad laissez-faire orientation.

The new Minister for Economics, Karl Schiller, argued strongly for new legislation that would give the federal government and his ministry greater authority to guide economic policy. The Bundestag in 1967 passed the Law for Promoting Stability and Growth, labeled the "Magna Carta" of medium-term economic management.

The 1967 law, which remains in effect although it is not as energetically applied as in Schiller's time, provided for coordination of national, state, and local budget plans in order to give fiscal policy a stronger impact. The West German government received the authority to limit divergences between the policies of the separate states and to adjust taxes and tax accounting procedures in order to influence private investment and consumer spending. The law also set a number of optimistic targets for the four basic standards by which West German economic success was henceforth to be measured: currency stability; economic growth; employment levels; and the trade balance. Those standards became popularly known as the *magisches Viereck*, the "magic rectangle" or the "magic polygon."

Karl Schiller, the man who shaped the new combination of law and structure, claimed the mantle of successor to Erhard as the architect of West German economic policy. But he followed a dramatically different concept. He was one of the rare German Keynesians. He brought to his new tasks the unshakable conviction that government had both the capacity and the obligation to shape economic trends and to smoothe out and even eliminate the business cycle. His tactics succeeded in fighting the 1966-1967 recession and he was widely praised when the West German economy again resumed its growth during the late 1960s.[7]

Schiller's chosen formula was *Globalsteuerung*, or "global guidance," a process by which government would not intervene in the details of the economy but would establish broad guidelines that would foster uninterrupted non-inflationary growth. Schiller particularly concentrated on fiscal policy, like any Keynesian, but he wanted to influence other aspects of economic activity as well. He persistently emphasized that he did not wish to abandon fundamental principles of the *Soziale Marktwirtschaft*, such as the importance of entrepreneurship and of monetary stability. He wanted, as he put it, to create a "synthesis of the Keynesian message and the Freiburg imperative" (see Chapter 6). Such a synthesis was to provide overall economic direction without interfering with the dynamic power of private initiative.

The 1967 law created two instruments that Schiller used to considerable advantage, at least initially:

- The *Konzertierte Aktion* (concerted action). This process, which Schiller regarded as the single most important element of his policy, was to bring labor and management as well as other elements of the economy together under the chairmanship of the Minister of Economics. They were to be guided by his advice on such matters as wage demands on the one hand and pricing or investment practices on the other.[8]
- An annual government statement that would develop an overall concept for the economy in response to the reports of the Sachverständigenrat, thus reinforcing the objective and rational policy foundation that the experts offered.[9] The government would arrive at "orientation data" for the economy, intended to exert the force of logic on the members of the *Konzertierte Aktion* by making them aware of the need for balance between competing interests and by providing the statistical foundations for rational decisions.[10]

Schiller's elaborate construct reflected his belief that it was possible to establish economic policy through logic and to persuade others to accept the results of that logic, combining Keynesian doctrine and instrumentalities with a cooperative and dynamic private structure. His initial success made him and the SPD popular with the electorate. The SPD emerged from the 1969 election strong enough to leave the grand coalition and to govern largely by itself with only the support of the Free Democratic Party (FDP). Willy Brandt became Chancellor.

The SPD's victory gave the party the opportunity to expand the West German social security system, substantially increasing the size of the social budget and its relative cost. Social program costs grew by over 10 per cent a year during much of the 1970s, introducing into the budget an unalterable obligation that reduced fiscal flexibility despite its anticipated anticyclical effect. This came back to haunt Schiller and the government.

By 1971, when the downturn had been fully overcome and the rise in the West German growth rate threatened to turn the economic revival into an inflationary boom, Schiller found little enthusiasm in the government or in the SPD for the types of restrictive measures that he or any Keynesian would have advocated, including fiscal restraint, as well as higher interest rates, and currency revaluation. Deficit financing and social programs proved impossible to reverse or to curtail. Privileges had become entitlements, programs had become fixtures, and innovators had become bureaucrats.

Even the *Konzertierte Aktion* did not function as Schiller had hoped. Although the process itself was not to break down formally until the pullout of the trade unions in 1977, well after Schiller had left office, he already found by 1970 and 1971 that it was becoming unwieldy and unresponsive to his guidance. Neither labor nor business remained ready to let the Economics Minister dictate their policies, especially toward restraint.

The West German government learned to its disappointment that the budgets of the states and municipalities, which should have acted in coordination with national policy, did not function in the anticyclical manner either. States and municipalities wanted to spend more when times were good and to cut back when times were bad, reinforcing rather than moderating the economic cycle.

Schiller also found it impossible to manage German economic policy autonomously at a time when the entire global economy was roiling in the final stages of the Bretton Woods system and the U.S. dollar was under constant challenge. The widening international expectation that the D-Mark would have to be revalued created waves of speculative fever. Foreigners bought German currency in ever-growing amounts, making it even more difficult to restrain domestic monetary supply and to curtail inflationary pressures. Schiller favored revaluation, as Erhard had, but German business remained resolutely opposed.

When changes in fiscal, monetary, and exchange rate policy were finally made, they were too small and they came too late. The budget deficit was out of control. The inflation rate rose above 5 per cent. Schiller himself had to resign in 1972, ostensibly because he rejected the government's increasing disposition to interfere directly in the economy but mainly because of growing doubt about his policies. At the end of his tenure he found himself virtually isolated within the party and the government, leaving it to the Bundesbank to throw the brakes alone and to his successors to implement some of the very measures that he had advocated.

The economy did little better without Schiller. The global environment remained unstable and unpredictable. Domestic policy remained controversial and uncertain. Different authorities worked at cross-purposes. The Bretton Woods fixed exchange rate system collapsed, to be succeeded by interim arrangements and finally by currency "floating." Shortly thereafter came the first "oil shock" that unleashed both inflationary and recessionary forces across the globe.

Trying to offset external disruptions or at least to neutralize them, the Bundesbank began framing monetary policy in terms of monetary targets—-annual ranges established for the growth of central bank money. This policy was reportedly advocated by Helmut Schlesinger, the Bundesbank monetary expert who was to become president of the Bundesbank in August 1991. It theoretically permitted the D-Mark exchange rate to move more freely than before with fewer domestic effects. The bank wanted its policies less subject to the whims of those who were increasingly using the D-Mark to speculate against the dollar.[11] But nothing could insulate West Germany entirely. Although it actually weathered the global economic storm better than most other countries, Germany still felt its effects. Willy Brandt had to resign because one of his closest assistants was discovered to be an East German spy, but also because there was a widespread feeling that he had not overcome economic problems.

Helmut Schmidt, Brandt's successor, had earlier opposed some of Schiller's policies and had succeeded him as Economics and Finance Minister. He was intensely interested in economics. Despite his other responsibilities and problems as Chancellor, he assumed day-by-day command of the government's economic policy. He also took a number of initiatives to enhance international coordination, measures which he believed essential in the new system of flexible exchange rates (Chapter 8).

During 1974 and 1975, the Federal Republic suffered a severe recession brought about in part by the steps that had been taken to counter the inflation of 1972 and 1973 and also by a general global downturn. West Germany's GNP in 1975 fell by 1.4 per cent (in constant prices), the first time since the founding of the Federal Republic that it had fallen so sharply. The West German trade balance also fell as global demand declined and as the terms of trade deteriorated because of the surge in petroleum prices.

By 1976, the worst was over. German growth resumed and the inflation rate began to decline. Although neither reached the favorable levels that had come to be taken for granted during the 1950s and early 1960s, they were accepted as tolerable after the turbulence of the previous years. Schmidt began to be known as a *Macher* ("achiever") and the government won reelection in 1976, albeit narrowly. The coordination that had developed between the government and the private sector, and Germany's relatively strong economy when compared to others, also led Schmidt and his party to claim that they had built *Modell Deutschland*, the "German model."

Schmidt and the Bundesbank knew, however, that Germany's escape had been a narrow one. They tried to keep a tight rein on the economy and on monetary growth to prevent a revival of inflation and to protect the D-Mark. They were prepared to sacrifice growth, if necessary. Unemployment rose to over one million in 1975. Government budget controls broke down in the face of rising social welfare expenditures, especially unemployment compensation. The cumulative fiscal deficit rose by 50 per cent (from DM 160 to DM 240 billion) in the six years between 1974 and 1980.[12] The

Konzertierte Aktion broke apart, as many in the SPD and the trade unions wanted a more expansionist policy.

Schmidt's restraint began to draw critical attention not only within Germany but outside. U.S. President Jimmy Carter, who thought that West Germany was not growing at a rate commensurate with its potential, wanted West Germany to act as the "locomotive" of international recovery by stimulating its own economy further and by reversing—or at least reducing—the current account surplus that had again risen by the mid-1970s.

A number of Schmidt's economists thought in the spring of 1978 that West Germany should restimulate its economy, but Schmidt delayed any action because he wanted to be able to tell Carter at the July Bonn summit that he was acting in response to Carter's wishes. By mid-1978 the West German economy was already in recovery. Schmidt nonetheless still decided upon more expansionary fiscal measures to follow his meeting with Carter. The West German economy continued expanding through 1979 and much of 1980, helping Schmidt win reelection.[13]

Subsurface trends were, however, working against West German prosperity even during the recovery. Unemployment remained high as German employers were reluctant to hire due to high non-wage labor costs. The upturn proved to be uneven and unrewarding, as the problems of the mid-1970s rapidly returned. Some German economists criticized Schmidt, saying that he should either have acted in the spring of 1978 or not at all.

The second oil shock hit the Federal Republic just as broad price levels were already rising. It jeopardized Germany's external position as well as internal economic stability. The speculative waves that had surged toward the D-Mark during the latter years of the 1970s reversed quickly. The Bundesbank had to raise interest rates to protect the D-Mark. The economy suffered from signals that were as contradictory as those of the 1970s: the lingering effect of the expansion policy; the secondary waves generated by the petroleum price increase; a rapid deterioration in the current account; and a series of sudden and very sharp measures to restrict credit. These culminated in early 1981, as foreign exchange fluctuations approached crisis levels and as the D-Mark fell sharply against other European currencies. It was the worst possible situation: growth fell, unemployment rose, but inflation did not abate:[14]

Year	GNP Growth Rate	Unemployment Rate	Price Index Rise
1979	4.0	3.7	4.0
1980	1.5	3.7	4.8
1981	0.0	5.3	4.0
1982	-1.0	7.6	4.4

Deep pessimism about the legendary economy and its faded economic miracle prevailed. When West Germany in 1980 actually suffered what many regarded as the ultimate indignity—-a massive trade deficit of around DM 25 billion—-many analysts concluded that the economy had reached a kind of maturity and could never again be expected either to grow or to export as before. Not a single element of the "magic polygon" was moving in the right direction. Chancellor Schmidt's reputation as a *Macher* was tarnished.

As the depressing statistics poured in, more and more German political and economic leaders began to say that the economy's problems could not be blamed only on outside events or on imperfections in demand management but they reflected more fundamental problems. Echoing some of the discussion that was taking place in the United States, they began proposing policies that would emphasize the supply side of the demand-supply equation.

The German economic institutes and the Sachverständigenrat in particular began to advocate supply-side policies and to speak ever more forcefully about what they had for some time condemned as the structural problems of the German economy, especially the apparently unstoppable expansion of the state sector. They blamed the federal government in particular, charging that its budget deficits, its high taxes, and its heavy hand had caused the economic problems.[15] They complained that government programs had helped raise annual costs per worker from DM 14,639 in 1970 to DM 33,576 in 1980, and that legislatively mandated non-wage costs had risen from 51 to 75 per cent of wages during the same decade.[16]

The most damaging blow to Schmidt and his government came from his own coalition partner, the FDP, and specifically from the Economics Minister, Count Otto Lambsdorff. In conjunction with two of his state secretaries in the Economics Ministry, Otto Schlecht and Hans Tietmeyer (who is to become Bundesbank president in 1993), he wrote a paper reinforcing the assertions that the government's policies were themselves to blame for Germany's problems. He charged that the government had departed from the principles of the social market economy. He recommended an urgent return to market principles and to a more modest government role. In effect, he called for a reversal of the entire thrust of government policy since the rise of Karl Schiller in 1967.

When Lambsdorff's paper was—perhaps deliberately—leaked, it created a sensation, not only because of the sharp criticism of the government by a minister within the cabinet but also because it demonstrated that the junior coalition member of Schmidt's government was ready to change partners.[17] It was the death blow for Schmidt. It was also the death blow for the German experiment with Keynesianism.

By the fall of 1982, Schmidt was as isolated as Schiller had been. The FDP left his coalition and formed one with Helmut Kohl, the leader of the CDU/CSU, to direct what was termed *Die Wende*, the "turning" or the "reversal."[18] The government proceeded to implement new policies and within a year won a popular vote in support of the new course.

DIE WENDE DURING THE 1980s

The new coalition announced that its policies would be primarily designed to curtail the role of the state, along somewhat similar lines to those being pursued in the United States by the administration of President Ronald Reagan. But the policies could be carried out more effectively in West Germany because the German system has less division of authority and responsibility between the executive and the legislative branches of government. Also, in Germany the same parties controlled the government and the Bundestag.[19]

Within its broad policy, the new government had four main objectives:

- To reduce taxes, so as to increase investment incentives and to raise government income over time.
- To reduce the federal German deficit by cutting expenditures as well as taxes.
- To reduce government restrictions and regulations, curtailing state intervention in markets.
- To improve the flexibility and performance of the labor market.

The government did reduce taxes and the state role in the economy. Taxes were cut in three steps, in 1986, 1988, and 1990. Those cuts reduced the nominal tax burden slightly and brought the highest marginal tax rates down from 56 to 53 per cent. Despite the tax relief, or because of it, tax income rose throughout the decade. Because of tighter budget controls, the deficit fell. It declined unevenly, but enough to permit the government to proclaim a Fiscal Year 1989 public sector surplus if the social security surplus of DM 24 billion was included in the calculations.

A number of elements combined with tax relief to reduce the size of the government sector during the 1980s.[20] The government carried through a series of privatization measures, selling almost DM 10 billion in shares of such diverse institutions as Veba, VIAG, Volkswagen, Lufthansa, Salzgitter, and others. It sharply reduced the number of government regulations and strengthened the *Kartellgesetz* to give itself greater powers to act against business practices or mergers that might restrict competition. It did not, however, succeed in cutting West German subsidies to industry, agriculture, and so on, as those expenditures rose both as an actual amount and as a share of GNP. It was, therefore, an imperfect achievement.[21]

Because the actual dimensions of the state sector remained difficult to calculate precisely, statistics differed but all agreed on the trend. Some estimated the decline in the state role between 1982 and 1990 to have been from 50 to 45 per cent of GNP and others estimated the decline to have been from 47.5 to 44.6 per cent. Bundesbank statistics showed a reduction in public sector expenditures as a per cent of GNP from 52 to 46 per cent between 1982 and 1989.[22] Whatever statistics one chose, one could clearly see that the *Wende* had achieved one of its principal objectives.

The CDU/CSU showed a difference in style as well as a difference in policy from its predecessors. Chancellor Kohl, whose slow and portly bearing concealed one of Germany's most alert political minds, did not want to be destroyed by economic problems as Schmidt and others had been. Therefore, although he was definitely in charge of the *Wende*, he did not usually present himself as either the originator or the executor of economic and financial policy. He chose to control events from behind the scenes. Other principal figures, like Economics Minister Lambsdorff or Finance Minister Gerhard Stoltenberg, also made relatively few public statements. But the Chancellor's and the government's lower profile also had a purpose, as he and others were trying to demonstrate that the government was not and should not be the principal actor in the economic process.

The West German economy began to resume growing at a gradual rate, in part because of the policies of the *Wende*, in part because of a widespread global recovery centered in the United States, and in part because of competitive advantages in European Community markets. The share of foreign trade and foreign transactions in the West German economy grew strongly, enabling the economy to benefit from foreign as well as domestic demand even when the Bundesbank began to restrain domestic demand during the latter years of the 1980s.

The sources of German growth alternated during the 1980s. During 1983 the main engine of growth was a sharp increase in domestic investment and private consumption as a sign of confidence in the new government and in an upturn. Foreign demand provided the main source between 1984 and 1985, as the high U.S. dollar made German goods more competitive internationally. By 1986 and 1987, domestic demand again fueled growth. After that, however, foreign demand played an ever more important role in boosting production, in part because of a European investment boom anticipating the EC Single Market.

The distinction between foreign and domestic demand as a source of growth became increasingly blurred as the decade advanced. By 1990, it became almost impossible to calculate as intra-European trade expanded and moved increasingly from finished goods to components and subcomponents. Many imports became parts for goods that would in turn be sold abroad. As intra-European investment grew, many German sales "abroad" were to German firms that had established plants in European Community states. But West German statistics on *Aussenbeitrag*, the export contribution to German GNP, continued to be kept, and they showed a powerful role for exports in German growth during the second half of the decade.

German export growth, and especially the West German balances of trade and of current account, were also helped by extraneous factors, such as the lift given to West German terms of trade by the persistent decline in global commodity prices during much of the 1980s. Even during years when German import volume rose faster than export volume (as from 1986 to 1988), the current account balance improved.[23]

West German monetary policy eased during the mid-1980s as the inflation rate, which had reached 7.3 per cent by October 1981, gradually declined. German monetary growth stayed generally on course from 1980 to 1986, remaining around the 5.5 or 5 per cent rate set by the Bundesbank. In 1986 and 1987, however, despite the Bundesbank's anti-inflationary commitment, the money supply rose at a rate of 8.8 per cent, which was far in excess of the intended 4.5 per cent rate. The excess was caused largely by German efforts to forestall revaluation of the D-Mark against the franc and the lira within the European Exchange Rate Mechanism, and money growth returned closer to planning levels after those currencies appeared to stabilize. As the monetary growth of the mid-1980s and the German export boom began to make themselves felt in 1987, the Bundesbank began a slow but persistent increase in interest rates that carried to the end of the decade and beyond.

Although the policies of the *Wende* changed the mood of the West German economy and reinstilled a measure of confidence, progress came unevenly and haltingly. During most of the 1980s, the figures on growth and inflation improved but slowly, and the figures on unemployment barely moved at all. German businesses, still uncertain about the future after the severe recession, raised production by installing additional machinery instead of hiring more workers. There was little job growth until the end of the decade. When the statistics did change, however, even modestly, it was at least in the right direction, and they improved more toward the end of the decade:[24]

Year	GNP Growth Rate	Unemployment Rate	Price Index Rise
1982	-1.0	7.2	4.4
1983	1.9	8.8	3.3
1984	3.3	8.8	2.0
1985	1.9	8.9	2.2
1986	2.3	8.5	3.1
1987	1.6	8.5	2.1
1988	3.7	8.4	1.5
1989	3.9	7.6	2.8

DECLINING SECULAR GROWTH PATH?

As the 1980s advanced and West German growth remained slow if steady, some of the questions of the 1970s were asked again by Germans as well as foreigners. The main thrust of those questions was whether West German growth was on a fundamentally declining path from which there was no prospect of escape beyond an occasional bounce, and whether Germans might perhaps have to reconcile themselves to a static standard of living which could be comfortable but would no longer be rising. The questions were based on statistics like the following, which showed a secular decline in the growth rate since the 1950s, an upturn in unemployment since the

1960s, and a gradual increase in inflation except during or after a severe downturn:[25]

Years	Real Growth Rate (GNP)	Unemployment Rate	Inflation Rate
1950-1954 (a)	8.7	8.5	2.0
1955-1959 (a)	6.0	3.8	1.9
1960-1964	4.6	0.9	2.7
1965-1969	4.0	1.2	2.1
1970-1974	3.0	1.3	6.1
1975-1979	3.9	4.4	3.7
1980-1984	1.0	7.0	4.3
1985-1989 (b)	2.8	8.8	1.0

(a) Excluding the Saar

(b) Partly estimated

The questioners asked whether the West German slowdown was perhaps a part of, and perhaps even at the core of, "Eurosclerosis," a term that became increasingly modish as the decade advanced.

Similarly unimpressive trends seemed evident in productivity growth, an area in which the German record was better than that of most other states but still not as good as it needed to be for a country with a declining native population:[26]

Increases in Productivity					
Dates	West Germany	U.S.	U.K.	Japan	France
1951-64	5.1	2.5	2.3	7.6	4.3
1964-73	4.4	1.6	2.6	8.4	4.4
1973-79	2.9	-0.2	1.2	2.9	2.8
1979-87	1.5	0.6	2.1	2.9	1.8

Statistics reflecting total production around the world also seemed to mirror a decline in West German output and vitality. Those statistics showed that the West German share of total Gross World Product in 1965 had been

6.6 per cent. By 1975, it had grown to 7.9 per cent. Twelve years later, in 1987, it had fallen to 7.4 per cent, largely because of the more rapid growth of Japan and other Asian states.[27] Even adding a reasonable estimate for the GNP of the former East Germany would not have brought the all-German share above 8.2 per cent by 1989, and would leave all of Germany with barely a greater share of world production than West Germany alone had reached 15 years earlier.

The most troubling statistic, however, was the unemployment rate, which appeared to have settled at yet another and higher plateau. It was one of the problems that was most insistently addressed in the discussions about the structural problems of the economy. A growing number and proportion of the jobless were long-time unemployed.[28] Businessmen and investors complained that various social regulations had made it so difficult to reduce staff that they did not dare to hire and that they also hesitated to start or expand ventures.

Few Germans contested these statistics and their implications. One, Kurt Biedenkopf, who was to become Minister-President of Saxony, argued that the West German economy was not stagnant but was, in fact, more efficient than any of its competitors. Given that Germans work fewer hours than workers in any other major country, he argued that West German productivity per working *hour* was well ahead of others. He argued that Japan's productivity was only about half of Germany's and America's only about two thirds of Germany's.[29] But most Germans and even more foreigners remained skeptical about German prospects.

THE END OF THE DECADE AND THE UPTURN OF THE ECONOMY

As the worries about stagnation intensified, West Germany's economy finally began to grow more rapidly in 1989. Part of that boom was tied to the overall growth of the European and the global economy, but part of it was a specifically German achievement.[30]

The growth rate for West German GNP rose to 3.9 per cent during 1989, the highest level of the decade. Productivity rose by 3.4 per cent. The unemployment rate fell to 7.6 per cent, despite an influx of workers from abroad. Orders received by manufacturers rose by 11 per cent. Unit labor costs rose only slowly, at 0.3 per cent.

The most important element of West German economic performance in 1989 was that it broke the secular downtrend line that had been established over almost 30 years. It could thus help to answer the many questions that had been posed by Germans and others. West German growth rates were again on an ascending path. Moreover, the West German growth rate for 1989 was higher than the average of all Western industrial states, after having lagged that average for most of the decade.[31]

The 1989 results appeared to vindicate the West German supply-side revolution. Tax rate reductions had led to greater vitality and revenues.[32] Investment was growing. Labor was finally being pulled in from the sidelines as well as from the black economy and unemployment fell even during a year of rising immigration. Although the cumulative public sector deficit had gone above the DM one trillion level, the public sector was growing more slowly than before.

West German export growth proved especially remarkable in the second half of the 1980s, culminating in 1989 and 1990. The current account surplus during 1989 rose to DM 104 billion, or 4.5 per cent of GNP, compared with DM 88 billion, or 4 per cent, during 1988. The increase in the current account surplus took place largely because of the boost in international demand for investment goods, and it was strong enough to offset a 7 per cent rise in imports. The last five years of the 1980s had given West Germany the largest sequence of trade surpluses in its history.

With its 1989 performance, the West German economy ended the decade on a strong note. Having begun the 1980s under the cloud of the second oil shock and of stagflation, it entered the new decade in a positive mood and with considerable confidence as one of the most influential economic powers in the world.

The Bundesbank, as well as a number of German economists, perceived two major potential problems even during the widespread euphoria. The first problem that disturbed the bank was that the boom appeared to be fueled more by foreign rather than by domestic demand. The second problem was the potential for inflation. The investment boom had compelled German industry to boost capacity utilization rates by 3 per cent over 1988. The Bundesbank warned darkly about the "increased risks to stabilization policy" posed by this high rate.[33] It continued to raise interest rates, although the effect of this on foreign demand was more likely to manifest itself indirectly (by forcing others to follow) than directly.

In particular, however, the Bundesbank reacted to the rise in the cost of living that had occurred despite the bank's efforts to restrain prices by progressive interest rate boosts. After having climbed very little during 1987 and 1988, the cost of living rose by 2.8 per cent in 1989. The producer price index in turn rose to 3.1 per cent.

The year 1989 assumes considerable importance in any analysis of the future prospects of the German economy because it was the last year of the West German economy as a separate and separable institution. From 1990, the positive and negative distortions generated by German unification were to set in, and by the mid-1990s the European Community's Single Market is expected to obliterate what remains of the distinctions between separate West European economies. But 1989 statistics showed that the West German economy could break out of the stagnation cycle to which it had been widely relegated during the 1980s, and that there was some prospect of improvement over the long term.

The record of the West German economy for four decades had represented a signal achievement. The first decade, that of the 1950s, had been that of the economic miracle. The second decade, that of the 1960s, had seen consolidation and the first signs of trouble. The 1970s had brought the oil shocks, the social programs, the rising deficits, and finally a loss of control. In the 1980s, the *Wende* at home and the more stable environment abroad had combined to put Germany back on its feet and on the path of growth.

Recovery had been slow in coming, and all the questions had not been answered, but progress and prosperity had returned. The government and the Bundesbank could legitimately be pleased. When Chancellor Kohl's coalition was reelected at the end of 1990, it was in part because of its economic policies.

UNITY AND THE BEGINNING OF THE 1990S

Whatever questions might have remained about West Germany as a separate entity were not to be answered and can never be answered. The West German economy ceased to exist around the end of 1989, as soon as East Berliners and East Germans could come across the Wall, although it formally ceased to exist only on July 1, 1990, when monetary union of the two Germanies took place.

From the beginning of 1990, and progressively throughout the year, the West German economy began to reorient itself toward economic and political union with what had been the GDR. The economy turned gradually and massively from its primary West European and global orientation toward an increasingly intense concentration on the requirements and the opportunities of unification.

Although statistics on West German economic progress continued to be published separately during 1990 and 1991, they became increasingly meaningless and even misleading as the year progressed because they showed the impact of unification only in the West and not in the whole country. By the same token, statistics on Eastern German performance, which had always been questionable, became so irrelevant that they ceased being published. A new and uncharted process had begun, and none of those who watched it could pretend that they knew the course that it would follow or the date on which it might be completed. Nor could they even be sure of what was happening below the surface statistics although they had to act as if they knew.

Unification had a number of effects in Western and Eastern Germany, some of them mutually reinforcing and some of them mutually offsetting.

The main immediate effect on the West German economy was to increase production at a rapid rate throughout the year. The GNP grew at a rate of 4.6 per cent for 1990, with the highest rates of increase coming during the second half and continuing at only a slightly slower pace into early 1991. Prices, however, remained relatively stable, as the cost of living grew at only 2.8 per cent despite some high wage settlements in some industries.[34]

Employment rose during the year, from 28 million to 28.7 million, and the unemployment rate sank to 7.2 per cent. Notably, the number of registered unemployed in Western Germany only declined by about 300,000, showing that at least half of the new jobs in Western Germany had been taken by persons who had moved or were commuting from Eastern Germany. Similar trends continued during 1991.

The dramatic improvement in the Western German figures resulted from the opening in Eastern Germany of a large new market of 16 million persons. Many East Germans at first wanted only West German consumer products and Western food. Eastern German products found no such markets in the West, although it was not clear whether this reflected consumer preferences or the problems that Eastern German producers faced in working with the inflexible and protective Western German distribution system.

Eastern Germans worked in the West and put their money into Western German banks, Western German insurance companies, and so on, giving a sharp boost to the Western German economy. By the end of 1990, as many as 250,000 Eastern Germans were commuting to work in the West, and that number was estimated to have grown to 350,000 or even 400,000 by the middle of 1991.

This meant that Western Germany not only had a vast new market but a growth of over 1 per cent in its work force, as sharp an increase as since the days of the economic miracle. It also had an increase in its capital base, because Eastern German deposits were placed in Western German banks that had come East, and those deposits moved back to the central German financial market at Frankfurt. Not all Western German states gained equally from the sharp rise in GNP, with the fastest growth coming in the states that were close to Eastern Germany or were economically linked to it (like Bavaria, Berlin, Hamburg, or Hesse).[35]

As consumers and workers in Eastern Germany shifted their preferences to the West, and as the long-standing problems of the GDR came home to roost, the economy in Eastern Germany imploded. Nobody could be certain of the exact extent of the collapse, but there was a broad expert consensus that industrial production had fallen by about 50 per cent before the end of 1990, with the gross regional product having decreased by perhaps 20 to 25 per cent.

If those statistics were correct, the widely reported German boom of 1990 had to come into question. Even if one were to assume that the true economy of Eastern Germany represented only 10 per cent of the new all-German economy, a decline on the order of 20 to 25 per cent of its regional economy would suggest that the 4.6 per cent GNP growth in Western Germany should perhaps be read more accurately as only a 2 or 3 per cent growth rate for all of Germany in 1990. They showed a less auspicious start for the united German economy than the West German figures.

The five West German economic institutes began to attempt a merger of the two sets of statistics. They revised their estimates for German growth downward, projecting a growth rate of only 1.5 per cent for 1991. In Western Germany, growth would slip from 4 per cent in 1990 to 2.5 per cent in 1991, and in Eastern Germany there would be an additional decline of perhaps 10 per cent in 1991.[36] But no estimates could be regarded as reliable because of rapid shifts in market and labor preferences.

The Bundesbank looked mainly at the Western, not the Eastern, German statistics. Its annual report at the end of 1990 and its first reports for 1991 cited the potentially inflationary effects of the rapid growth rate in the West. The bank expressed concern about the booming level of domestic demand. It was pleased that the yearly inflation rate had been only 2.5 per cent, but warned that interest rates would have to remain high to keep "domestically fabricated" price rises under control.[37] It was also disturbed by the fiscal stimulus created by a large German budget deficit and by the indisputable evidence that production was not rising as fast as demand in Eastern Germany.

Unification also affected Germany's international position. During 1990, the German trade and current account balances declined, as follows:[38]

German Trade and Current Account Balance in Billions of DM, 1990

	All Germany		Western Germany only
	1989	1990	1990
Exports:	641	668	650
Imports:	507	558	552
Trade Balance:	134	110	98
Current Account:	104	72	

The figures showed that German exports as a whole had risen strongly, by DM 27 billion, during 1990, although a major part of that increase had been contributed by exports from the former East Germany. Imports, however, had risen almost twice as fast, by DM 51 billion. The German trade and current account surpluses of the past decade were rapidly fading.

The trend continued in early 1991, with united Germany actually having a net foreign trade deficit during January and February of the new year. Predictions of a significant surplus, even if a smaller one than during the late 1980s, appeared to be vanishing, as all projections had to be recalculated in terms of the effects of unification. By mid-1991 it seemed likely that united Germany would have at most a modest trade surplus, if any, for the first full year of its existence, and that it would almost certainly have a current account deficit.

Those who had long wanted West Germany to be a locomotive for the world economy could take some pleasure in seeing the rise in German imports and the decline in exports. The shift appeared to be widespread, with German exports declining and imports rising in almost every category. The OECD indicated that it expected the situation to continue, with German exports continuing to remain relatively low during the first several years of the 1990s while imports would rise, although it expected a positive German current account balance to return by 1992. It attributed these trends to German unification, to the weaker dollar, and to the prospects that several of Germany's trading partners would suffer from slow growth or recession.[39] If that projection were to hold true, and if the Germans were prepared to accept a low export surplus and perhaps even a negative trade balance,

Germany might be a locomotive for some time. But the previous German experiment with being a locomotive, during the late 1970s, had ended badly, and there was no assurance that the 1990-1991 experiment would end any better.

Domestically as well as internationally, the first half of 1991 showed the many conflicting pressures under which the German economy was operating. The growth rate in Western Germany dipped to 2.5 per cent compared to the latter half of 1990, although it remained at over 4 per cent compared to the first half of 1990. If one included the sharp decline in Eastern Germany, however, growth was at best slow. The decline in Eastern Germany would have been more serious if Western German funds were not subsidizing the region to the extent of two thirds of its Gross Regional Product, thus effectively supporting a share of Western German growth. The inflation rate rose to 3.5 per cent by mid-1991 and was expected to crest even higher, perhaps at 4 per cent. Some Germans warned of a return of 1980-1982 "stagflation." (For more detail on 1991 trends under separate headings, see Chapters 5 through 10.)[40]

AN EVALUATION AT THE TURN OF THE DECADE

With 1990 and 1991 being the beginning of a new era for the German economy, they have given some signs regarding the main features of the new era.

The first and perhaps most notable feature is a potentially immense capital requirement. German unification will call for much more new capital than even the most sober pessimists had anticipated. No precise calculation can be made, but the sums continue to rise as the problems are studied more closely. A total of DM 1 trillion over ten years has been mentioned frequently and may be too low. West Germany during the 1980s had been generating enough capital (an estimated DM 200 billion or more annually) to meet such needs, and united Germany can do so as well, but other sites of German investment will feel the results.

Second, state claims against the economy have begun to rise rapidly as a united Germany needs large increases in public expenditures to help finance unification. The Bundestag had to pass three supplementary budgets in a row during the second half of 1990 to cover the growing expenditures necessary to finance unification. The Bundesbank grew alarmed and raised interest rates to force the government to raise taxes. The government thereupon did decide on a number of tax increases and expenditure cuts to keep the deficit from becoming too great and perhaps growing out of control. Some of those tax increases were scheduled to be temporary and others were permanent. Some, like an increase in the value-added tax, were mandated by European Community agreements. Nonetheless, the federal budget deficit rose to DM 46.7 billion in 1990 and was officially expected to rise to DM 66.4 billion in the 1991 budget, even after a tax increase. The institutes at first projected a total public sector deficit of DM 70 billion in 1990 and DM 90 billion in 1991 but had to revise those estimates upward. Unofficial estimates ranged much higher, and internal Finance Ministry documents by mid-1991 spoke of a total 1991 public sector deficit of DM 200 billion.

If some of the news has been worrisome, some of it has been good. The Western German economy has been able to meet the new production demand and to exceed its normal capacity usage without undue price increases because of the new supply of labor coming from the East. The Eastern Germans are obviously prepared to work, and to work hard, despite some rather condescending West German expectations. And, over the long run, the outlook for large sales to the new East European and Russian markets can be positive, although they will require massive credits.

The dilemma for Germany and for its economic planners and managers is that the country has grown accustomed to a certain framework of activity and to a certain steady pace. That pace, which has consisted of relatively slow but steady incremental growth, based largely on exports and on productivity increases, has not excited Germans or others. It was often even criticized, especially during the 1970s and 1980s. But it has created a stable and comfortable prosperity that has made Germany a good place to live and has given it considerable influence abroad. It was also superbly suited to the German style and to German wishes and needs after generations of turmoil and loss. Nonetheless, it placed Germany in a situation in which it was better at being pulled than at pulling, especially because the Bundesbank quickly tried to reduce any demand that appeared to exceed supply.

Thus, after German unification, something else may be needed. And the Germans, as well as those associated with them in various forms of cooperation, have to examine whether and how to cope with the new situation. To answer that question, a close look at the functioning of the German economy is warranted, with much of that look based on the way the institutions and the economy of West Germany have functioned.

NOTES TO CHAPTER TWO

1. Ludwig Erhard, *Wohlstand für Alle* (Düsseldorf: ECON Verlag, 1957), 3rd edition, 1990, p. 18. This book by Erhard, which has been translated into English as *Prosperity through Competition,* was first published in 1957 with the assistance of Wolfram Langer when Erhard was still Economics Minister, and was republished when East Germany was freed.
2. General Clay liked to recollect the conversation when he had called Erhard to his office to challenge Erhard's decision to abolish controls. Clay told Erhard, "All my advisers tell me that what you have done is insane." Erhard replied, "All my advisers tell me the same thing." This sign that Erhard was not cowed by bureaucrats or "experts," as well as his commitment to a free economy, may have played a significant role in persuading Clay that Erhard deserved support.
3. For reviews of the 1948 events that established the West German economy, see Axel Borrmann, Karl Fasbender, Hans-Hagen Härtel, and Manfred Holthus, *Soziale Marktwirtschaft* (Hamburg: Verlag Weltarchiv GmbH, 1990), pp. 54-63; Jean Edward Smith, *Lucius D. Clay: An American Life* (New York: Henry Holt, 1990), pp. 483-486; Henry Wallich, *Mainsprings of the German Revival* (New Haven: Yale University Press, 1955), pp. 1-21.
4. Material on the first phase of the "economic miracle" is drawn from Karl Hardach, *The Political Economy of Germany in the Twentieth Century* (Berkeley: University of California Press, 1976), pp. 180-187, and statistics are drawn from the Sachverständigenrat and from Ludwig Erhard, *Deutsche Wirtschaftspolitik* (Frankfurt: Knapp, and Düsseldorf: Econ, 1960).
5. Edzard Hermberg, "The German Economy in the World Economy," paper presented at the U.S. Embassy, Bonn, July 10, 1982, p. 4.
6. *Ibid.,* p. 5.
7. This discussion of Schiller's attitudes and policies is drawn from the earlier listed sources and also from the following: Fritz Ulrich Fack and Peter Hort, *Soziale Marktwirtschaft* (Freiburg/Würzburg: Verlag Plötz, 1985), pp. 63-67; and Christopher S. Allen, "From Social Market to Meso-Corporatism: The Politics of West German Economic Policy," *German Studies Review,* DAAD Special Issue, 1990, pp. 15-17.
8. Hardach, *op. cit.,* pp. 201-202.
9. For excerpts of the 1963 law establishing the Sachverständigenrat and of the 1967 amendment, see Sachverständigenrat, *Weichenstellungen für die neunziger Jahre* (Stuttgart: Metzler-Pöschel, 1989), pp. 202-204 (hereinafter cited as *1989/90 Report*).
10. Peter Katzenstein, *Policy and Politics in West Germany* (Philadelphia: Temple Univ. Press, 1987), p. 91.
11. OECD Special Study, *Why Economic Policies Change Course* (Paris: OECD, 1988), p. 45.

12. Fack and Hort, *op. cit.*, pp. 67-69.
13. For a detailed analysis of Schmidt's 1978 decision to respond to Carter, see Robert D. Putnam and C. Randall Henning, "The Bonn Summit of 1978: A Case Study in Coordination," in *Can Nations Agree? Issues in International Economic Cooperation* (Washington: Brookings, 1986), pp. 12-140.
14. Statistics drawn from the Ifo *Spiegel der Wirtschaft, 1990* and the Sachverständigenrat, *1989/90 Report*, passim.
15. OECD Special Study, *loc. cit.*, pp. 53-55.
16. Fack and Hort, *op. cit.*, pp. 69-70.
17. Ibid., pp. 70-71.
18. As with many German words and terms, the full implications of *Die Wende* are almost impossible to convey in English by the direct translation of "the turn" or "the turning," or even by "the reversal." A *Wende* has a strongly corrective connotation, suggesting not only a change of policy but also a process of purification, an abandonment of erroneous ways, and a course toward something new and better. Its meaning can perhaps be best expressed in English by the term "new departure." To convey the full sense of the German word, I shall continue to use it in the text.
19. The following sources have been used for this description of German economic policy and performance during the 1980s: Sachverständigenrat, *1989/90 Report*, pp. 103-119; Karl H. Cerny, "Between Elections: The Issues, 1983-1987," Cerny, ed., *Germany at the Polls: The Bundestag Elections of the 1980s* (Washington: American Enterprise Institute, 1990), pp. 191-196.
20. For a summary of these steps, see OECD, *Germany, 1989/1990* (Paris: OECD, 1990), pp. 38-43.
21. *Ibid.*, p. 43; for a detailed analysis, see Martin Hellwig and Manfred Neumann, "Economic Policy in Germany; Was There a Turnaround?", *Economic Policy*, Special Report, 1987, pp. 103-145.
22. *Monthly Report of the Bundesbank*, January, 1990, p. 39.
23. It should be noted, however, that the overall volume of West German *exports* during the decade of the 1980s rose by more than a half, whereas the overall volume of *imports* rose by only a third.
24. Statistics drawn from the Ifo *Spiegel der Wirtschaft*, publications of the Sachverständigenrat, and Bundesbank or OECD reports.
25. Horst Siebert, "Principles of the Economic System of the Federal Republic," paper presented at a German-American conference in Washington, D.C., October 23-25, 1989.
26. Nick Crafts, "British Economic Growth before and after 1979: A Review of the Evidence," Discussion Paper No. 292, Center for Economic Policy Research (November, 1988), cited in David P. Calleo and Claudia Morgenstern, *Recasting Europe's Economies* (Lanham: University Press of America, 1989), p. 119.
27. IMF statistics cited in "The World Economy," *Financial Times*, September 26, 1989. Statistics on such topics are difficult to evaluate because they can

be affected by shifts in exchange rates, but in this instance appear to reflect real trends.

28. The proportion, which held steady at about one third of all unemployed between 1984 and 1988, suggested structural as well as cyclical difficulties. *Wirtschaftspolitik* (Bonn: Bundeszentrale für Politische Bildung, 1990), p. 287.

29. Kurt Biedenkopf, "The Federal Republic of Germany," David Calleo and Claudia Morgenstern, eds., *Recasting Europe's Economies* (Lanham, Md.: University Press of America, 1990), pp. 90-93.

30. Data relating to 1989 come from the following sources: Deutsche Bundesbank, *Report of the Deutsche Bundesbank for the Year 1989* (Frankfurt: Bundesbank, 1990), passim; OECD, *Germany, 1989/1990*, passim.

31. FRG, *Sozialpolitische Umschau*, June 25, 1990.

32. George Melloan, "Has Anyone Noticed the German Tax Reform?" *Wall Street Journal*, October 29, 1990.

33. Comments and statistics for the first six months of 1990, unless otherwise indicated, are from the Bundesbank report on the German economic situation in the summer of 1990 contained in *Monatsberichte der deutschen Bundesbank*, September, 1990, pp. 5-11, 19, and 29.

34. The statistics for 1990 come from the following: Bundesministerium für Wirtschaft, *Jahresbericht 1991* (Bonn: Bundesministerium für Wirtschaft, 1991); "Die Wirtschaftslage in der Bundesrepublik Deutschland um die Jahreswende 1990/91," *Monatsberichte der Deutschen Bundesbank*, February 1991, pp. 5-46; and FRG, *Aktuelle Beiträge*, No. 6, 1991, February 11, 1991.

35. *Handelsblatt*, February 6, 1991.

36. Semi-Annual Forecast for the German Economy by the German Economic Institutes, October 29, 1990, *Wirtschaftswoche*, November 2, 1990, pp. 43-45.

37. *Ibid.*

38. FRG, *Aktuelle Beiträge, loc. cit.*, p. 5.

39. *Frankfurter Allgemeine Zeitung*, January 4, 1991; *Financial Times*, June 4, 1991.

40. Bundesministerium für Wirtschaft, *The Economic Situation in the Federal Republic of Germany, Monthly Review*, June 1991, pp. 1-3; Deutsche Bundesbank, *Monthly Report of the Deutsche Bundesbank*, June 1991, pp. 1-47; OECD *Economic Outlook*, No. 49, July 1971, pp. 59-64.

Three

Germany, Inc.? The Bundesbank and the Associations

Former Chancellor Helmut Schmidt used to describe himself on occasion as the *"Vorstandsvorsitzender der Aktiengesellschaft Deutschland,"* a phrase that was often translated into English as "Chief Executive Officer of Germany, Inc." Schmidt never liked that translation, in part because he believed that it conveyed a much more direct authority than the German text intended, and in part because the translation—especially the "Inc."—implied a much more centrally directed economic structure than he wanted to suggest. Instead, he insisted, he was a chairman of a board, a loosely organized and sometimes unruly board, whose members might have a common general objective but many strongly held and contradictory ideas about how to reach it.

Whatever the positive or negative implications of the phrase or of its translation may have been, and whatever its merits or its faults, it does pinpoint one of the fundamental characteristics of the West German economy—that Germans do have a sense of being collaborators in a common enterprise even as they may compete for their place within it or may argue ceaselessly about the specific policies that the enterprise should pursue.

West Germany's economic success has been achieved through a combination of two seemingly irreconcilable processes: On the one hand, a highly developed form of competition in which different firms struggle hard to make the best possible product and to maintain market share; on the other hand, a framework of relationships in which the fundamental principles—sometimes known as the *Rahmenbedingungen*—are broadly understood and accepted by all the players.

What emerges from this combination combines competition and conciliation, attack and restraint, struggle and compromise, in a combination that contributes markedly to the totality of West German success but that would be hard to duplicate elsewhere. Understanding for it is acquired more by habit than by instruction, and it is difficult and perhaps even impossible for outsiders to grasp in its entirety.

When Germans are asked to discuss this phenomenon, they often observe that participants in the German economic process constantly struggle against each other but that they try to reach a consensus before they fight and that even as they fight they are always looking for an opportunity to settle the struggle. They describe themselves as "social partners" even as they differ. They are very conscious of being in a small country that can only survive if all work together.

Germans do not like to describe the process to foreigners because they fear that it will be misunderstood. One German said that the process was like cycling: You either know it or you do not; until you know it you cannot understand it even when you see it done; once you know it, it becomes a part of you. He added that it is something that you can only learn by doing, and that you may have a fall or two before you master it. Yet, if the process seems difficult when you do not know it, it is really very simple once you do.

The system functions through formal and informal interactions that reach from the pinnacles to the foundations of the public, semipublic, and private hierarchies, effectively mingling the three into a coordinated although not a single entity. Those interactions establish common responsibilities and mutual dependencies. No single element in the German process can succeed if another fails. Nor is any element likely to gain prestige and power by attacking and attempting to destroy another participant directly. Instead, prestige and power usually come from making decisions that will benefit and may even involve all.

This chapter and the next will describe and analyze the functioning of that Germany, whether "Inc." or not. This chapter concentrates more on organization and the next more on process, but both represent only different perspectives on the same subject. For the organizations are shaped by the process even as the process is shaped by the organizations.

THE GOVERNMENT

The requirement for cooperation begins at the most senior level of the government, which has almost always been a coalition government bringing together one or another mix of political parties. The three principal political figures responsible for economic policy are the Chancellor, the Minister of Economics, and the Minister of Finance. The three positions have only rarely been held simultaneously by members of a single party. They are usually divided among two or sometimes three.

Any German economic policy must, therefore, reflect the interests of at least two political parties, with all that this may mean in terms of compromise and conciliation. The coalition negotiations to form a new West German government after a national election are never more delicate or more difficult than when they touch on economic policies. Yet those negotiations must elaborate a common program, decide on the persons charged with executing it, and prepare the legislative and administrative agendas to bring the program to life.

The main German parties that are likely to be in coalition have different economic philosophies and they pursue generally different objectives. The Christian Democratic Union (CDU) and the Christian Social Union (CSU) are conservative, business-oriented, but with a long tradition of support for social welfare programs. Their policies are similar but not identical, and they may become more distinct because the CSU has not been successful in establishing itself in Eastern Germany. The Free Democratic Party (FDP) is liberal in the English sense, very much in favor of the free market and of a minimum of government regulation. The Social Democratic Party (SPD) is in the tradition of German social democracy, a party that believes in combining political freedom with large social programs and with government involvement in the economy. It is impossible for any of the three parties to be in a government with the others without yielding something. But each wants to share in the government to exert at least some influence, and they are all ready to compromise to some degree.

The office of the Chancellor reflects the need for compromise and conciliation but also the Chancellor's personal style. The Chancellor has only a small economic staff at the Chancellery. He has an Assistant for Economic Affairs, directing and coordinating the work of a number of suboffices that deal with different ministries and different functions. One suboffice may handle finance, another planning, a third European integration, and so on, depending on the exigencies of the moment. The persons in the various offices may be career government bureaucrats or may be brought in from outside.

The operation of the office, as might be expected, depends largely upon the personality, the interests, and the wishes of the Chancellor. To cite only two recent examples:

- Under Helmut Schmidt, the Chancellery office of economics shaped, directed, and coordinated the economic policy of the entire government economic apparatus. It also kept contact with the business and financial community, including the Bundesbank, and helped Schmidt with his long-range planning. Schmidt also used his assistant for economic affairs to circumvent the bureaucracy or the Bundesbank when he thought it necessary.

• Helmut Kohl operates very differently, using the Chancellor's office for limited day-by-day coordination but not attempting to use it to manage the economic policy of the government. He uses the political, not the bureaucratic, structure to make policy, working through the CDU/CSU and the FDP or through personal contact with ministers, other political leaders, Bundestag members, and state or regional officials.

Schmidt, an economist by training and a bureaucratic operator, centered his policy at the Chancellery. Kohl, more politically oriented, treats economic matters as political issues and uses the Chancellery bureaucracy more as an information center than as an operational staff.[1] Each does what he wishes, and the office is structured to give that flexibility.

In the cabinet, roles are more fixed, although they may also change in accordance with personalities and political parties. There has been a fundamental shift in responsibilities since the founding of the Federal Republic. The *primus inter pares* within the cabinet used to be the Minister for Economics, traditionally empowered to shape the government's basic economic policy under the Chancellor's broad guidance. It is the position made famous in West Germany's early years by Ludwig Erhard. Erhard himself had enormous responsibilities and opportunities during the postwar years, when the foundations and guiding principles of the postwar German economy had to be laid.

After the 1960s, however, the Economics Minister became less important within the German policy process. Schmidt took the first crucial step to undercut the authority of the Economics Ministry when he took the office of Money and Credit with him from the Ministry of Economics to the Ministry of Finance in 1972. This transferred one of the Economics Ministry's most important functions. The role of the Economics Minister was further diluted as new ministries were established for the environment, for energy, for research, and for several social programs.

The Economics Minister can still exercise great influence when he is a respected personality in his own right, with a solid position in German politics, as when Count Otto Lambsdorff was Minister. It also has a very important role in the formulation of general economic policy. It is still a principal channel for contact with industry, labor, and semipublic associations, but several ministers have complained in bitter frustration that they were not able to carry out the policies they wanted.

Kohl in 1991 appointed a young FDP politician, Jürgen Möllemann, as the Minister of Economics in the first elected all-German government. Although the German political and financial press snickered, regarding Möllemann as too young and inexperienced, he moved into the position with vigor and with clear concepts regarding economic policy and German economic unification. He won great respect for a number of actions, including a threat to resign if subsidies could not be cut by DM 10 billion in 1992 and by equal amounts in the next two years. He has also taken a number of other strong positions, and he may be able to revive the Ministry's prestige and authority.

As the Minister of Economics has waned, the Minister of Finance has become the single most influential cabinet member for economic policy. This Minister is responsible for the German federal budget, which has become ever more important as the government's share of national income has grown and as governments have increasingly used the budget to set priorities and to guide national economic activity. The Finance Minister also accompanies the Chancellor to the annual financial summits and is the main German spokesman in the G-7 meetings. He has thus been in a position to manage not only domestic but also international financial policy for Germany, and to coordinate the two in his office. The position has not always been strongly staffed, as many financial issues are left in the hands of the Bundesbank, but has also had some eminent personalities. As of this writing, it is held by Theo Waigel, himself an important political figure because of his leadership role in the CSU.

In West German coalition governments, the two ministries have often been held by politicians from different parties although both Schiller and Schmidt held them simultaneously. The FDP has held the Ministry of Economics during most of the 1970s, 1980s, and 1990s, whereas the major coalition parties—whether SPD or CDU/CSU—have held the Finance Ministry. That combination has given the major coalition partners an incentive to promote the image of the Finance Minister even further, especially when the news was good. Helmut Kohl used Waigel to take the lead in managing the economic aspects of German unification in 1990, giving Waigel and the CSU a useful and popular platform before the full range of problems that might emerge from unification had come to be widely understood. This division between the parties has been continued in a united Germany.

Because West Germany and united Germany have a federal system, *Land* (state) and local governments also have important functions. This also reflects the German tradition. Germany, whether as empire or republic, had always been decentralized before the Nazis. It always combined a mix of national, state, and local structures with carefully defined and deliberately circumscribed powers.

Land and even local authorities are involved in many economic functions, such as social services, development and energy policy, education—including vocational training, public housing, environmental protection—or industrial policy. They also share certain tax revenues that are centrally collected but distributed among the central, state, and local authorities in accordance with carefully negotiated ratios. Under those ratios, before German unification, 42.5 per cent of personal income tax revenue was allocated to the federal government, an equal share was divided among the states, and 15 per cent was divided among local authorities. Corporate tax revenue was shared equally between Bonn and the states. The states and localities also collect certain taxes directly. Real estate taxes, for example, are entirely collected and allocated to the local communities.[2] The final allocation of taxes that may be agreed for a united Germany remains to be decided, but it will probably remain along the same broad lines because the pattern of responsibilities that different levels of government are expected to carry is not likely to change. But there have been many arguments over this subject. The Western German states have not wanted to share revenues on an equal basis with the new states but have instead offered temporary subsidies. The new states, in turn, have insisted that they actually need a larger share of federally collected revenues than the old. They specifically claim that they should have the right to get additional funds under a system that provides for transfers from wealthy German states to those less privileged.

Different West German *Länder* have followed different economic policies. The Minister-Presidents of two West German states, Bavaria and Baden-Württemberg, have stressed industrial development policies that departed radically from those of others, putting their states into the front line of German technological development. On the other hand, the states of North Rhine-Westphalia and of the Saarland have helped to subsidize coal and steel production, and have only later attempted to encourage new industries.

The possibility for separate *Land* policies has already encouraged some of the states of the former GDR to try their own development policies. They have invited industry from other countries to invest in their states and have also done some export promotion. They will probably be even more inclined than the other states to chart their own way as soon as they can.

THE BUNDESBANK

At the center of West German success have been a number of institutions that are not formally part of the government structure but that have considerable power and influence over general economic policy. Those institutions exist throughout the entire economy, from banking through industry, agriculture, and labor. Some have a more official character than others. Some carry out more formal or formally assigned functions than others. Some may have a private or semiprivate function. All, however, have highly public roles.

The single most important of those institutions is the German Federal Bank, the Deutsche Bundesbank. More than any other German economic institution, it has acquired almost universal recognition and even notoriety. It has the dominant voice in West German monetary policy. Through that voice, it has established and maintained a firm policy in favor of solid currency value within West Germany, united Germany, and increasingly within the European Community and even the world at large. When the Bundesbank speaks, the Chancellor will listen, as will others in the German government, Europe, and throughout the world.[3]

If a central bank's reputation is its most valuable asset, the Bundesbank is among the world's most highly endowed institutions. Its contribution to the economic and political stability of West Germany and Western Europe in the postwar years is almost legendary, and is given due respect even by those who disagree with some or many of its policies. Even persons who know little about Germany and even less about German economics have heard of the Bundesbank and of its passion for (or, as some would say, obsession with) stability.

The Bundesbank often appears to be *the* maker of German economic policy, although its exact powers are carefully set forth and circumscribed in the 1957 law establishing the bank. Even when the Chancellor overrules the Bundesbank on questions that are within the competence and the responsibility of the government, he normally does so in a way that does not undercut the confidence which global markets and foreign investors must have in German financial policy.

The Bundesbank's carefully cultivated and ferociously protected image of rectitude emerges from its specifically articulated mandate, set forth in the *Gesetz über die Deutsche Bundesbank*, as "the preservation of the value of German currency." The creators of the Bundesbank regarded that mandate as so important that it was clearly intended to override the bank's other principal task, "to support the general economic policy of the federal government." Even the latter was carefully limited by the specific provision that the bank "shall be independent of instructions from the federal government."[4] The mandate to preserve the value of the German currency has become so deeply enshrined in the thinking of the bank's leaders, and has become such a widespread element of global financial planning and action, that the Bundesbank can often influence others without having to act.

The bank is more independent than most central banks, especially in Europe, as intended. It has more authority in the realm of monetary policy than either the French or Italian central bank or even the British. The model on which it was most closely based, at least in its structure although not in its formal mandate, was the U.S. Federal Reserve Bank. But it exercises more functions than the Federal Reserve, in part because it carries out some exchange responsibilities that are assigned to the U.S. Treasury in the American system.

Unlike many central banks, in which board or council members are chosen by the national government and may serve at its pleasure, the Bundesbank has the majority of its Zentralbankrat (Central Bank Council) nominated by *Land* governments. They do not serve at any government's pleasure, including that of the *Land* that nominated them.[5] The members of the Zentralbankrat who are in the bank's Frankfurt directorate, the Direktorium, are appointed by the German President upon the nomination of the Chancellor, but they do not constitute a majority. Even those members, however, are not subject to government direction.

The German government does have an important role, if it wishes to exercise it. Government representatives can and do at times attend the meetings of the Zentralbankrat, although the government cannot block the bank's actions but is authorized only to delay them for no longer than two weeks. The government can, however, influence the bank's actions through indirect or public pressure. There are also informal contacts between the government and the bank, and it is not unusual for senior officials at the Chancellery and the Finance Ministry to know in advance what the Central Bank Council may be expected to decide at its next meeting.

The Bundesbank has normal central bank powers and functions. It issues currency, decides upon discount and other interest rates, makes open market policy, conducts open market transactions, and establishes minimum reserve requirements. It makes as well as carries out policies regarding government deposits, swap transactions, currency exchange, currency market intervention, and sale or purchase of certain securities. Its principal instruments are (1) the discount rate for loans to other banks, (2) the Lombard rate for short-term funding, (3) open market operations, and (4) minimum reserve requirement policies. It determines interest rates by the influence that its actions have upon markets.[6]

The former president of the Bundesbank, Karl Otto Pöhl, was the longest-serving central bank chief in Europe. He was originally appointed by Schmidt, was reappointed by Kohl, and could have served until 1995. When he was first appointed, he was regarded as a radical because he had been a journalist and a Social Democrat, but he achieved a reputation as a solid money man although he was something of a pragmatist. He was never regarded as one of the true conservatives on the Zentralbankrat. Although he said that he was resigning in July 1991 for personal reasons, many Bundesbank students believe that he resigned because he found that too many government decisions undercut the bank's capacity to carry out its policies and because he was increasingly frustrated by the array of problems that the bank was facing.

Pöhl's successor for two years, Helmut Schlesinger, is regarded as a tried-and-true hard money man. He has been a career Bundesbank official who was promoted to the Direktorium and to the vice presidency of the bank, an expert monetarist whose views on the importance of a stable D-Mark on occasion carried the Central Bank Council against Pöhl. He was often believed to have the conservative state bank chiefs solidly on his side. His appointment was regarded as a sign that the government wanted to support the bank's basic mandate even if it did not approve of all the bank's policies. His attitude throughout his career has been that the function of a central bank is to hold a steady course geared to preserving monetary stability rather than to engage in anti-cyclical monetary policy. He warned several times during 1991 that rising wage rates and stimulative government fiscal policy were creating a significant risk of inflation that required counteraction by the bank.

Schlesinger has periodically exasperated foreigners, and especially Americans, who have had to deal with him. He was reported to have been the leader in the Bundesbank's decision to raise the repurchase rate several times during 1987, and those rate increases as well as Treasury Secretary James Baker's denunciation of Schlesinger were widely believed to have helped precipitate the October 1987 Crash (see Chapter Eight). Nonetheless, before the end of that year Schlesinger was reappointed to a five-year term as vice president.

Schlesinger's successor in the summer of 1993 is to be Hans Tietmeyer, who made his mark in the Economics and Finance Ministries as a career official and then as state secretary. Kohl, whom he had served as Sherpa, appointed him to the Direktorium in 1990 in the international finance post, one of the Bundesbank's most important positions. It had been held by

Leonhard Gleske, who had acquired a reputation for quiet sagacity through several international crises. Tietmeyer was principal author of a number of important documents, including Count Lambsdorff's 1982 paper, and was a widely respected figure in Germany and abroad even before joining the Direktorium.

Kohl might have wished to make Tietmeyer Bundesbank president in 1991 but that would have aroused speculation about the bank's independence from political pressure and might have complicated Tietmeyer's task. Thus, like Pöhl, Tietmeyer was first to serve an apprenticeship on the Direktorium before becoming the head of the bank.

The Central Bank Council of the Bundesbank before German unification had 18 members, including the 7 members of the bank's Direktorium in Frankfurt as well as the 11 presidents of the West German *Land* banks. The representatives of the state banks outnumbered the Direktorium and could outvote it, although public and foreign attention usually concentrated on the Frankfurt establishment and on the Direktorium. The state bank presidents were reputed to grumble periodically that the Direktorium had become excessively influenced by international considerations and had sometimes neglected Germany's true interests.

One of the delicate questions arising out of German unity was a possible reapportionment of the seats in the Zentralbankrat to be decided within a year after unification, or by October 1991 (but not resolved as of this writing). If each of the five new *Länder* of the former GDR were to have a state bank, and if each of those banks were to be represented on the Zentralbankrat, the Zentralbankrat would have 23 members and the Frankfurt Direktorium could theoretically be outvoted by 16 to 7. Even if all 10 seats available to the Direktorium were to be filled, the balance of power would still be 16 to 10 against them. This would have called into question the bank's internal power balance and perhaps ranked international considerations too far down the list of the bank's priorities. There was also some question whether a Zentralbankrat of 23 or even 26 would be too large and unwieldy to be efficient and effective.

A number of arrangements were proposed to overcome the potential imbalance between the center and the states in the Zentralbankrat. One proposal, quickly denounced as a Frankfurt power grab, would have reduced the total number of state banks to seven, giving the president the deciding vote in case of a tie. A number of the smaller banks understandably opposed amalgamation proposals,[7] and the German upper house, the Bundesrat, voted to give each *Land* a central bank.

As the debate unfolded during 1991, it became increasingly clear that a decision on the number of state banks could affect the policy orientation of the bank. Because the Eastern German states need to have the most rapid development possible, they might be inclined to favor lower interest rates to encourage investment and growth even at a potential risk of somewhat greater inflation. The Western German states would presumably be less ready to take such risks. Some of the proposals for amalgamation of state banks seemed deliberately intended to weaken the influence of the new states, as several of their banks were to be merged with Western state banks so as to lose an independent voice.

After considerable discussion, the government by mid-1991 appeared to lean toward a compromise proposal that would leave fewer than 16 but more than 8 state bank representatives on the Central Bank Council. But the allocation of those seats remained a difficult issue, especially because even the compromise suggestions appeared to leave the new states of Eastern Germany under-represented. The policy implications were uncertain and might only be measurable over time.

Despite the Bundesbank's reputation, it is not all-powerful. Helmut Schmidt overruled it in 1978 and 1979 in moving toward the European Monetary System (EMS). Similarly, in 1990, the West German government decided in favor of a one-to-one exchange rate for certain transactions between the D-Mark and the former East German Mark, against parts of the Bundesbank's recommendation. The government's decision was based on a widespread consensus that the bank's views, while perhaps economically sound, could have provoked an immediate crisis of confidence in East Germany and immensely complicated the delicate task of reforging a German state quickly, before the Soviets might change their minds about unification.

The Bundesbank remained very concerned about the way that the government was managing German unification. It continued to express frustration when the government delayed raising taxes to cover the mounting costs, and after tax increases complained that the government had not done enough to contain the deficit by spending cuts. The bank made a point of raising interest rates one month before the December 1990 all-German elections to show its displeasure and presumably to strengthen the D-Mark before the strains of unification became apparent. It continued a very tight monetary policy during the first half of 1991 and tightened further at its first Zentralbankrat meeting after Schlesinger became president. At that meeting, it raised both the discount and the Lombard rates, although not as much as some had expected.

The Bundesbank has, on the whole, acted with considerable consistency and without public rift despite occasional arguments, but rumors persist that individual members of the Central Bank Council and even of the Direktorium do not always agree. Not only are the presidents of the state banks reputed to be generally more conservative than the Frankfurt members, but analysts who make a point of studying and predicting Bundesbank policies insist that they can detect differences among individual state bank presidents and Direktorium members through finely articulated shadings in their public pronouncements.

THE BUNDESKARTELLAMT

The Bundeskartellamt (Federal Cartel Office) is the West German and now all-German institution specifically instructed and empowered to prevent a return to the monopolies and cartels that periodically controlled much of the German economy between the 1870s and 1940s. The policies of the office, like the office itself, have always been controversial, with some Germans wanting it to have greater power and others believing that it was already abusing its existing authority and was preventing German companies from cooperating more effectively to compete abroad. Its original responsibility had been to preserve competition in the West German economy, but it quickly perceived that it might be even more needed as Germany was uniting.

The Bundeskartellamt was established in 1957. Many, including Ludwig Erhard, believed that it had not been given enough authority to restrict cartels and other monopolistic practices. The Western Allies had insisted that the fledgling Federal Republic have such a law, but German business associations used their influence to undercut its authority to the point where it has sometimes been described as a "Swiss cheese with countless holes." Erhard had favored a much stronger law but had been overruled by Adenauer, who was less of an economist but who had developed strong political links with the business associations opposing the law. Some of the holes in the Swiss cheese were closed in 1973, when the Bundestag passed a merger law (*Fusionsgesetz*) intended to block monopolies in advance so that the Bundeskartellamt would not always have to act after the fact.

In retrospect, the laws and the office have performed a central and useful function but they have not been able to prevent a gradual shift toward ever larger companies in West Germany. The number of mergers in West Germany increased rapidly during the later 1980s, rising to over 1,000 per year.[8] Nor has the Bundeskartellamt been effective in curtailing the countless informal contacts and discussions that have characterized the West German system (like other European systems) and that would be suspect and perhaps illegal in the United States. But the very existence of the office and of the anti-cartel legislation may have helped to hold back any tendency toward cartels, or at least to shift cooperation into other channels that are less damaging.

The Bundeskartellamt has several means to implement its policies and make them known. It can announce the types of activities, mergers, or acquisitions that it will approve or disapprove; it can issue specific decisions to block or suspend mergers; and it can impose penalties. It has, however, preferred to adjudicate problems rather than to act by decree. It has normally consulted with the partners to a proposed merger before making or issuing a decision. It often tries to use such consultations to prevent improper mergers or to impose preconditions, instead of trying to block mergers precipitously or to undo them after the fact.

Because of its nonconfrontational tactics, the Bundeskartellamt has often been denounced as ineffective. Critics have pointed out that the office has actually blocked very few mergers or other forms of cooperation.[9] They also assert that hidden monopolistic or oligopolistic practices are creeping back into the German economy. But others argue that the very existence of the Cartel Office has enhanced competition, and that the consistently low number of rejections by the office reflect its predilection for solving problems through nonjudicial processes.

Despite its title, the Bundeskartellamt does not have the final authority over German mergers and acquisitions. That authority is reserved for the political level, the Minister of Economics, who has on more than one occasion overruled the Bundeskartellamt. After the Bundeskartellamt had raised a number of searching questions about the legality and propriety of Daimler-Benz's 1989 acquisition of Messerschmidt-Bölkow-Blohm (MBB), and after it had even disapproved the acquisition, the Minister of Economics approved the merger on condition that Daimler-Benz and MBB sell off majority control in a small marine and technology division. The West German government justified the step by recalling that it had specifically sought the merger to support MBB—which was engaged in military production and could not be permitted to collapse—with Daimler-Benz's financial resources.

The MBB case illustrates the complex web of considerations that affect German decision-making on economic matters. Unlike most antitrust offices, especially that in the U.S. Department of Justice, the Bundeskartellamt must take account of economic, institutional, and political as well as legal considerations. It can and does use its influence to create a climate that restrains potentially improper actions, and it has acted in specific cases with an eye to that general objective. It thus preserves the effective functioning of the competitive system. But it must also be sensitive to broader considerations, which an American legal scholar described as a "healthy safety valve."[10] Beyond issuing decisions, it orchestrates a wide-ranging dialogue on the management of antitrust policy in the present international climate.

The Bundeskartellamt faces a particularly difficult task in the integration of the East and West German economies. Many large Eastern German firms cannot survive unless they can merge with large Western German firms. The process may, however, create new enterprises whose very size and combination of resources could open the way for monopolistic or oligopolistic temptations. Moreover, most acquisitions of defunct Eastern German firms would be made by Western German firms in the same field, enhancing the purchaser's competitive position. Powerful economic and political pressures for such mergers exist, if for no other reason than to help revitalize Eastern Germany.

The Bundeskartellamt also faces problems on the European front, as a new European cartel office was formed in the European Community during 1990 and a special European task force was formed to elaborate a common policy. The Germans were generally skeptical whether the new office would act with sufficient severity against prospective mergers, although the head of the new office is himself a German, Claus Dieter Ehlermann. German officials expressed concern that the European evolution toward a single market would lead to mergers between companies from different states operating in the same industrial or commercial area, compromising some of the theoretical efficiency benefits of a single market.

OTHER OPERATING INSTITUTIONS

Many other organizations had specific functions within the West German economy and are continuing to exercise them in a united Germany, in some cases suitably augmented. The organizations in question are formally recognized in the German Basic Law or in subsequent legislation and regulation. They are commonly known in Germany as the *Verbände*. Over 1,200 are represented in Bonn. Each has played an assigned role, and together they have contributed to a broad framework of cooperation mingled with competition.

Among the main organizations are the following:[11]

- The Bundesverband der Deutschen Industrie (BDI), the Federation of German Industry, which is the central organization representing the interests and policies of German industry. It is an association of associations, combining 34 organizations that have represented different parts of West German industry. Those 34 associations were in turn organized into over 500 trade and regional associations before German unification, and they have been pulling together additional associations since unification. The associations represented approximately 80,000 firms totaling over 8 million employees in West Germany, and in a united Germany they may represent about 100,000 firms and 10 million or more employees.

Because of its role in organizing and representing German industry, the BDI has immense influence. Any German government, even one with a Social Democratic majority, would consult with it before making any policy or introducing any legislation that would directly affect German industry or the German economy as a whole. So would key members of the Bundestag, especially as German legislators are becoming more independent in their attitudes and do not follow the government lead on economic policy as much as before. The director general of the BDI, Ludolf von Wartenberg, was himself a member of the Bundestag and a secretary of state in the Economics Ministry.

- The Deutscher Industrie- und Handelstag (DIHT), the German Industry and Trade Association, which is an umbrella organization of the German chambers of commerce. It represents the interests of all business, but especially small business, on a regional as well as sector basis. It organizes the chambers of commerce, which have such highly visible responsibilities as helping to manage vocational training programs, running stock exchanges, and helping to formulate regional economic policy.

The DIHT had 69 domestic chambers in West Germany and added a number of others in the former GDR although the final count will depend on the final industrial and commercial arrangements in Eastern Germany. Membership is obligatory for any German firm, no matter what its size or business, and membership is on an individual or a firm basis, not on an association basis as in the BDI.

The chambers are public law bodies but they are not representatives of the government. They have many roles, whether formally assigned by law and regulation or whether emerging out of the interests of the members or of their groups. They promote the well-being of their industries, consult on legislation that may come before the German federal or state parliaments, interact with government institutions at all levels, and become intimately involved in many aspects of the functioning of the German economy.

Some of the powers of the chambers of commerce in Germany would be exercised by government authorities in almost any other country. They participate in the German vocational training program, issue licenses and work permits, set store hours, solve disputes between members, issue certificates of origin, and so forth. They are legally entitled to make their views known in a variety of governmental fora, from the local to the national level, and they thus have direct as well as indirect influence over many elements of the German economy. Their functions are central to the operations of the German system, as they have been throughout much of German history.

The chambers constitute an important link not only in the formal but also in the informal coordinating mechanisms that operate throughout the German economy. Whereas the BDI may be more visible in national policy matters and may influence national government decisions more directly, the chambers and the DIHT have a more pervasive presence at the local and regional level as well as at the national level. They shape and even set most of the regulations that determine how German commerce and industry will act, helping to establish the day-by-day rules under which production and trade will take place.

- The Bundesvereinigung der Deutschen Arbeitgeberverbände (BDA), the Federation of German Employers' Associations. It coordinates the collective bargaining strategy of West German employers, administers the strike fund, gives legal advice, and deals with matters relating to social policy. It had 44 branches and 13 local organizations in West Germany, representing over 80 per cent of all employers, and has been establishing proportional levels of representation in Eastern Germany. Eight member federations organize enterprises in industry, handicrafts, commerce, banking, agriculture, transportation, insurance, and publishing.

A broad division of labor exists between the separate German employers' associations. The BDI, for which the closest American parallel is the National Associations of Manufacturers, mainly addresses matters of broad economic policy. It is, however, much more influential than any parallel American organization. It has been a powerful force for the development of a strong and competitive German industry and has also played a major role in Germany's foreign economic policy, but it has also been a force for restraint and mutual understanding within the competitive environment. It has helped shape Germany's policies in the European Community and has been a voice for an open trading system, strongly urging German efforts to settle the differences that were blocking completion of the Uruguay Round. It has a strong voice in German parliaments, especially at national and *Land* levels.[12]

The DIHT might be compared to the U.S. Chamber of Commerce. It represents regional interests as well as the interests of medium-sized and smaller enterprises. It exercises a great deal more influence and even authority locally.[13] The BDA concentrates on labor and social legislation and also acts as the representative of German employers with the trade unions.[14]

These organizations also represent part of the continuity of the German experience. The BDI was formally established in 1895 out of several predecessor organizations. The BDA was formed in a similar manner in 1913. The chambers, which emerge out of the German guild tradition of the Middle Ages when they often formed what amounted to an important source of local authority, were formally established around 1800 during the Emperor Napoleon's rule over Germany.[15]

* Deutscher Gewerkschaftsbund (DGB), the Federation of German Trade Unions, an umbrella organization that joins 17 trade unions along industry lines that match those of the BDA. The most powerful trade union, the IG-Metall, had almost 2.5 million steel and iron workers as members in West Germany and stands to gain a number in Eastern Germany. Founded in 1891, it is the largest single trade union in the world. In 1990, it won an agreement in West Germany for a gradual shift to a 35-hour work week by 1995.

The Western Allies favored the development of free German trade unions after World War II to succeed the political mouthpieces that the Nazis had created, and such free unions were reestablished already during the first phase of the occupation. Their creation led to fierce and often violent struggles between Communist and non-Communist factions, especially after it became clear that the unions in the Soviet occupation zone were under Soviet control. Western, and especially American, labor strongly supported the free German trade unions and helped them to prevail. As the trade unions under the GDR regime were unable to survive German unification because of their political taint, West German trade unions under the DGB aegis began to organize and represent East German workers even before unification.

Other trade unions are the Deutscher Beamtenbund (DBB), the civil servant trade union, the Deutsche Angestelltengewerkschaft (DAG), the white-collar trade union, and the Christlicher Gewerkschaftsbund (CGB), the Christian trade union. The armed forces also have a trade union, the Deutscher Bundeswehr-Verband. Trade union membership was not obligatory in West Germany and is not obligatory in united Germany. Fewer than one half of all West German workers were in the trade unions in 1989. German unification led to a rise in trade union membership in absolute and percentage terms because the East German workers were accustomed to union membership. They hoped that membership in the trade unions would give them influence in the many microeconomic decisions that needed to be made with respect to industries and companies, and they appear to have been correct because the trade unions have been a major force to prevent quick closure of even inefficient Eastern German plants.

The West German trade unions began representing the East German workers vigorously as soon as unification came about, to a degree that disturbed unification planners because wages in Eastern Germany began to rise faster than productivity and may have helped deter investors. But the trade unions did not only want to help the Eastern German workers. They also wanted to prevent mass migration and commuting by Eastern workers to the West, depressing wages in Western Germany. They won a number of agreements that will raise East German wages to rough parity by the mid-1990s, with the precise terms varying from industry to industry. But their actions may, in fact, accelerate migration rather than prevent it, as excessively high labor costs are a factor forcing East German plants to close.

The trade unions in West Germany have had a dual function. On the one hand, they have negotiated for their members with employers and have represented their members' interests in general. On the other hand, they have integrated the workers into the economy as a whole, using their economic successes to undercut the traditional socialist argument that the workers in Germany were exploited. They have accepted and defended the principles of the social market economy although they also long sought a "third way" between capitalism and socialism. Some observers have complained that the trade unions in West Germany were not as militant as they should have been, but the trade unions have replied that their policies have helped provide the average West German worker with one of the highest standards of living in the world. There are, in fact, periodic signs that the trade unions may become more militant, and some have seen such signs again in the strike threats issued by IG-Metall in 1991.

The trade unions play roles in the German economy that go well beyond strike calls and pay matters. At all levels, but especially at the state and local levels, they work closely with business and especially with the chambers of commerce in formulating local regulations, arranging for vocational training and other programs, and making certain that the system recognizes the workers' interests on almost a daily basis. Observers of the German economic and labor scene frequently note that no action is taken without the approval of the trade unions whether within any company, any chamber of commerce, or any local jurisdiction. In that sense, the trade unions form as much a part of the total functioning and guidance structure of the economy as the industrial associations.

One of the most important results of German trade union action has been one of the world's most comprehensive social security systems. West Germany itself has had more than 1,500 social insurance funds to administer its social welfare system. Going back to the German Empire's era of national social legislation, they operate insurance funds against illness, accident, and old age. Except for the health insurance funds, which number over a thousand and function under separate authority, the system is highly coordinated although the separate funds are nominally independent. The level of funding of the West German social insurance program has been high ever since the 1970s, with the total sum to be paid out in 1990 amounting to DM 703 billion—or one third of the German GNP. Contributions come in roughly equal shares from employers (31 per cent), workers (29 per cent), and the state (39 per cent).[16]

In part because of the legacies of the Nazi era, but mainly because of the different historical roots of German social security systems, most welfare funds are not managed by the state but independently, although the state helps finance the programs. Only the unemployment funds, administered under the supervision of the Ministry of Labor, are under government control. The East German social security system, which was state-managed, has been amalgamated into the West German system, but complex questions of contribution and payment rates required lengthy and delicate negotiations.

- The Deutscher Bauernverband (DBV), the German Farmers' Union, has organized about one million farmers or about 90 per cent of all West German farmers and has now added many of the former East

German farmers. It has exercised a powerful influence on German and European agricultural policies, keeping prices well above world levels. The proportionate influence of German farmers can be expected to grow as the larger East German farm sector, with the agricultural states of Brandenburg and Mecklenburg-Vorpommern, comes into the all-German economy.

Other groups have existed in West Germany and now exist across all of Germany. They organize and represent every German economic interest group. Altogether, the staffs of these associations at the national, regional, and local level have been estimated to number over 60,000, and their expenditures well over 1 billion DM in Western Germany alone. Those personnel and cost levels are rising in a united Germany but have not been reported.

FUNCTIONS AND QUESTIONS

As can be seen from the above discussions of the individual associations, these groups operated as inside participants in policy formation and execution. Some—like the BDI, the DIHT, or the DGB—have more influence than others. But they all share in the legislative and administrative processes. They may, as appropriate, become involved in drawing up commodity lists—a powerful position of great protectionist potential—and they sit on inter-ministerial committees in an advisory capacity. Because the German system has not given members of the Bundestag independent status, the groups have primarily concentrated on developing contacts with the national, regional, and local bureaucracies, and with party factions as a whole. They establish active and direct contacts with members of the German national, state, and local legislatures, especially at the committee level. They also have direct contact with the political parties. The combination of these contacts offers the groups important opportunities to influence German domestic policy as well as its international role.[17]

Lobbying in Germany is different from that in the United States. The BDI and its associations, or the DIHT, DGB, and others, speak for industries or for an entire productive sector rather than for separate firms. Moreover, different industries, associations, and other organizations do not concentrate on trying to influence individual legislators but on influencing party decisions that will commit entire blocs of votes in the German parliament. The lobby groups usually meet with Bundestag committees and their staffs rather than with individual legislators—except for the most influential. They try to influence parliamentary party groups as a whole, as German parliaments generally vote along party rather than individual lines. When they do address individual legislators, they do so primarily not to persuade those legislators in themselves but to persuade them to use their influence within the parliamentary group as a whole.

There is much less lobbying for separate favors in Germany than in the United States. Except in very rare cases, in which the government also has an interest, German firms will not obtain special legislative allowances or exemptions as they regularly do in the U.S. Congress through an individual legislator or staff member. In fact, German firms regard some of the forms of lobbying that American (and some foreign firms) use in Washington as highly questionable. Lobbies can make contributions to an individual German legislator's campaigns, but such donations are not tax deductible. Nonetheless, the West German parliament and the separate parties have had their share of scandals about the way money has been used and about what it has bought.[18]

The German institutions are, however, far more than lobbies. They act as sector and regional coordinators. Some do not only exercise a voice toward the government but also represent a forum where German industrialists or others can meet legally and talk about business affairs. Some serve as planning institutions, collecting and disseminating information on anticipated sales, production capacities, and investment goals. Others negotiate and settle conflicts between different industries (as within the structure of the BDI), although some conflicts may go higher and may need to be resolved by the Minister of Economics.[19] They also help to settle disputes and to administer the German economic mechanism. One of the most damaging sanctions against aberrant behavior by any participant in the German economic process is disapproval by his or her peer group members if their behavior was not *anständig* (proper).

The groups have established extensive contacts with appropriate European Community offices, adding to the general reputation of Brussels as the world lobbying capital. With more and more European-wide regulations being written in Brussels, the groups attempt in many ways to make their voices heard. They work with the EC bureaucracy within the Commission and through political formations at the European level, and they also attempt increasingly to work through the European Parliament although that institution remains weaker than its national counterparts.

Because the groups exist not only to coordinate and to reconcile the interests of their members but also to exercise influence and even pressure upon firms or legislators, their policies have been controversial and periodically criticized.

Some of their functions, especially their ubiquitous opportunities to lobby the Bundestag and the bureaucracy, have raised more questions than others. They have been accused of establishing a feudal society or of exercising an almost "colonial" influence upon West German governments at various levels, especially because their functions now go increasingly beyond local and even national matters into the realm of international politics through the European Community. They defend their actions by arguing that they have compelled the West German and now the all-German political system to give proper attention to the needs and interests of all participants. But they are still expected to carry out their functions with an eye not only to their particular interests but also to the general good.

More seriously, critics have charged that the Verbände do not only represent their members but also coordinate between them, potentially preventing competition by assigning priorities and responsibilities and even market shares—especially in export markets. They do not do that on the basis of formal legal authority and they do not take actions that have a legally compulsory effect, but they can exercise a powerful collegial pressure for conformity and cooperation that gives German management an element of the "Germany, Inc." image. Similarly, chambers of commerce govern so many aspects of economic activity that they can not only restrict trade but limit entry by regulation or by fiat. They have been influential in making it difficult and even illegal in some instances for stores to offer discounts or to remain open longer in the evenings or on weekends.

The associations vigorously reject any and all charges which suggest that they act in restraint of trade or to curtail competition. Instead, they argue that their only function is to establish sets of rules under which all parties to the economic process have an equal chance. They insist that German firms compete intensely with each other even if they do act jointly to protect common legislative or other interests, and that German goods would not be able to compete effectively across the world if German companies did not find themselves under constant pressure to excel at home.

OBSERVING AND EVALUATING INSTITUTIONS

Beyond these operating institutions are others that have been established to review and evaluate the performance of the West German economy and to offer proposals on how that performance could be improved. The most important of those has been the Sachverständigenrat zur Begutachtung der gesamtwirtschaftlichen Entwicklung, the Council of Economic Experts, which is informally known as *Die Weise*, the "wise men." The Council, consisting of five senior economists and their staff, was established in 1963 to prepare annual and special reports and to offer advice on ways to achieve economic stability and growth.[20] Their annual reports carry weight in the German government and parliament, as well as in the German economic establishment and the press, and they require formal government comment under the 1967 Stability Law. They are among the most searching reports of their kind in any nation, with extensive analyses and statistical appendices. The "wise men" have also been asked to conduct special studies of specific topics as they may arise. They produced one of the most farsighted—but widely ignored—reports on the potential economic consequences of German unification.

The members of the Sachverständigenrat firmly and even sternly perpetuate the legacy of the social market economy. They consistently criticize deviations from free competition and from the free interplay of market forces. They oppose an excessively large state role as well as subsidies and protectionism. They praised the European Community when it lowered trade barriers within Europe, and they have just as consistently denounced the Community when it raised barriers to trade from outside Europe. Their reports have sometimes forced the German government to issue lengthy and somewhat embarrassed explanations, as they have consistently reminded the participants in the German system that the system will function best when it remains true to its original principles. Their advice is not always welcomed and is sometimes ignored, but that has not deterred them.

The members of the Sachverständigenrat take particular pride in asserting that they initiated the global "supply-side" revolution. They already recognized in the mid-1970s that Keynesian policy formulas were not working as predicted. They began advancing the supply-side notion in their 1976/77 report, before Ronald Reagan even became U.S. President. They then saw their ideas progressively accepted during the late 1970s and vindicated in the *Wende* after 1982.[21]

West Germany also created five economic institutes, supported by the Bonn government but independently staffed, to prepare joint or separate reports on the German economy as a whole or on specific topics. The institutes have provided a useful resource for study and evaluation of the West German economy or of international economic developments. Although publicly funded, the institutes are not mouthpieces of the government and may at times say things that the government finds uncomfortable.

The five institutes of West German origin are the Institut für Weltwirtschaft in Kiel, the Ifo-Institut für Wirtschaftsforschung in Munich, the Deutsches Institut für Wirtschaftsforschung in Berlin, the Hamburger Weltwirtschaftliches Archiv, and the Rheinisch-Westphälisches Institut für Wirtschaftsforschung in Essen.

After German unification, several East German economic institutes were evaluated, and the former Ökonomisches Forschungsinstitut of the GDR State Planning Commission in Berlin has become the sixth German economic institute in the united Germany.

Although all the institutes are mandated to follow German economic affairs in broad terms, each may specialize in certain areas. The Berlin DIW, for example, has concentrated mainly on East-West and all-German issues, reporting in detail on the GDR economy before its demise. The Kiel Institute has concentrated on international economics and has published a number of special studies on the structural problems of the West German economy. The Ifo Institute in Munich publishes periodic surveys of business opinion and also publishes, in the *Spiegel der Wirtschaft*, an annual statistical survey of the West German economy. The HWWA in Hamburg specializes in international trade matters as well, and the RWI in Essen analyzes developments in the coal and steel industries as well as global matters.

West Germany also created a body of economic legislation that helped to establish, piece by piece, one of the most complex and far-reaching bodies of Western economic law. That legislation, introduced by different parties as they were in the government, now constitutes a web of law and regulation that is intended at the same time to perpetuate a free market system, to protect participants who may prove to be the losers in the system, and to regulate a number of economic activities. Although it is not as wide or detailed as U.S. regulation, it is extensive enough and is assiduously enforced.[22]

West German legislation and regulation was essentially carried over into East Germany under the State Treaty governing economic unification. It thus functions now in a united Germany. Having been designed for a modern, efficient, wealthy, and essentially stable economy, it now paradoxically constitutes one of the principal barriers to the early revival of Eastern German economic activity. Many pieces of legislation—especially those governing social welfare arrangements—are proving to be ill-suited to conditions in Eastern Germany, where new ventures need more freedom and less regulation. Some investors in Eastern Germany have openly admitted ignoring regulations that would delay start-ups and complicate operations, although they say that they will begin strict compliance as soon as it is possible and reasonable.

NOTES TO CHAPTER THREE

1. Some of this discussion is drawn from a presentation made by Phyllis Berry on the role of the Chancellery in German policymaking, American Institute for Contemporary German Studies, March 21, 1991.

2. Kurt Gönner, Siegfried Lind, and Hermann Weis, *Betriebswirtschaftslehre: Industrie* (Bad Homburg vor der Höhe: Max Gehlen, 1988), p. 473.

3. The best sources of information on the Bundesbank, from which this discussion is mainly drawn, are the publications of the bank itself. They are among the most thorough of any central bank, containing not only an impressive array of statistics but many articles describing the performance of the German economy as well as specific financial issues. In the course of the articles, the Bundesbank also tells much about itself. Also see Ellen Kennedy, *The Bundesbank* (London: Chatham House, 1991), and Roland Sturm, "The Role of the Bundesbank in German Politics," *West European Politics*, April 1989, pp. 1-11.

4. Kennedy, *op. cit*, p. 13.

5. John B. Goodman, "Monetary Politics in France, Italy, and Germany: 1973-85," Paolo Guerrieri and Pier Carlo Padoan, eds., *The Political Economy of European Integration* (New York: Harvester Wheatsheaf, 1989), pp. 192-193.

6. Kennedy, *op. cit.*, p. 27.

7. For details of this discussion, see *Frankfurter Allgemeine Zeitung*, January 17, 1991; *Süddeutsche Zeitung*, January 21, 1991; and *Die Zeit*, February 8, 1991.

8. A legal and societal explanation regarding the functioning of the Bundeskartellamt, especially in comparison with U.S. practice, is contained in Dudley H. Chapman, *Molting Time for Antitrust* (New York: Praeger, 1991), pp. 381-386 (draft); for statistics showing the larger productive share of the principal firms in any sector of the West German economy, see Gilberto Granados and Erik Gurgsdies, *Lern- und Arbeitsbuch Ökonomie* (Bonn: Verlag Neue Gesellschaft, 1985), pp. 287-288.

9. For a statement of this argument, see Fack and Hort, *op. cit.*, pp. 26-30.

10. Chapman, *op. cit.*, p. 383.

11. Katzenstein, *op. cit.*, pp. 24-30; for a comprehensive review of the organizations, their activities, etc., see "Interessenverbände und Interessengruppen," *Informationen zur Politischen Bildung*, #217, October, 1987.

12. Ferdinand Müller-Rommel, "Interest Group Representation in the *Bundestag*," Uwe Thaysen, Roger Davidson, Robert Gerald Livingston, eds., *The U.S. Congress and the German Bundestag* (Boulder: Westview, 1990), pp. 314-357.

13. *Industrie- und Handels-Kammern der Bundesrepublik Deutschland: Aufgaben und Gesetz* (Bonn: Deutscher Industrie- und Handelstag, 1990).
14. For an extensive discussion of the role and history of the BDI and other employers' associations, see Gerard Braunthal, *The Federation of German Industry in Politics* (Ithaca, N.Y.: Cornell University Press, 1965).
15. Elmar Lange, *Marktwirtschaft* (Opladen: Westdeutscher Verlag, 1989), pp. 244-246.
16. FRG, *Sozialpolitische Umschau*, Nr. 198/1990, May 14, 1990.
17. Michael Kreile, "West Germany: The Dynamics of Expansion," Peter J. Katzenstein, *Between Power and Plenty* (Madison: University of Wisconsin Press, 1984), pp. 200-201.
18. See, for example, *Der Spiegel*, May 6, 1991, pp. 87-98.
19. *Ibid.*
20. Katzenstein, *Policy and Politics in West Germany*, pp. 63-64.
21. *Handelsblatt*, March 8/9, 1991, p. D1.
22. The most important pieces of legislation are collected in Kurt Gönner and Robert Wiegel, *Gesetzsammlung für Wirtschaftsschulen* (Bad Homburg vor der Höhe: Max Gehlen, 1986). Summary comments on legislation are in Heinz Lampert, *Die Wirtschafts- und Sozialordnung der Bundesrepublik Deutschland* (Munich: Olzog, 1988), pp. 225-290.

Four

A German Style? Management, Labor, and the Banks

There is a story, perhaps apocryphal, of a group of West European tourists vacationing together at a Turkish lake resort which is engulfed one afternoon by a terrible storm. The storm destroys a long pier that the group has used for boating and fishing. The tourists are distraught, fearing that their vacation is ruined. But Turkish men from a nearby village work all night to repair the pier, and it is rebuilt by the next morning.

The hotel guests marvel at the speed and determination of the villagers. A British tourist, unable to resist a little joke, observes to a German who is with the group: "Aren't these people remarkable? Now, if you Germans had been in charge here, you would have spent at least four weeks analyzing the problem, three months making drawings and immersing yourselves in dozens of volumes of turgid regulations, and three more months recalculating the whole business. You wouldn't have had that pier up again for a year."

"Yes," replies the German, "you are right. But, of course, once we do build it, no storm will ever take it down."

This story, like the review of the German organizations in the last chapter, poses a question. Is there, in the interaction and the behavior of Germany's economic institutions and its people, something that might indeed be termed a German "style"? Is there, perhaps, even the shadowy "Germany, Inc.," suggested, but then discounted, by Helmut Schmidt?

MANAGEMENT

German management, like the German economy as a whole, blends conservatism and dynamism in combinations that are not always predictable and that may vary from industry to industry and from company to company. It goes back to the German guild and merchant tradition, but it also has a sense for the future and for the long term that many others might envy and emulate.[1]

The German style of competition is rigorous but not ruinous. It eschews and condemns what Germans call the *"Ellbogen-Mentalität,"* the "elbow mentality." Although companies may compete for the same general market, as Daimler-Benz and BMW do, they generally look for market share rather than market domination. Many compete for a specific niche. German companies despise price competition. Instead, they engage in what German managers describe as *Leistungswettbewerb*, competition on the basis of achievement, of excellence in their products and services. They usually compete on a price basis only when it is necessary, as in the sale of bulk materials like chemicals or steel. But even then they try to show that their prices are based on, and justified by, specific product attributes.

The German manager at every level concentrates intensely on two objectives: product quality and product service. He wants his company to be the first and the best, and he also wants it to have the best products. The manager and his entire team are strongly product-oriented, confident that a good product will sell itself. But the manager also places a high premium on customer satisfaction, and Germans are ready to style a product to suit a customer's wishes. The product is also usually accompanied by very specific service guidelines, which the customer is expected to follow not only to save money but also to protect quality and preserve the product. Germans do not believe in planned obsolescence. They expect their products to be good and to be respected.

German manufacturers take great pride in their commitment to quality and service. They enjoy repeating stories about German managers and companies who worked under intense pressure, sometimes for years, to remain competitive in quality goods.[2] They tell legendary tales of German service representatives appearing in remote jungles or deserts virtually overnight in response to a call or cable. The watchwords for most German managers and companies are quality, responsiveness, dedication, and follow-up. When you buy the product, you buy the company, and the company does everything to be proud of its products.

Product orientation usually also means production orientation. Most German managers, even at senior levels, understand their production lines and processes. They follow production methods closely. Just as there are countless stories about German quality and service, there are countless stories about German managers who know their shop floors intimately and who are profoundly shocked when visiting American managers want to see financial statements and "the bottom line" rather than to inspect the floor and the machinery.[3] A German manager believes deeply that a good quality production line and a good quality product will do more for the bottom line than anything else that he (or increasingly she) can do.

If there is a third theme beyond quality and service, it is cooperation—or at least coordination—with government. German industry works closely with government. German management will be sensitive to government standards, government policies, and government regulations. Virtually all German products are subject to norms—the *DIN-Deutsche Industrie Normen*—established through consultation between industry and government but with strong inputs from the associations, the chambers, and the trade unions. The concept of private initiative operating within a public framework lies firmly imbedded in the conscience of West German managers. They believe in the link between a cooperative society and individual freedom, and in the implications of this for self-restraint as well as for competition.

The role of government remains an open question for many German managers, especially in larger firms. The West German federal and *Land* governments have always taken a direct interest in business activity. But no clear line has been drawn to separate those areas where the government can help an enterprise from those where it cannot. Nor, outside the rules of the Bundeskartellamt, do business firms and state or federal agencies attempt to delineate their roles and the dividing line between them. It remains an open area, subject to judgment and to evolution. Non-Germans competing in Germany sometimes complain about what they term a "clubby" atmosphere in relations between German companies and their government, but it is probably no more intimate than the links between companies and government in Japan or the links between specific firms and specific legislators in the United States.

The German management style is not litigious. Neither the government, the trade unions, nor the business community encourage litigation where there is no clear sign of genuine and deliberate injury. Firms do not maintain large legal staffs. Disagreements are most often talked out, sometimes over a conference table, sometimes over a beer, and sometimes in a gathering called by a chamber of commerce or an industrial association. Differences are usually settled quietly, often privately. Frequent litigation is regarded as reflecting more on the accuser than on the accused.

Problem-solving takes place within a context of cooperation even in the course of competition and potential confrontation. Few deviate from those principles, which are regarded—in this as in other areas of management behavior—as a *Selbstverständlichkeit,* something that is obvious to every-body and understood by all. The kind of hair-trigger rush to the courts that has come to mark American business practice is not part of the German style. With one third the population of the United States and one fourth the GNP, Germany has less than one fifteenth the number of lawyers. German manag-ers believe that they can come up with much better solutions among them-selves than through a court which takes the decision out of their hands.

German managers are drawn largely from the ranks of engineers and technicians, from those who manufacture, design, or service, although more non-engineers have been rising to the top in recent years. They are better paid than other Europeans (except the Swiss), but on average receive about two thirds of the income that their American counterparts expect. They do not receive the millions and tens of millions of dollars that some American managers receive.

Managers in most West German enterprises usually work their way gradually to the top. University graduates, even if they have studied man-agement, are rarely admitted to senior levels quickly. Instead, they spend time in the factory, with the sales staff, or in other departments of the firm. The new aspirant absorbs the way things are done, the company production and management style, and the history and philosophy of the firm. He or she is expected to learn things, not to change them. The process of bringing managers up through the ranks may inhibit innovation, but it breeds a genuine understanding of what a company produces and of the workers who produce it.

Managers can normally expect to advance progressively within one company for their entire career if they are successful. They are not expected to advance by moving from one company to another too often, preferably not more than once but absolutely not more than twice in a career.[4] German companies do not like to see their management staff leave them and they try to prevent it from happening. There have been debates in Germany about the advantages and disadvantages of what the Germans call "job-hopping" as against company loyalty, but the consensus remains that loyalty pays off in the long run except for persons who have very marketable skills and who—unlike most Germans—are prepared to move themselves and their families frequently.[5]

One distinct advantage of a lifetime career within a company is that a German manager does not need a visible bottom-line result quickly. Manag-ers do not need to be concerned about how their careers might be affected by a company's or a division's progress, or lack of progress, for each year and certainly not for each quarter. German companies do not issue quarterly reports as American companies do, and many issue no reports at all. Small shareholders receive less information, and have fewer rights, than in the United States, although there have been movements to protect shareholders more actively.

Because a manager becomes an expert on the company, its products, customers, and workers, that expertise is in itself regarded as an asset to the firm. The virtue of the periodic shakeup, of the stimulus provided by new blood, is not widely perceived in Germany, especially because most German firms do well without it.

In return for stability and security, a German manager is expected to take responsibility, even under German enterprise laws that require double signatures on many documents. German management is leaner than American. Organization is tight and usually efficient. There are fewer layers of management in German firms than in the United States, even in large enterprises, and fewer ways to obfuscate responsibility. German senior managers are fired more often than those of some other nations when their companies have trouble.[6] German firms with rare exceptions lack the large networks of public relations, legal, marketing, etc., staffs that characterize many American firms.

With fewer levels of coordination and fewer staffs not directly connected with production, finance, sales, or service, there is a greater simplicity and directness of purpose than one may encounter in many American firms. There is more commitment to the success of the firm as a whole rather than to a specific division or cell within the firm. There is also a measure of informality even within a hierarchical structure, especially as junior managers may meet with seniors far more often than they do in American or multinational companies.

Because management has not been generally regarded in Germany as a separate science, it has until recently not been separately taught. A number of German universities have courses in business administration, or *Betriebs-Wirtschaft*, producing a *Betriebs-Wirt* degree. The German vocational system also trains in business administration, producing a *Diplom-Kaufmann* as a graduate. But those schools strive to provide knowledge of current enterprise operations rather than of management as a separate discipline. German bookstores carry shelves of books on various aspects of operating a business, but few German texts on management technique in itself. Those books are usually in English and written by Americans. They are read and even studied with considerable interest, but the personal flexibility, career mobility, and pressures for early and singular achievement that lie at the core of American management doctrine and practice have little parallel in Germany.

Germans sometimes observe wryly, and not entirely in jest, that one reason for the economic achievements of the Federal Republic has been that Germany does not have a graduate management school like those at Harvard or Stanford universities. Some believe that management as a separate discipline breeds selfishness, disloyalty, bureaucratic maneuvering, short-term thinking, and a dangerous tendency to neglect quality production.

Despite this, a group of German industrialists founded Germany's first private university for business administration, the Hochschule für Unternehmensführung, at Koblenz in 1984. They did this in part to preserve the German system of thinking by making it unnecessary for Germans to go abroad to study management, but also to give German students an understanding of management methods. Koblenz does, however, require a year of foreign study in the degree program.

There is also a "European Business School" at Offenbach, somewhat more oriented to producing managers for small and medium-sized *Mittelstand* firms than for the large companies where Koblenz graduates would normally go. Graduates from either school are sought by German business, as are graduates of some German universities making special efforts to introduce management studies. But these developments do not yet represent a major shift in German managerial thinking or practice. The schools do not teach techniques that would undercut the German commitment to quality production or to direct lines of responsibility.[7]

German taxation, based on the system that has existed in West Germany, also induces toward long-term planning. German tax legislation and accounting practices permit German firms to allocate considerable sums to reserves, often in ways that do not appear as separate assets on the balance sheet. The tax authorities accept reserve allocations for accelerated depreciation, bad debts, or other contingencies, provided the reserves are available to the firm and related to its business. This has enabled and even encouraged West German management to enlarge such assets.[8]

The ability to subtract such costs from profits means that West German enterprises have paid only somewhat more tax than the West European average. Actual tax rates may average about 30 per cent, whereas on paper they appear at over 50 per cent. The lower actual rates and the reserve resources enable companies to acquire assets with a minimum of debt and to confront a deflationary economic environment with considerably better prospects than many non-German firms. They also, however, can tempt corporations to place funds into such reserves rather than into new product lines that might be more productive even if they are more risky. To encourage investment in Eastern Germany, the all-German government had to provide special tax and investment incentives that would outweigh the advantages of large reserves.

The German inclination toward long-term planning is reinforced by German capital gains tax rules. Tax laws exempt capital gains income if the assets are held for more than six months or, in the case of real estate, for more than two years. This especially militates against short-term speculation or asset manipulation. It also combines with the general tax system to place a premium on long-term increases in asset value rather than on income growth in itself.

German business managers and the Bundesbank do not always think alike. The bank complicates the task of export-oriented German managers by keeping the D-Mark so strong that export prices rise with the currency. This puts producers under constant pressure and helps explain German productivity growth. On the other hand, a German manufacturer can be confident that inflation will not distort production costs, turn the terms of trade against him, or encourage allocation of resources to nonproductive assets. The real cost of funds to German manufacturers is normally much lower than to those in other countries (often half or less than half of that in the United States), although it began to rise in 1989 and 1990. These factors have been crucial in permitting the kind of effective long-term planning evident in West Germany. The fixed income that many German companies receive from invested reserves only adds to their opposition to inflation.

The German system exercises a reverse pressure on the Bundesbank as well. Because German firms do not normally engage in price competition and because they have such large reserves, prices rarely fall quickly and sharply even during a recession. The West German cost of living has fallen in only one year since 1960. Moreover, the long-standing existence of several subsidized manufacturing sectors in West Germany (see Chapter 5) has introduced structural barriers to price declines. The Bundesbank therefore knows that it cannot count on a swift price response when it tightens credit and that it must anticipate inflationary forces more than other central banks..

Relations between German managers and workers are often close. The German manager, and even the president of a middle-sized German firm, usually knows many workers or at least the foremen. Some of those workers or foremen may be seen in the senior manager's or in other managers' offices, with the foreman or the worker making suggestions and the manager listening carefully. Managers respect good workers as a military officer respects good soldiers and especially good noncommissioned officers.

The German manager does not forget his or her obligations and responsibilities after normal working hours. The manager must also reflect and foster the company's role within the community. A manager's relationship with the workers and their families is close within a small or a *Mittelstand* firm, especially in a small town. In companies of that size, it is normal and expected that the company or the division manager or his wife will appear at a worker's funeral or at the funeral of a worker's wife or husband. If a worker falls ill, the manager is expected to send flowers. Even in the giant and rather impersonal steel, coal, or chemical firms, where relations between management and labor are much less intimate and more confrontational than in small companies, supervisors are expected to maintain some personal contact with workers, although relations of German supervisors with foreign workers have not been as close as with German workers.

The German manager, as he or she rises, also develops good ties with other managers by participation in trade associations. At meetings of local and national organizations, the managers come to know each other. They especially come to know others in their trade. They do not regard conversations about business as collusion, as Americans might. Instead, they regard it as a discussion of common interests and problems. They also regard it as normal to discuss their problems with government or labor officials in informal settings.

Out of this compendium arises what might be termed a German management style, with the following characteristics:

- Collegial, more than hierarchical or individualistic.
- Oriented to achieving consensus, not issuing orders.
- Conscious of the employees, and respectful of their expertise.
- Closely attentive to the company's product, to quality, precision, and service.
- Loyal to one company and its long-term prospects.
- Long-term, not short-term, oriented, and to innovation by evolution, not revolution.
- As a price for this, less apt than American or Asian managers to react quickly to new developments.
- Committed to foreign market position, even at the cost of temporary losses.
- Involved in the affairs of the local and national business community.
- Committed to work, but not at the expense of other activities; "quality" work, not "quantity" work.[9]

With rare (and widely commented) exceptions, the German management style is deceptively modest, even to the point of using titles that conceal true powers and responsibilities.10 But, although there are few "stars" among German managers, a number of senior managers are very widely respected within their profession and they do not hesitate to make decisions or to present their views at any level.

Certain aspects of German management style have grown out of the West German experience since 1945, but most go back much further in German history. If a German manager from the 1890s were to be brought by a time machine to the 1990s, he might find certain things to be strikingly new and different—such as the speed and reliability of transport and communications, the presence of women in at least some management positions, the greater distance from government and from other companies, or the European Community—but in many ways he would feel right at home. He would understand the mix of formality and collegiality within the firm and within the industry, the yearning for stability and long-term planning, the search for foreign markets and the concern about terms of trade, and above all the commitment to quality, service, and responsibility.

THE *MITTELSTAND*

The glory of West German production has not been in the big West German firms that are well-known around the world, such as Daimler-Benz, Volkswagen, Siemens, Allianz, or Bayer. It has been in the small and medium-sized firms that comprise what the Germans call the Mittelstand. Although that term has a political and social as well as management connotation, it has been widely accepted to mean companies that employ less than 500 workers.11 Those firms constitute 98 per cent of all German companies, hire 80 per cent of all German employees, are responsible for a significant share of exports, and provide one of the foundations of the German middle class.

West German medium and small firms have been consistently better at innovation than larger firms, either in their production techniques or in the products themselves. They have often created more new jobs than larger firms, and were often hiring even as large companies were laying off workers. Between 1970 and 1987, employment in West Germany grew at the firms of the Mittelstand but decreased in the largest companies.12

The West German government supported and furthered the Mittelstand, in part for political reasons but also because it made a crucial contribution to the German economy. The government established special provisions that permit those firms to cooperate if they do not thereby hinder competition, and after the Wende it also provided favorable tax and depreciation arrangements. In 1989, the West German government provided special funds to promote research and development in *Mittelstand* companies.[13] The united German government is now trying to encourage *Mittelstand* companies to invest in Eastern Germany.

The precise profitability and financial situation of *Mittelstand* companies is unknown. Many of them are family-owned or privately held firms, and few publish detailed reports (if, indeed, they publish reports at all). But every indication suggests that the firms are conservatively managed, profitable, and in strong financial condition.

The fact that the *Mittelstand* firms are small does not mean that they are insignificant or that they are parochial. Many have large export earnings. Some of the specialized companies, like those that make printing equipment or laser drills, have worldwide niche markets in which they are so outstanding that they have no real competition.

THE LABOR STYLE

German labor has as much of a unique style as German management. The abilities and the attitudes of the West German labor force have contributed at least as much to the success of the West German system as have those of West German management, and perhaps even more so. One of the main tasks of German unification will be to integrate the labor system used by East German workers into the system used in West Germany.

Although Karl Marx was a German, many modern West German workers have departed radically from Marxist thinking or from the Marxist model, especially in a small or medium-sized firm. They regard themselves as serious professionals, and are normally treated as such. They live in comfortable circumstances, hardly as the factory workers of old. They may travel abroad, own foreign property, or otherwise lead lives that had formerly been reserved for the middle class.

Even the workers in large companies have lost a good deal of their class spirit, but the conflict and tensions between management and labor rise almost in direct proportion to the size of the company and the degree to which the company relies on unskilled as against a skilled labor force.

West German workers have consistently had the highest level of education of any group of workers in the West, with much of that education acquired after they finished formal secondary school training.[14] About one and a half million West Germans, or almost half of the 15-19 age group in both sexes, have annually received vocational training within a range of about 400 designated occupational specialties, often on the basis of contracts with preselected employers.[15] Like many German programs, this one has a long history going back to the craft guilds of the Middle Ages.

Worker training usually lasts two to three years and may last longer for highly specialized vocations. Shorter programs have occupied almost another 20 per cent of the 15-19 age group, so that at any given time about 70 per cent of any German age contingent between 15 and 19 years of age may be engaged in one or another form of vocational training. East Germany had a similar program, with 385,000 persons engaged in training during 1988, and the training of East German workers was nominally more advanced than that of Western labor, although many could not use their advanced training because East German industry did not use the necessary equipment.[16]

The German vocational training system has come under some criticism for allegedly being too rigid or for permitting industrialists to exploit cheap laborers by pretending to educate them.[17] It has also had difficulty adjusting fully to the needs of the East German trainees who have a very different background. But it has helped create one of the firmest foundations of German economic success.

Many of the generalizations that can be made about West German labor have not applied equally to the foreign workers who have come to constitute about one tenth of the West German labor force. Nor could they have been applied to the foreign workers in the former East Germany. The foreigners often work in the very large companies at menial tasks under difficult conditions, at assembly lines or in mining and chemical operations with little prospect for advancement. Many came to Germany temporarily, expecting to return as soon as they had saved enough money. Many do not become consumers. Many do not believe that they are part of German society, and they are not encouraged to believe it. But they have often remained much longer than they expected and some have even settled. This has been a difficult choice in a land that has no tradition of immigration. Some foreign workers or—more often—their children are beginning to move into the mainstream of the German work force, but it has taken a long time.

Liselotte Funcke, who was asked to undertake special responsibilities for foreign workers by the West German government, complained bitterly in a 1991 report that foreign workers in Germany were not given equal chances at training, promotion, or integration. She wrote that foreigners often found themselves in dead-end jobs and that their children were not given equal opportunities with Germans.[18] Legislation that has been passed may facilitate full integration, at least in the second or third generation, but progress has been painfully slow. Only about one third of foreign young people in Germany enter the labor training programs, as opposed to the overwhelming proportion of Germans who enter them, although the percentage among the foreigners has been gradually increasing over the years.[19] Mrs. Funcke resigned her position in June 1991 to protest what she regarded as inadequate support from the government. As she resigned, she reiterated her demand for a firmer government commitment to the integration of foreign workers.

Although there are many fields to choose from in German vocational training, most apprentices have selected about 20 specializations. The young men prefer training in manufacturing, crafts, carpentry, electronics, or painting. The young women prefer training in sales, industrial purchasing, office or banking work, or medical assistance. Even while they are in training, the students may receive up to DM 1,200 in salary a month, although most receive less than that, down to DM 255. It is a constant complaint among German women that they receive lower vocational training salaries then men, although the men insist that this is because men tend to concentrate in the higher-paid specialties (such as carpenter, construction worker, mechanic, etc.).[20]

The West German vocational training system has been administered jointly by the West German states, various economic sectors, the chambers of commerce, trade unions, and German business. The training system and the examinations are designed and produced cooperatively by employers' associations, trade unions, and the public sector of schools and various levels of government. The trainee normally signs on for a certain company and training course and then works at that firm for three or more days a week, in positions that change with his or her skills. The remainder of the five-day week is normally spent at a state vocational training center. More than two thirds of German help-wanted advertisements list specific vocational qualifications, and persons who cannot show that they meet those qualifications need not apply.

After finishing vocational training, German students can go to technical universities or polytechnical colleges located all over Germany, or to public health or nursing colleges, and they can move on to advanced specialization courses in programs for continuing education. Those systems exist separately from the academic colleges and universities but may be as demanding.

Not all industries require the same level of technical training. Machine tool manufacturers need designated craftsmen or skilled production workers for over 80 per cent of their blue-collar positions, but automobile manufacturers or the chemical industry can do with fewer.[21] For persons who want to maintain, change, or improve their skills, the West German state spent DM 6.3 billion in 1989 for special retraining programs.[22]

The programs in West Germany have been expensive for industry as well as government. One estimate holds that West German industry pays about DM 35 billion annually to support the program.[23] Siemens in 1989 spent DM 700 million on such programs, with more than 20,000 employees enrolled at any given time. The philosophy governing the expenditure of time and money was articulated by the head of personnel at Volkswagen, who said: "Training costs money; not to train costs a great deal more money."[24]

West German youth unemployment remains among the lowest in any industrialized state, largely because of the training programs. They offer a popular and widely accepted transition from school to work. It is not considered a disgrace or a fall from social status to enter such a training program instead of further academic studies. One of the reasons is that skilled workers can move gradually into supervisory positions and perhaps even into management, especially in small firms but sometimes even in larger companies.

The high level of training of German workers has produced a "quality time" labor productivity formula. The German worker spends fewer hours a year at work than any competitor, averaging an annual 1,708 hours compared to 1,763 in France, 1,778 in Britain, 1,912 in the United States, and 2,166 in Japan.[25] Yet West Germany has had the highest share of world trade in goods with a high skill content: 20 per cent, as against 17 per cent for Japan, 15 per cent for the United States, and 7 per cent for France.[26]

The main problem for industrial training in West Germany has been the slowly declining numbers of young persons entering the work force. Between 1985 and 1995 the number of 20- to 25-year-olds is expected to fall from 3.5 to 2.3 million in West Germany.[27] The somewhat larger proportion of young people in the East German population as well as the expected decline in the size of the German armed forces will provide some compensation for this, but probably not enough. The number of persons entering West German job training programs has been declining steadily since 1986 and the number of program vacancies reached new highs in 1989 and 1990.[28] Despite this shortfall, or perhaps because of it, German industry appears all the more determined to maintain the programs in order to make certain that as many young employees as possible are properly trained.

CODETERMINATION

Mitbestimmung—codetermination—under which German workers or their representatives sit on the governing boards or the factory councils of most German firms, is a classic example of how the German system reconciles apparent opposites and points them to a common purpose and in a common direction. The apparent opposites are labor and management. The common purpose is the success of the company. The common direction is efficient production.

When *Mitbestimmung* was first introduced in West Germany after World War II, partly under pressure from British occupation authorities at the direction of the new British Labour government, many foreign and even some German businessmen feared that German firms would become impossible to manage under the system. American investors in Germany had deep reservations, as did American officials.[29] But *Mitbestimmung* landed on fertile soil, where it was understood for what it could do to promote rather than hinder production. Rudimentary forms of codetermination had existed in German thought and practice for over a hundred years before the arrival of the Allied occupation authorities. The 1848 Frankfurt Assembly planned for factory councils in which workers would be represented. The German Empire's 1916 draft law obliged all employers to establish committees with worker participation. More relevant to the postwar experience was the absolute determination of West German government, management, and labor to avoid repeating the management-labor conflicts that had helped to destroy the Weimar Republic.

The present system of *Mitbestimmung* did not come about as a single step. It evolved and expanded through five different West German laws, beginning in 1951 and continuing in 1952, 1954, 1972, and 1976. The first three laws were passed with the Christian Democratic Union as the principal partner in the German governing coalition and the latter two with the Social Democratic Party in that role.

Each of the separate laws established codetermination over different types or sizes of organizations:

- The 1951 law brought codetermination to the *Montan* industries, those producing coal, iron, and steel in the European Coal and Steel Community.
- The 1952 law covered small corporations and small limited-liability companies, those with more than 500 but less than 2,000 employees.
- The 1954 law covered civil servants, such as federal, state, and municipal employees as well as railroad and postal workers.
- The 1972 law, perhaps the most sweeping, covered all firms with at least five employees.

- The 1976 law covered corporations and limited-liability companies with more than 2,000 employees, but that had not been covered under the *Montan* law.

Through the combination of those laws, 85 per cent of all West German employees have been included in some form of codetermination, and a roughly similar percentage of all German employees will probably be covered in united Germany after the industrial reorganization is complete.

Codetermination takes place basically through two structures, the *Aufsichtsrat* (supervisory board) in a large enterprise or the *Betriebsrat* (factory council) in the smaller companies. Many large firms have both.[30]

The *Aufsichtsrat*, as the senior body of any large firm, must have one-third worker representation for an enterprise between 500 and 2,000 employees, or one-half worker representation for an enterprise with 2,000 employees or more. Even when there is parity, however, the deciding voice is with management in the event of a tie. Membership on the supervisory board gives the employees a strong voice in overall company policy as well as good information about the health of the company. It does not, however, involve them in detailed management decisions, which are reached by the *Vorstand* (management board) at a level below the *Aufsichtsrat*. The *Aufsichtsrat* thus gives employees a voice in broad policy matters but not operational issues.

The *Betriebsrat* is at the operational level, almost opposite in an organization chart from the *Aufsichtsrat*. It is composed exclusively of employees and can vary with the size of the company. It exists in most German firms and gives their employees a voice in—but no direct control over—such matters as personnel planning, production shifts, company moves, construction, and other operational questions. It has no management authority but offers employees a running opportunity to make their views known and felt on a wide range of management problems. It is in many ways a more important form of codetermination than the *Aufsichtsrat*, despite its relatively lower ranking within a company's organizational chart, because it deals with many issues of immediate concern to the workers and because it is a far more prevalent form of worker participation. Over two thirds of all German firms have a *Betriebsrat*, and only about a quarter have an *Aufsichtsrat*. Where a firm is large enough to have both, the workers are twice represented—at the top and in the center of the operation.

Under the provisions of the codetermination laws, employees have real influence. They can and do participate in decisions on such diverse questions as hiring and firing, closing or relocating a plant or the firm itself, merging with another firm, basic direction of the company, or new production processes. Their participation is not as complete as the trade unions wished. The workers' representatives on the supervisory board represent not only the blue-collar workers but also the white-collar workers, and the chair of the supervisory board who has the deciding voice is chosen by a majority of the shareholders' representatives in large corporations.[31]

The degree of influence, and the spirit in which it is exercised, varies in relation to the size of the firm and to its line of business. In larger firms, especially those in which there is more unskilled than skilled labor, codetermination can soften but not fundamentally alter the tensions that can and do arise between labor and management. In smaller firms, the spirit has been more cooperative and codetermination has indeed become a form of common management.

The manner in which codetermination has been carried out in West Germany has been at least as important as the texts of the laws governing the institution. Few issues, especially those of fundamental importance, are brought to a vote. They are resolved as much as possible by a process of compromise and conciliation. In a long period of widespread prosperity and little industrial upheaval, bitterly divisive issues like mass firings or plant closings have rarely arisen. But *Mitbestimmung* has not been tested in a financial crisis, a depression, or a restructuring that might make whole sectors or industries obsolete.

One study of the effects of 20 years of codetermination concluded that it had led to "a mutual incorporation of capital and labor by which labor internalizes the interests of capital just as capital internalizes those of labor," and in which labor usually prefers having labor-management conflicts resolved by negotiation or arbitration instead of by conflict.[32] The *Betriebsrat* has, in fact, often assumed a de facto "co-management" role.[33] Berthold Beitz, managing director of Krupp, was quoted as saying that German business would have had to invent codetermination if it had not been legislated.[34]

The result of 40 years of codetermination has been the kind of bargain that is typical of how the German economy is managed, and that accounts to a considerable degree for its success. Management can largely direct the functioning of the company. It makes investment, financial, operational, and market decisions, but it makes those decisions through a mechanism in which labor can articulate its views. Labor can make certain that the conditions under which the workers must operate are socially acceptable, and can also make certain that the workers benefit from the company's well-being. But labor in turn has a stake in ensuring that the demands and actions of the workers do not jeopardize the firm itself or cost them their jobs.

Under *Mitbestimmung*, therefore, labor and management become more partners than opponents in the continuation of their company and in a gradual process of evolution that maintains the firm and the positions that they hold and for which they have been trained. Critics can say that labor has been co-opted and has fallen into a tender trap in which it has been less effective than if it had been able to criticize management and capital from the outside. But most German labor leaders have favored the practice, and German labor clearly feels comfortable with it. It is almost certainly one of the principal reasons why Germany loses far fewer man-days to strikes than almost any other country.

THE ROLE AND THE POWER OF THE BANKS

Like management and labor, banking has formed an integral element in the establishment and the success of the German economy. Banks provide most of the investment capital in West Germany because of the high German savings rate and because most Germans prefer to put those savings into a bank rather than into stocks or bonds. German companies have a much higher ratio of debt to equity than American companies, although not as high as Japanese companies.

As with many other German economic phenomena, this bank role is not new. Banks have played a central role in German financial and economic history, especially in commercial and industrial growth, since the Middle Ages, and they provided the capital for German industrial expansion during the nineteenth century.[35] Their role in West Germany has, however, generated some controversy because of their immense influence across the spectrum of German industry.

German banks function as universal banks, able to offer a full range of banking, saving, foreign exchange, and investment services to their depositors and clients. They may hold funds or other assets, broker securities, underwrite equity issues, give advice on asset placement, manage accounts, and so on. About a quarter of German banks are commercial. Most of the remainder are savings banks, mainly owned locally or regionally and operating under public statutes, or cooperatives that may perform such specialized services as agricultural, crafts, or mortgage lending. German banks are not as large as the major Japanese banks or as such American giants as Citicorp, but they are sizable by continental European standards and they are growing.

The three best-known and most important West German universal banks, the Deutsche Bank, the Dresdner Bank, and the Commerzbank, have been omnipresent throughout West Germany and West Berlin. They also moved rapidly to expand into the former East Germany as soon as the Wall collapsed. They were among the first West German institutions to establish offices on former East German territory, moving in even before plans for monetary union were announced. They opened hundreds of new offices. They sent thousands of bankers from Western to Eastern Germany to manage their offices and to train permanent personnel.

But the "big three," as they are often known, are not the only large banks in Germany. A number of other banks, including regional banks, may even be more important than the "big three" within their areas of operations. The DG Bank, which operates out of Frankfurt, has a higher nominal capital stock than that of the Commerzbank. The Düsseldorf Westdeutsche Landesbank, owned in part by the state of North Rhine-Westphalia, has a higher nominal capital stock value than that of the Deutsche Bank. The value of the combined nominal stock of the three major banks in Bavaria is even higher, and those banks are omnipresent in Bavaria and have helped finance the industrial boom in Southern Germany. Other major banks exist in other states, often owned in part by the states themselves with additional capital coming from state-wide savings associations or other local institutions.[36]

The role of the banks in the West German economy has raised questions. Many political figures, including FDP leader Count Otto Lambsdorff, have charged that the banks have accumulated excessive power by sitting on supervisory boards and by holding bonds or shares of many large German enterprises. West German newspapers and magazines, including business journals, periodically make the same charge.[37]

It has been estimated that banks directly or indirectly hold more than 25 per cent of the voting capital in a quarter of Germany's largest corporations and have about 28 per cent of all members of the supervisory boards.[38] They are empowered to vote not only their own shares but also, by proxy, shares that they may hold for their clients. This *Depotstimmrecht* is controversial in Germany, especially as banks tend to vote with management for all the shares that they represent. Although there are indications that the banks' ownership proportion of major firms has been reduced over time as other sources of investment funds have become more available, the combined influence and presence of the banks must be regarded as considerable. They often join supervisory boards not by virtue of a share holding but because they have sold bonds for a corporation or made loans to it.[39] They are said to pool information on the basis of which they steer investments throughout the economy.[40] But they may have different interests from those of the enterprise itself.

A periodic Commerzbank listing of ownership of 10,000 large West German publicly and privately owned and traded companies indicates that the role of the banks has spread across the spectrum of the West German economy.[41] According to the 1988 listing, the Deutsche Bank owns shares in 77 different firms, the Dresdner Bank in 55, and the Commerzbank itself in 48. Other state-wide and smaller banks may be less broadly invested, as are major German companies (Siemens, 39, Bayer Leverkusen, 31, Preussag, 23, and Krupp, 17). The Commerzbank listing does not show the bond or loan holdings of the banks, nor the votes they exercise in proxy, and thus understates the banks' influence on industrial corporations. It does show, however, that in pure ownership terms alone the banks have a strong voice in a significant number of major German corporations, many of which operate internationally.

The positions that banks have taken range across the broad spectrum of German production and services. The Deutsche Bank owns 28 per cent of Daimler-Benz and 10 per cent of Krauss-Maffei. It has significant share ownership in major insurance and reinsurance firms, such as Allianz Holding and Munich Re (which in turn have other holdings including in each other), in the Karstadt department store chain, the Philipp Holtzmann construction company, Hapag Lloyd shipping, Heidelberger Zement, and many other firms in such diverse fields as industrial holding, utilities, agricultural trading, regional and sector banking, mortgage financing, real estate or capital asset management, and venture capital.[42] This has given the Deutsche Bank, as well as other banks on a smaller scale, a wide reach into every aspect of the German economy, especially because their asset management and venture capital holdings penetrate into many other firms as well. But banks do not necessarily have exclusive relations with certain firms. Although Deutsche Bank may own shares in Allianz, Allianz owns 23 per cent of Dresdner Bank and is in turn owned in part by Dresdner.

The positions that the banks hold in German firms afford wide opportunities to influence industrial decision-making although they are far from the kinds of true monopoly positions that the earlier German cartel arrangements offered. Nor is it unusual for any two or all three of the major German banks or of important regional banks to own shares in the same enterprises, especially in venture capital and capital management firms. They can thus exercise joint influence as well as monitor the broad policies that their competitors are pursuing. They can, of course, also determine the kinds of industrial ventures that they will support or reject, and can thus shape the future as well as the present course of German enterprise.

A mid-1980s study by the West German Monopolkommission, looking only at major companies, concluded that the influence of the banks in West Germany's 100 largest corporations was quite significant. It reported that the banks held a major voting share in 32 of these corporations through the combination of their own capital shares, the seats that they held due to loans they had made, and the votes that they were authorized to exercise for what it called the *Streukapital*—the shareholders who, either because their equity participation was small or for other reasons, would permit the banks to vote on their behalf.[43] As a sample, it showed that the three major banks could vote significant percentages of the following major German corporations, whereas all banks together had even greater voting authority:

Firm	Major Bank Voting Shares	All Bank Voting Shares
Siemens	32.52 %	79.83 %
Daimler-Benz	61.66 %	69.34 %
Volkswagen	7.98 %	19.53 %
Bayer	54.50 %	95.76 %
BASF	51.68 %	96.64 %
Höchst	63.48 %	98.34 %
Thyssen	32.62 %	59.11 %
Average (of these and 24 other firms)	45.44 %	82.67 %

Of the 45 per cent that the three major banks could vote on average, approximately 21 per cent could be voted by the Deutsche Bank, 15 per cent by the Dresdner Bank, and 9 per cent by the Commerzbank.[44]

The power of the banks also manifests itself in the seats they hold on the boards of Germany's most important corporations, and here Deutsche Bank again leads the field. Hilmar Kopper, the head of the bank, sits inter alia on the board of Daimler-Benz and of Klöckner-Humboldt-Deutz. Other members of the Deutsche Bank board sit on the boards of such giant firms as Bertelsmann (publishing), Hapag-Lloyd, Continental (tires), and Hösch (steel), as well as of many smaller firms in which Deutsche Bank also has an interest.[45] This gives the bank not only a considerable fund of information on the state of the German and even the global economy, but also enables it to influence the directions that much of German industry will take.

A poll conducted in mid-1989 suggested that the influence of the banks had grown during the 1980s, even if their share ownership had perhaps declined. When 500 firms were asked whether the power of the banks had risen or fallen during the decade, 49 per cent of the firms replied that it had risen and 45 per cent replied that it had remained constant. Only 3 per cent replied that it had fallen.[46] The poll also showed that the banks tended especially to exercise their influence when it came to financial decisions, company financial structure, and investments. About one fifth of the firms complained that the influence of the banks on their firms' decisions was too great, with the main complaints coming from companies in trade and construction. Forty per cent of the respondents also expressed the view that the power of the banks should be limited.

Two specific proposals for limitation of bank power have been made. One is that banks be prevented from owning more than 5 or 10 per cent of the shares of any other enterprise. The German *Monopolkommission* first made this proposal in 1976 after completing a study of bank investments. It reiterated the proposal in 1978, and others have periodically advanced the same suggestion.[47] Another is that West German banks should no longer serve both as investment and commercial banks because they may make their commercial loan decisions on the basis of their investment portfolio, refusing loans to entrepreneurs who might compete against firms in which the banks have major investment shares.[48]

The same proposal for splitting bank functions emerged from another study which concluded that West German banks that functioned both as investment and commercial banks had so much information that they could not avoid the temptation to base their loan decisions on their investment interests.[49] It observed that the main reasons why enterprises with significant bank shares had high profits might not be the help and advice that banks could offer them but the refusal of the banks to finance competitors. If that was true, then banks would be acting in restraint of competition and using their interest to hold back the German economy as a whole. This would prevent new blood from entering German industry and would jeopardize Germany's international position.

Alfred Herrhausen, the chief of the Deutsche Bank who was assassinated by terrorists in 1989, replied to criticisms of "bank power" by stating that the power of the banks had been wildly overestimated.[50] By widening the base for discussion to the entire breadth of the German economy instead of only to the major firms, he could state that a Bundesbank study had shown that German banks held only 8 per cent of all securities at the end of 1988, and that this share was dwarfed by the 40 per cent held by the entrepreneurs themselves. He reaffirmed that banks had reduced their participation in German industry since the 1960s, often voluntarily, and he insisted that the banks did not seek the securities of German industrial firms in order to play a role in the production process itself. He also pointed out that the bankers who took part in the meetings of the supervisory boards were for the most part not acting for themselves but for their shareholders, for their depositors, and for those who had given them their proxies.

Both Herrhausen and the critics of the banks appear to be correct. The German banks do not appear to want to seize industrial power or to make production decisions. They would be hard put to exercise monopoly power, and their actions on individual boards would clearly be subject to enough scrutiny—at least by other board members—that improper actions would become widely known. Nor are the banks and the roles that they play normally regarded as unhelpful. If one fifth of all firms object to the influence of the banks, the other four fifths do not.

In fact, the German concept of the *"Haus Bank,"* or "house bank," in many ways represents an extension of management. The house banker not only participates in meetings of the supervisory board. He or she (or they—as a firm can have more than one house banker) would be expected to follow the affairs of the company closely between board meetings, offering services and financing where appropriate or necessary. The bankers and the managers would also expect to meet frequently (often in the banker's office). Over time, the bank and the firm could begin to think alike, each shaping the thinking of the other.

The real question, thus, is not whether German banks have and exercise "power" as such, but the direction in which they may exercise the influence that they do have. That direction is normally quite predictable. With respect to bonds or loans, they want the firms to be able to meet their interest payments and ultimately to pay off the debt. Even when they own stock in a company, German banks (except in their venture holdings) normally do not seek rapid capital gains as much as steady income growth at low risk. They may treat the shares that they own more as if they were bonds than stocks. They want appreciation that will exceed the inflation rate, preferably by more than the real interest rate, but they do not encourage management to look for gains at the cost of greater risk.

Those who want to see a more dynamic German entrepreneurial spirit could well complain that banks by their nature have to make decisions on a different basis than those on which an entrepreneur should operate, and that the banks should not be so central to the business process. The frequently stated justification for large bank holdings to the effect that they prevent hostile takeovers may mask the more pertinent argument that large bank holdings do not challenge managers more than they wish to be challenged. Whatever else may be said or thought about it, the complex web of bank power and influence does not serve the Schumpeterian ideal of dynamic entrepreneurship.

All available evidence suggests that German business is on the whole prepared to accept the power and influence of the banks and to see it perpetuated, despite the criticisms of bank power that have emanated from the FDP and also on occasion from German trade unions. There are, in fact, a number of advantages for many business firms in the association with the banks and in the system under which the banks are the primary financing agents for business:

- Instead of having to dilute ownership and perhaps control by going to the markets for new funds, a firm can turn to the banks and can expect smooth long-term relations with bankers prepared to understand its problems and unlikely to challenge management.
- Bankers can exchange information more discreetly and sometimes more quickly than markets can (if perhaps not as efficiently).
- Bankers are usually prepared to accept lower dividend payments than stockholders.
- Large bank ownership percentages can block hostile takeover attempts. This protects managers, although it also obliges them to work with the bank.

Large bank holdings may even serve national political ends. When Friedrich Karl Flick wanted to sell his blocking minority (25 per cent plus) share in Daimler-Benz in 1975 and the Shah of Iran expressed an interest in buying it, a combination of Daimler-Benz, the West German government, and Deutsche Bank arranged for the shares to be bought by a trust, Mercedes Automobil Holding, created especially for the purpose and financed by Deutsche Bank. That trust still holds slightly more than 25 per cent, as directed, and in combination with Deutsche Bank's other holdings and other votes it serves to protect the company from unfriendly takeovers (although Kuwait owns 14 per cent).[51]

Whatever criticisms might be made of German banks for their power and influence, it appears unlikely that they could be criticized for reckless behavior or for casual lending practices. They occupy some of the highest capital-adequacy rankings under the Basel rules, negotiated through the Bank for International Settlements (BIS), which will by 1993 require a capital ratio of at least 8 per cent of bank assets on a risk-adjusted basis. Although the West German requirement has to date been only 5.6 per cent, Deutsche Bank already maintains a ratio of over 11 per cent, Dresdner Bank over 10 per cent, and Commerzbank 8 per cent.[52] Entry into Eastern Germany and into Eastern Europe might squeeze those ratios in two ways, by creating higher risks or by stimulating the banks to higher loan ratios as they move into new areas. But by early 1991, the West German banks that had gone into East Germany had raised far larger amounts of cash from deposits than they had granted in loans, and it appeared unlikely that they would seriously jeopardize their ratios at least in Eastern Germany.

The large ratios could, however, raise questions as to whether the banks are really being as competitive as they could be, or whether they are providing as much capital as a fast-growing or modernizing economy might need. No bank would be able to hold 11 per cent in reserves if all its competitors were holding much less and were proving more profitable. In order to follow such policies, banks must be able to make certain assumptions not only about general economic conditions or about potential borrowers but also about each other.

German banks operate, like everything else in the German system, with an eye to history. They justify their generally conservative policies by recalling the great German financial crisis of 1931, when the German banking system collapsed and what remained of the 1920s prosperity collapsed with it. The German banking crisis was not caused by Germans. It resulted from the global stock market crash and more directly from the failure of the Austrian Creditanstalt and from the veto that the World War I victors exercised against mutually supportive German and Austrian credit arrangements as well as against suspension of reparations. But it still left a mark on the minds of German bankers, reinforcing their tendency to remain cautious in their attitudes and in their practices.[53]

NON-BANK FINANCING

Critics of German banks have consistently complained that West Germany offered little alternative means of financing. Ever since the collapse of the Berlin stock exchange after Hitler's seizure of power in 1933, West Germany has lacked a major international market for bonds and equities. Nothing in Germany rivals New York or Tokyo, and the London market also does more overall trading than Frankfurt. London even trades almost one third of all German shares.[54] There have been a number of smaller regional exchanges in West Germany, and some are opening in the former GDR, but unless and until Berlin is revived or Frankfurt boosted there is not likely to be any major German exchange.

German regulators have been sensitive to the lack of such a market, especially because a major exchange in Frankfurt could reduce the costs of trading and could also provide more liquidity for the German system. German companies raise far less funds from the markets than their EC competitors, a factor that might slow their growth in a competitive environment.[55] During the late 1980s and early 1990s, a number of steps were taken to make Frankfurt as well as other German exchanges more attractive. These included an options and futures market, improved electronic links between regional markets, some computerized trading, longer opening hours, freedom for firms to issue commercial paper, and the elimination of a small but annoying German turnover tax on securities transactions.

Real questions remain, however, about German competitiveness and attractiveness in the international finance field. There have been persistent rumors and periodic revelations that German banks and exchanges tolerate and even encourage a level of insider trading that puts outside investors at a genuine disadvantage and that would be illegal anywhere else. A major scandal, even implicating Deutsche Bank, erupted in mid-1991, showing that some of the informal banking and exchange rules were not working and were not obeyed. To compound the problem, the German Constitutional Court ruled in June 1991 that investment income could no longer be kept confidential and subject to voluntary disclosure but had to be declared and taxed after January 1, 1993, thus raising fears of capital flight from Germany by persons who had kept their assets there in order to avoid paying taxes.

Most firms do not seek equity financing, and even if they do they often work through banks to obtain it. West Germany has had 370,000 GmbH companies (*Gesellschaft mit beschränkter Haftung* — limited-liability companies or closed corporations) as against 2,300 corporations (*Aktiengesellschaften*, or AG's). Of those, only 619 had their shares quoted on the markets at the end of 1990.[56] Investors usually prefer bonds to stocks, although there are signs that the younger generation may change this.

There are some signs that West German firms appear to be turning increasingly to exchanges for funds, and the volume of such placements has increased over the last several years. In the first six months of 1990, West German firms placed a total of DM 13.4 billion on German exchanges, more than twice the amount of the corresponding period a year earlier. Several placements were made by large German banks and corporations. West German exchanges also offered DM 1.4 billion in new issues.[57] Those were still very modest figures by the standards of New York or Tokyo, but they suggested that Germans were taking steps toward greater use of non-bank capital sources. Those steps, however, go against such strong currents within German tradition and practice that little can be expected to come of them soon. German equity markets will more probably supplement the German banks as sources of capital than replace them. And most funds for investment in Eastern Germany are coming from established banks or firms, not through stock offerings, although there are some management buy-outs.

Whatever changes in German thinking might emerge with respect to sources of capital, none is evident with respect to the use of capital. The link between finance and production remains central for German bankers and industrialists. Finance serves the purposes of production (or such related purposes as commerce). The two are intimately linked, and finance as a separate purpose in its own right is not considered as important as in the United States.[58] In this atmosphere, scandals can and do occur, such as the Neue Heimat revelations of the early 1980s, but the main object of finance is to help produce and not to speculate or to maneuver. Financial systems are the servants, and not the masters, of German industry, commerce, and banking, as they have been throughout German history.[59]

German bankers and businessmen recoil in horror at the mere mention of some American financial operations of the 1980s, such as leveraged buy-outs, debt dumping on buy-out victims, "junk bonds," and the like. The Germans categorically reject the assertions made by some American financiers that such maneuvers force management to become more efficient. Instead, they point to the legacy of decimated corporations, the mountains of questionable and perhaps unrecoverable debt, and the whiff of suspected criminality. They will do everything in their power to make sure that nothing of that kind happens in Germany.

STEADY GROWTH

At first glance, the German economy seems a bankers' economy. From the powerful Bundesbank, whose policies have given Germany a world currency, through the "big three" and the other banks that influence and perhaps determine the policies of the major corporations, to the corner *Sparkassen* where Germans place their savings every week or month, the banks are at the core of the German system and of the German style. Because the German financial system has offered few instruments for raising investment or operating capital, the banks have a large voice, and perhaps even the final say, regarding which enterprises will live and which will die, what will be produced and what will not, and what direction the economy will take. They are also already deciding what happens in Eastern Germany.

But the German style is more than the banks, and more than any single grouping. It includes bureaucrats, parliamentarians, investors, association directors, managers, labor leaders, and many workers, in a broad consensus about how the economy should function and the directions it should take. The banks do not create that consensus. They express it. So do other elements of the German system, including even the government and the Bundesbank.

Each of the major participating elements on the German scene has at least an equal interest in pursuing broadly similar kinds of policies, and they reinforce each other by acting in ways that the others find acceptable, non-threatening, and non-disruptive. When they meet, when they speak, when they correspond, or when they act, they function on the basis of common principles that are so widely understood that it would be unnecessary, pointless, and perhaps even improper to talk about them.

Just as German banks are a force for stability, for conservatism and for prudent and circumspect management, so are German managers and German workers. All are skilled, highly competent, highly dedicated, and well trained. They have a commitment to the preservation and improvement of what exists and to change through evolution and not through revolution. Most managers do not want to move and do not want to take too much risk. Skilled laborers and foremen prefer to see their crafts and their skills preserved and refined rather than to have a new technology or a new venture make them obsolete. They are content with the ascent that the system can promise and which it has granted.

The *Mittelstand* reinforces the tendency toward incrementalism. Small firms, even when well capitalized, do not want to stray too far afield, especially if they know and respect their competitors and if they have a fairly well established production and market niche that is unlikely to be challenged.

One could legitimately conclude from this that the German system can stifle change. That is correct, but not completely so. For change can and does take place. It occurs gradually, not always obviously, under the mottos of stability and permanence, with the least dislocation possible, and often under competitive pressures from abroad. No German, and no observer, can be certain that it occurs fast enough to cope with the needs of today and tomorrow. German managers themselves occasionally speculate that it might be too slow, but they are themselves not sure how best to change the system and its incentive structures.

These tendencies are reinforced by societal and geographic realities. The German economic establishment is singularly cohesive, much more than that which existed in Germany before 1914 or that which exists today in the United States. It has come a long way from the "cartel of anxiety" that appeared in the postwar years, both in competence, breadth, and self-confidence.[60] It is usually estimated (by non-Germans) to consist of about 250 to 300 bankers, industrialists, aristocrats, politicians, senior lawyers, and labor or *Verbände* chiefs. It includes little new money and no fast money. Senior figures may differ in political orientation or affiliation, but they usually come from similar backgrounds and have broadly similar political and economic interests.

The gaps that separated the *Junkers* of the Prussian estates or the Berlin intelligentsia from each other or from the small holders of the Rhineland have either dissipated through the rigors of flight or been submerged in larger institutions including Europe. They remain in historical recollection, in regional accents, and in some personal and political preferences, but not in basic economic or political philosophy or in modes of behavior.

The shape, size, and infrastructure of West Germany have contributed to cohesion and mutual understanding. Lufthansa and the Bundesbahn adhere to such precise schedules that any director or manager can count on going to two or three meetings any day in different German cities, and a good driver with a German sedan on the *Autobahn* can usually guarantee average speeds of over 80 mph and fixed arrival times except in some particular stretches during ski or vacation seasons. United Germany will not be that different. Dresden, Leipzig, and Berlin, the upcoming industrial centers, are not far from each other or from Western Germany. Regular flights began serving them within weeks after unification.

It is not unusual for German senior managers or others to see each other half a dozen times a week in meetings that may have different agendas but that all deal with similar problems and pose similar options. They may call each other often between meetings. They think alike, usually act alike, and will probably not be displaced by persons, groups, or forces that may think or act differently. If unification proceeds as planned, and the infrastructure in Eastern Germany is built up to the Western German level under Western German guidance, the pattern of thinking may spread but will not change. Only a failure of unification to bring prosperity might jeopardize the cohesion of German thought.

The informal and often unspoken rules under which the system is managed are not contained in formal regulations, although many regulations exist. Germans regard, describe, or prescribe some forms of action or behavior as *"anständig"* (decent) or as *"selbstverständlich"* (so obvious as not to warrant further explanation). Faced with forms of what they regard as improper behavior, they say *"Das tut Man nicht,"* or "That is not done" as well as *"Das ist nicht ernst,"* or "That is not serious." This thinking imposes standards for both behavior and performance, with participants measured not only on whether they do well but also on whether they play within a set of unwritten but widely understood rules.

German prescriptions for behavior may often be exercised more in entry rules than in regulations. The German system is very highly regulated, but individual managers and bankers may have much greater leeway in their decisions and practices than many Americans. In Germany, it is hard to gain entry in the first place, but one may be more free to act once one has gained entry. It is much easier to open a bank in the United States than in Germany, where the Federal Bank Supervisory Board in Berlin must pass on all applications and has been known to reject some. But, once one is a banker, one is not as subject to detailed supervision as in the United States. The Germans assume that anybody who is cleared to enter will perform and act in the proper manner.

The consensus can punish as well as reward. The informal cohesion of thought and practice can lift those who follow it and who succeed within the parameters of what is expected of them. It can cast down or aside those who fail, especially if they fail by taking paths that depart from the norm or challenge that norm. Some may be exiled, leaving those who deal with Germans in international organizations to wonder whether they are talking to an exilee or to a person with true influence. Some may be permitted to continue in their careers, but limited by consensus in their functions and in their responsibilities. Some may set forth on their own, with varying degrees of determination and success. They will not be ostracized, but the limits to their potential endeavors will be quietly and widely understood and respected.

The German system is not the Japanese. There is no central and powerful directing institution, such as the Ministry of International Trade and Industry (MITI), that gives the Japanese system its thrust and cohesion. Nor is there a formal coordinating mechanism or the infinitely complicated system of ritual and relationships that makes the Japanese system so exclusionary. Nor is there the system of competition at home and cooperation abroad. The German system is less structured, more consensual. Those differences, depending on how one may look at them, give each system different strengths and different weaknesses. But the German system shares with the Japanese a firm belief that the economy is not a place for individuals or groups to exercise their personal instincts or predilections to the possible detriment of others or of the society as a whole.

The structure of the German system makes it more conservative than the Japanese. Those who make up the German consensus, whether in management, banking, or labor, are those who want to keep things as they are, not to change them to their own possible detriment. Thus, Japan is more likely to be at the forefront of industrial development, and Germany more likely to dedicate itself to perfecting what it has long done.

The German style appears to have remained constant during the past several decades and even longer. Henry Wallich, an American economist who 40 years ago wrote a study about the postwar German economy, made a list of what he then termed the "economic consequences of German mentality." Many of the observations he made still ring true.[61] The sense of material values and the passion for work appear to have moderated over time, perhaps because Germans now have many of the material objects that they were then still seeking. As for the return to cartelization that he feared, the German consensual system has taken a rather different form. But the basics of the system have not changed.

A number of analysts have defined the German system and German modes of action variously as "corporatism," or perhaps "neo-corporatism" or "meso-corporatism," and also as "controlled capitalism."[62] Those definitions are subject to different interpretations, and every analyst may have his or her own. Indeed, as some of the definitions suggest, major German enterprises and trade unions do sometimes solve their difficulties and differences at the expense of the public, often in conjunction with a level of government, and major enterprises may exercise great economic or political influence through the government and otherwise. But one cannot apply such definitions unreservedly to the German system because they ring true in some ways but not in others, and they are certainly not unique to the German system. The distinct ingredient of the German system is its consensual nature, and any definition must place a strong emphasis on that element of the German style. Yet it would be a mistake to describe the consensual process as conspiratorial. It is too universal, too widely accepted, and too open within the parameters that Germans understand.

In answer to the opening question of this chapter, and to the speculations that might be raised by the term "Germany, Inc.," one can say that there is indeed a German "style." There are patterns of thought and action that could legitimately be brought together and so labeled. The style exists in management, in labor, in banking, in finance, in virtually all economic activity, and in behavior. German "Economic Man" is not American, Japanese, French, or British "Economic Man."

It is difficult to describe the German style without using terms that seem at first to contradict each other. It is forward-looking but not radical, conservative but not backward, coordinated but not centrally directed, competitive but not destructive, progressive but not venturesome, hierarchical and yet informal within established limits. It resembles other styles in some ways but is distinctive and even unique.

The German style has its strengths and its weaknesses. Its conservative, collegial, and collaborative mode of operation prevents mistakes and maintains consistent progress. It has fitted comfortably into the situation of a state and of an economy that want to maintain stability. It minimizes risk. It does not incline toward the establishment of new and different enterprises or industries. The Germans who have been creatively entrepreneurial, like Horst Dassler (Adidas), Werner Otto (Otto Versand), Ferdinand Porsche, or Axel Springer, still represent the exception rather than the rule.

Any examination of the German style, however, poses a question that German industry and German management have yet to answer: Can the mighty enterprise that the German economy now represents not only prosper but lead? Can it achieve the integration of Eastern Germany? Can it generate enough capital to finance all the many policies that Germany wants to pursue in Western and Eastern Europe, policies that may have an economic base but that can have a vital political reward? In a world without competition and without upheaval, steady growth may have been enough. In a different world, it may not be.

It is this question that forces a closer look at some of the problems that may result from the German style, and a look at German economic theory, history, and tradition.

NOTES TO CHAPTER FOUR

1. The discussion of German management style is drawn largely from the author's conversations with German managers, economists, and others, and from a number of written sources listed below. There was only limited literature on the German management style until the last few years, when the subject began to command some international attention. What has been written comes often from non-German sources. The German literature—largely in textbooks—concentrates more on management technique than on style. Some Germans have chosen to write in English for foreign editors. Other Germans who have written in German have conveyed information

about German management more by indirection than by direction and are cited elsewhere in the appropriate context. The literature also includes observations on labor attitudes and management-labor relations. Written sources include Christopher S. Allen, *op. cit.*, pp. 13-39; John Ardagh, *Germany and the Germans* (London: Hamish Hamilton, 1989), pp. 106-107; K.H.F. Dyson, "The Politics of Economic Management in West Germany," *West European Politics*, May, 1981, pp. 35-55; "Survey: West Germany," *The Economist*, October 28, 1989, pp. 26-30; Joseph Esser, "State, Business and Trade Unions in West Germany after the 'Political Wende,'" *West European Politics*, April, 1986, pp. 199-214; Karl Hardach, *op. cit.*, pp. 140-179; Herbert Henzler and Mark Young, *German and American Management: Similarities, Differences, and Problems* (Washington: American Institute for Contemporary German Studies, 1989); Gary Herrigel, "Industrial Order and the Politics of Industrial Change: Mechanical Engineering," Katzenstein, ed., *Industry and Politics in West Germany* (Ithaca, N.Y.: Cornell University Press, 1989), pp. 185-220; Katzenstein, "Industry in a Changing West Germany," Katzenstein, ed., *loc. cit.*, pp. 3-28; Horst Kern and Michael Schumann, "New Concepts of Production in West German Plants," Katzenstein, ed., *loc. cit.*, pp. 87-109; Michael Kreile, West Germany: The Dynamics of Expansion," Katzenstein, ed., *Between Power and Plenty*, 191-224; Heinz Lampert, *op. cit.*, pp. 132-290; Ezra Vogel, "Conclusion," George C. Lodge and Vogel, eds., *Ideology and National Competitiveness* (Boston: Harvard Business School Press, 1987), pp. 301-323; Peter Lawrence, *Managers and Management in West Germany* (New York: St. Martin's Press, 1980); Ira Magaziner and Mort Patinkin, *The Silent War* (New York: Random House, 1989), pp. 103-136; David Marsh, *The Germans* (New York: St. Martin's, 1990), pp. 185-203; Thomas Mayer, "Economic Structure, the Exchange Rate, and Adjustment in the Federal Republic of Germany," International Monetary Fund, *Staff Papers*, June, 1989, pp. 435-463; Tom Peters, "The German Economic Miracle Nobody Knows," *Across the Board*, April, 1990, pp. 17-23; Michael E. Porter, *The Competitive Advantage of Nations* (New York: Free Press, 1989), pp. 355-382; Klaus Werner Schatz and Frank Wolter, *Structural Adjustment in the Federal Republic of Germany* (Geneva: International Labor Office, 1987); Wolfgang Streeck and Philippe Schmitter, *Private Interest Government* (London: Sage, 1984); Henry C. Wallich, *op. cit.*, pp. 113-152. There is no currently useful literature on the former East German way of doing business.

2. See Magaziner and Patinkin, *loc. cit*, for one example.
3. Herbert Henzler and Mark Young, *op. cit.*, p. 12.
4. *Wall Street Journal*, April 18, 1990, p. R28.
5. For example, "Junge Karriere," *Wirtschaftswoche*, October 13, 1989.
6. *The Economist*, April 27, 1991, p. S-43.
7. Interview with Manfred Stassen, American Institute for Contemporary German Studies, January, 1991.

8. Gerhard Fels, Otto Vogel, eds., *Unternehmensbesteuerung am Standort Bundesrepublik* (Essen: Deutscher Instituts-Verlag, 1988); Otto Jacobs, "Deutsche Steuerlast kleiner, als die Interessenten sagen," *Handelsblatt*, December 24, 1990, p. 5.

9. Max Weber's thesis regarding the "work ethic" was not, however, based on Germany. It was based on Calvinism rather than on German Lutheranism. Lutheranism, at least as interpreted in Germany, does not demand total dedication to work at all times. It envisages and even encourages other activities as well.

10. The late Alfred Herrhausen, who as chief of the Deutsche Bank was one of the most powerful and influential bankers in the world, was formally titled the "Spokesman for the Supervisory Board." Other German senior titles may be equally understated.

11. Material on the *Mittelstand* is drawn from the following sources: Elmar Pieroth, "Ordnungspolitik für den Mittelstand," Klaus Weigelt, *Soziale Marktwirtschaft im Aufwind* (Herford: Busse-Seewald, 1989); Matthias Schmidt, "Neuorientierung der Mittelstandspolitik," *Wirtschaftsdienst*, No. 3, 1989, pp. 388-394; "West German Survey," *The Economist*, October 25, 1989, pp. 25-26.

12. FRG, *Sozialpolitische Umschau*, February 26, 1990.

13. FRG, *Aktuelle Beiträge*, May 29, 1989, pp. 1-5.

14. For descriptions of the German system of apprentice training, see Ardagh, *op. cit.*, pp. 112-115; Porter, *loc. cit.*; *West Germany: The Logical Choice for Investment in Europe* (Frankfurt: Charles Barker, 1985), passim.

15. The number of designated specialties, which used to be over 600, has been declining in recent years because of coordinated efforts to consolidate specialties so as to increase labor mobility.

16. GDR, *Statistical Pocketbook, 1989*, p. 41.

17. James Goodhart, "Critical Lessons from the German School," *Financial Times*, June 3, 1991, p. 8.

18. *Frankfurter Allgemeine Zeitung* and *Süddeutsche Zeitung*, March 27, 1991.

19. FRG, *Sozialpolitische Umschau*, January 14, 1991.

20. *Süddeutsche Zeitung*, March 25, 1991.

21. Horst Kern and Michael Schumann, "New Concepts of Production in West German plants," Katzenstein, *Industry and Politics in West Germany*, pp. 87-111.

22. FRG, *Sozialpolitische Umschau*, January 22, 1990, p. 1.

23. *Financial Times*, August 25, 1988, p. 13.

24. *Wall Street Journal*, March 18, 1991, p. 14.

25. Ardagh, *op. cit.*, p. 115.

26. *Financial Times, loc. cit.*

27. *Wirtschaftswoche*, January 12, 1990, p. 33.

28. *Handelsblatt*, October 18, 1990.

29. Katzenstein, *Policy and Politics in West Germany*, p. 143.

30. Katzenstein, *loc. cit.*, p. 144.
31. For short description and discussion of the codetermination system, see Ardagh, *op. cit.*, pp. 101-109; Karl Römer, ed., *Facts about Germany* (Gütersloh: Bertelsmann, 1987), p. 257-262; Gönner, Lind, and Weis, *op. cit.*, pp. 467-472; Katzenstein, *loc. cit.*, pp. 131-163.
32. Lampert, *op. cit.*, p. 253.
33. Katzenstein, *loc. cit.*, p. 146.
34. Lampert, *op. cit.*, p. 143.
35. Charles P. Kindleberger, *Financial History of Western Europe* (London: George Allen & Unwin, 1984), pp. 117-135.
36. Information about these and other banks is drawn from Commerzbank, *Wer gehört zu wem?* (Frankfurt: Commerzbank, 1988), passim.
37. For Lambsdorff arguments, see *Die Zeit*, October 27, 1989, p. 32. Appropriate *Spiegel* article cited below.
38. Kreile, *op. cit.*, p. 211.
39. For a review of different bank roles, see OECD, *Germany, 1985/1986* (Paris: OECD, 1986), pp. 45-49.
40. Josef Esser, *op. cit.*, p. 199.
41. Commerzbank, *op. cit.*
42. *Ibid.*, passim; John Dornberg, "The Spreading Might of Deutsche Bank," *New York Times Magazine*, September 23, 1990, p. 29.
43. Arno Gottschalk, "Der Stimmrechteinfluss der Banken in den Aktionärsversammlungen von Grossunternehmen," *WSI Mitteilungen*, May, 1988. pp. 296-299.
44. *Ibid.*, p. 301.
45. *Der Spiegel*, February 25, 1991, pp. 116-118.
46. The study, conducted by the Ifo Institute, was reported in *Wirtschaftswoche*, September 1, 1989, pp. 26-30.
47. Erhard Katzenbach, "Macht der Banken," *Handelsblatt*, July 17, 1989, reprinted in Deutsche Bundesbank, *Auszüge aus Presseartikeln*, July 20, 1989, pp. 1-2 (hereinafter cited as *Auszüge*).
48. Bernhard Schramm, "Macht der Banken," *Handelsblatt*, July 14/15, 1989, reprinted in *Auszüge*, July 20, 1989, pp. 2-3.
49. *Wirtschaftswoche*, September 1, 1989, pp. 28-29.
50. Alfred Herrhausen, "Macht der Banken," text distributed by the Deutsche Bank on October 25, 1989.
51. *Frankfurter Allgemeine Zeitung*. September 2, 1990, p. 6.
52. *The Economist*, January 5, 1991, pp. 59-60.
53. For reviews of developments regarding the German banking crisis, see John A. Garrity, *The Great Depression* (San Diego: Harcourt, Brace, Jovanovich, 1986), pp. 182-184 and 443-46; and Kindleberger, *op. cit.*, pp. 372-378.
54. *Frankfurter Allgemeine Zeitung*, April 27, 1991.
55. *The Economist*, April 27, 1991, p. S-42.
56. *The Economist*, April 27, 1991, p. S-42.

57. *Handelsblatt*, August 8, 1990, p. B10.

58. This concept is explored in Christopher Allen, *Financial Regulation in the Federal Republic of Germany and the United States* (Washington: American Institute for Contemporary German Studies, 1990).

59. John Plender, "Flotsam of Cut-throat Years," *Financial Times*, December 22/23, 1990, II, p. 1.

60. See Ralf Dahrendorf, *Society and Democracy in Germany* (Garden City: Doubleday, 1967), pp. 265-279.

61. Wallich, *op. cit.*, pp. 328-343.

62. For example, Christopher Allen, "From Social Market to Meso-Corporatism: The Politics of West German Economic Policy," pp. 13-39; Michael Hülshoff, "West German Corporatism at Forty," Peter Merkl, ed., *The Federal Republic of Germany at Forty* (New York: New York University Press, 1989), pp. 161-177; Ezra Vogel, *op. cit.*, pp. 301-323.

Five

Structural Burdens and the Role of the State

The four preceding chapters have shown the nature of the West German economy as well as the power of West German economic performance with its steady forward thrust across a broad spectrum of traditional industries. The chapters have also shown how the West German government, the trade unions, and the banks, as well as the public, semipublic, and private associations all joined in a broad consensus toward consistent and smooth growth. The major political parties supported or reflected that consensus although they consistently argued about power and policy. With unification now achieved, all those groups are now committed to transferring that system across all of Germany in order to make united Germany in the West German image.

The German system can, however, generate problems as well as progress. German economists have themselves increasingly pointed to those problems and have warned that even an economy as powerful as that of Germany could lose momentum if its priorities and efforts were misdirected, if its costs went out of control, and if it failed to keep up with the larger world.

Rumblings of West German concern came in waves throughout the decades of growth. They were always most powerful when growth slowed or when competitors seemed more successful. They emerged with particular force during the stagflation period of the late 1970s. They were revived during "Eurosclerosis" in the middle 1980s.

These concerns are even more pertinent in the 1990s and are drawing renewed and even intensified attention. The enormous requirements of German and European unity have given them new force. So has the prospect for a single European market after 1992. All these developments will, although for different reasons, raise the level of competition within Europe while also probably raising German costs.

The most searching analyses of West Germany's economic and structural problems were published in a series of studies that began during the 1970s, when the Bonn government asked each of the five economic institutes to evaluate the structure of the West German economy and to offer recommendations. The institutes replied, in painstaking detail and with a series of recommendations. Three cycles of evaluation followed in 1978-1980, 1981-1983, and 1984-1987, with the institutes complaining ever more insistently about what they described as the inadequate response of the federal, state, and local governments. Those governments in turn firmly supported the abstract objective of economic restructuring while protecting and deepening the very weaknesses that the institutes decried.[1]

Some institutes, such as those in Kiel and Hamburg, were more critical than others. The Kiel Institute even published a special study about its ten years of structural reporting and used the study to summarize what it saw as the failings of the West German economy and to reiterate its warnings.[2] The Sachverständigenrat has weighed in heavily, consistently using its annual and some special reports to warn about the same problems and to urge action.

At the core of the structural dilemma, sometimes hardly visible in the mass of technical and sometimes laborious detail, lies a very fundamental debate about the direction that the West German——and now the German economy——must take if it is to remain successful and prosperous. That debate includes a seminal discussion about Germany's place in the global division of labor, an issue of immense importance to an exporting nation like the Germans.

Those who have led the debate, and those who have insisted most firmly that Germany's economy had to change, have been those who have seen the world economy changing in directions that would increasingly relegate Germany to a second rank. They have seen the coming of a world in which the work performed by traditional German productive sectors, whether coal, steel, chemicals, agriculture, electronics, machinery, and so forth, could be done better and more cheaply elsewhere. They believed firmly that West Germany had to de-emphasize some of those sectors and abandon others in order to move with the greatest speed and the most powerful possible commitment into new areas that will lead the growth of the world economy. They now believe that united Germany must do so. The West German government was, however, never ready to pursue a course that could lead to mass dislocation and upheaval while German industry searched for new niches, new markets, new training and new production methods. There are some early signs that the pressures and costs of unification may persuade or compel the united German government to do what the West German government would not undertake, but it is not yet clear whether the government will go as far as the critics wish.

Those who oppose the arguments of the institutes fall into several categories. Some remain committed to the traditional sectors and believe that Germany can still perform competitively in those sectors, especially if enough effort is made to modernize and rationalize them or to find particular specialties. They believe that Germany has carved out a firm and unassailable place in the global division of labor and should hold it. Others support traditional sectors not for economic but for social and political reasons. Others believe that the issues must be raised and understood but that action can and perhaps should be postponed.

The debate between these various elements has been conducted in a highly scholarly tone which sometimes obscures the fact that the decisions to be made can profoundly affect Germany itself and the life of every German. The very existence of the debate itself reveals the deep concern that serious Germans feel about the country's economy, and the outcome to date reveals the balance that continues to exist between the powerful forces at work.

The West German structural problems, as defined by the institutes and by others, have fallen into several broad areas:

- Failure to modernize;
- Inadequate research, development, and new ventures;
- West German shortcomings as a place to produce;
- Excess subsidization;
- The burden of the state.

FAILURE TO MODERNIZE

The basic complaint about modernization, made almost uniformly by all five institutes, was that the West German economy did not remain at the forefront of global development and progress. The fundamentals of the German economy of the 1970s and 1980s, and perhaps even that of the 1990s, have not changed materially from the German economy of the past. The German economy is not advancing decisively into the ranks of the most advanced industrial societies such as the United States, Japan, and the smaller Asian economies.

West Germany might have combined the precision of the laser with the versatility of modern metallurgy to make the supreme producer product of the second industrial revolution, and it might have combined the speed and maneuverability of the racing car with the comfort of the sedan to make the supreme consumer product of the age, but it was not advancing into the next revolution as quickly or as strongly as it should.

The institutes expressed deep fear that the failure to modernize and to push into high technology would cost the West German economy its competitive position over the long term, especially in a world economy dominated by a fluidity of investment capital and technical talent that permits production lines to be shifted quickly from place to place and output to be radically altered in months or even weeks instead of years. They especially expressed concern about the German lag in the most modern technologies (which they have termed *Spitzentechnologie*) and in information processing. They warned that failure to develop and apply those technologies could give Germany's competitors permanent cost advantages. They also warned that only a few sectors of West German industry were keeping pace and that others were actually delaying progress by draining resources into traditional but less competitive production lines.

The institutes were not monotonously critical. They expressed pleasure that the West German economy was advancing strongly in at least some technologically advanced sectors. They accepted the argument frequently advanced by West German industrial managers, especially in machine tools and in the *Mittelstand*, that they and their firms integrate state-of-the-art technology into their production processes at least as rapidly as any foreign firms. But this did not satisfy the institutes because they feared that German producers and consumers seeking the most advanced technology would sooner or later have to begin buying it outside Germany and might not always be able to obtain the latest materials and methods. Over time, the institutes feared, a lack of dynamism risked feeding on itself, ultimately leaving Germany in a backwater while at least some other nations were rapidly moving forward. Some of the institutes warned that economic growth might begin a long secular decline if no basic changes were made.

A more far-reaching argument, made by the institutes as well as by private Germans, and certainly shown by the evidence, was that the new technologies could not only improve traditional production but could become new industries in themselves. The institutes cited the computer hardware and software industries producing tens of thousands of jobs as well as helping other industries to modernize. The West German business journal *Wirtschaftswoche* joined in the argument, warning that West Germany might continue to prosper superficially but would fall further and further behind until the time for recovery was past.[3]

The warnings of the institutes at first fell mostly, if not totally, on deaf ears. Despite ups and downs in economic production, West Germany's consistent ranking as one of the world's leading exporters helped calm concern about modernization. But the arguments produced considerable discussion in West Germany, and the whole matter of the German place in the international division of labor came increasingly under review.

INADEQUATE RESEARCH, DEVELOPMENT, AND NEW VENTURES

As part of their assertion that West Germany was not modernizing fast enough, the institutes also expressed concern that West Germany had not given adequate priority to research and development and that German capital had not been venturesome enough. They argued that West German funds did not go sufficiently into the kinds of research or into the start-up ventures that helped keep the United States at the forefront of international inventiveness even as traditional American industries declined. In particular, the institutes charged, Germany neither spawned masses of new firms nor generated the venture capital needed to get them started, despite some of the relatively modest venture capital funds established by the major West German banks.[4]

Even casual observers could see that the institutes had an important argument. Computer stores in West Germany and in united Germany display and sell American and Japanese computer hardware and some Italian and French products as well as largely American-made software, but they have few German computers. The only ones, made by Nixdorf and by Siemens after Siemens rescued and absorbed Nixdorf, may be of high quality but not at the very edge of what is available internationally at any given moment--although Siemens has a strong position in a number of technologies. Any listing of the world's largest information-processing or office-technology companies includes only Siemens as a German company among a host of American and Japanese companies and a smattering of other Europeans that are losing money and are either being taken over by Japanese or rescued by their governments.[5]

One of the most difficult elements of the German debate has been to attempt to fix the point at which the West German industrial sector as a whole ceased to have an adequate component of new entrepreneurs and new industries and began slipping more and more into a mold in which it maintained its existing profile. One study which attempted to compare the portions of German industry that were innovative as against traditional concluded that the pace of innovation began to slow during the latter 1960s and that the shift to a preservationist model took place in the early 1970s. At that point, the German economy was being subjected to many external and internal pressures (collapse of Bretton-Woods, global recession, oil shock, etc.), and chose to stress the maintenance of what existed instead of encouraging continual ventures into new areas.[6]

This has not meant that West German industry has not invested in research and development or continued to advance. European Community statistics have consistently shown that West Germany was either first or second in European R & D expenditures, with only France coming close enough to be a real competitor. But those same and related statistics also showed that the West German lead was shrinking during the 1980s and even earlier, and that Germany did not have the lead in computer-oriented R & D.[7] In particular, they showed that West Germany was not doing well at the global level, lagging behind the United States and even further behind Japan in the pace at which it was increasing its R & D expenditures. In some areas, as in machine-tool R & D, Germany was well ahead in Europe and ahead of the United States but only barely keeping up with Japan. In high-technology areas, Germany was trailing badly, and *Der Spiegel* warned of the "deadly pressure" of foreign competition.[8]

This problem was shown with particular force in another German study indicating Germany's shortfall in absolute research and development expenditures:[9]

Total Research and Development Expenditures

	Year	Amount (in bill. DM)	Percent of GNP
United States	1970	65	2.6
	1980	155	2.3
	1990 (est.)	365	2.7
Japan	1970	15	1.9
	1980	59	2.2
	1990 (est.)	144	2.7
West Germany	1970	14	2.1
	1980	36	2.4
	1990 (est.)	66	2.8

A similarly alarming trend was showing in inventions and patents. A German patent office study showed that West Germany by 1989 was falling behind in three of four major areas of domestic patent grants compared to Japan and the United States. It shared the lead with the United States for patents granted in automotive technology. In biotechnology, the United States led but Germany was even with Japan in second place. In microelectronics and office technology, however, West Germany had lagged in third place throughout virtually all the 1980s and was falling further and further behind both Japan and the United States.[10]

German businessmen and officials are often much more deeply worried about Japan than about the United States, especially in their private conversations. They think they can withstand American technological competition, especially because they believe that the United States will want to work together with European states in exploiting any advances that it may make. But they fear Japan, especially because they have already seen signs that Japan is not yielding its most advanced technology to foreigners, including even some German companies with which it has partnership or customer relations. They recognize that the Japanese lead in computer technology could ultimately give Japanese products an advantage across the entire spectrum of industrial technology in which West Germany has competed and united Germany would need to compete, as Japan could obtain a wide-ranging advantage by marrying its technology with a full array of industrial products.

Closer examination showed that not all the news was bad but that West German technological progress was uneven. West Germany certainly remained competitive in biotechnology and general medical research. The same could be said about Germany's competitive position in smaller robotic machine tools and in many areas of electronic and even specialized computer research. But this did not compensate fully for the lag in cellular communications, microtechnology, or computers.[11]

By the same token, some German companies were competing much better than others, spending more money on research and also increasing their sales. A number were also making international cooperative arrangements that would help improve their positions. Siemens and Daimler-Benz ranked first and second in European R & D expenditures for 1989. Bayer and Höchst were in the fifth and sixth places on the list with Volkswagen tenth. And German banks were increasingly working with German companies to shift more investment credits into R & D expenditures and into *Spitzentechnologie*.[12] But all that was not enough.

The role of government can make an important difference in industrial research, and it has made a difference for the Germans. One of Germany's initial handicaps in R & D was the difficulties that the West German federal government had in funding research after World War II, largely because official research and development funds could be appropriated only at the *Land* level. It was only during the late 1950s and the 1960s that the West German federal government could have a research budget of its own.[13] Even then, the tradition of *Land* involvement continued strongly although the federal government began to play an increasingly large role in research and development. With unification, several Eastern German *Länder* have begun developing research budgets of their own.

During the 1960s, West Germany began to conduct aerospace research, largely because that field appeared to offer some of the most promising technological breakthroughs. It developed or helped develop and produce military jet aircraft. Later, it also participated in European satellite programs and other space missions. There was strong German financial and scientific participation in a variety of European programs, such as ESPRIT, EUREKA, JESSI, RACE, or BRITE, programs that were designed to internationalize research at the European level to enable the smaller European states to compete against the United States and Japan.[14]

The West German government has also, of course, made efforts in Germany itself as well as at the European level. The West German Research Ministry received consistent budget increases during the 1980s. Its Minister during most of the decade, Heinz Riesenhuber, has tried consistently to shift the emphasis of German research and development into the areas that most worried the economic institutes. During 1989, he especially asked the German trade unions to recognize that more jobs would be lost by a failure to modernize than by modernization itself.[15] For 1990, he announced that much of the annual R & D program of DM 678 million would be devoted to making up the German lag in computer and data-processing technology, and that this would be done in conjunction with private industry as well as in government and private laboratories. One fifth of the budget, for example, was to go into the promotion of microtechnologies. The German government has also concentrated considerable support on the JESSI program for electronics research.[16]

The great open question regarding united Germany's technological progress is East Germany, where research had been ill-focused during the GDR years despite considerable expenditure. As West German resources had to shift heavily into re-industrializing East Germany, some Germans hoped that West German industry could make high-technology production in East

Germany its first priority, trying to re-create in Berlin, Saxony, and surrounding states the center of German technology that had existed there before World War II. Riesenhuber announced special programs to promote research in Eastern Germany. He also said that he wanted Western German firms to spend at least 5 per cent of their R & D budgets in East Germany.[17]

The institutes in their reports pointed also to another problem, the German lag in establishing new ventures. The Kiel Economic Institute was again the most highly critical of West German performance, asserting that West Germany was not creating the kinds of small venture companies or funds that were needed to give expression to new ideas.[18]

The Kiel argument went to the core of the total functioning of the West German system and was never adequately met by West German industry or by the government except as part of a general approach to structural difficulties. Many German businessmen and economists continued to believe that this problem was not as important in Germany as it might appear on the surface. But West Germany, and Germany as a whole, has not found a way to create an environment in which small entrepreneurs in new fields arise in large numbers. Start-ups are harder and the penalty for failure is greater, especially in comparison with the United States.

WEST GERMAN SHORTCOMINGS AS A PLACE TO PRODUCE

During the mid-1980s, an intense debate began in West Germany about yet another structural problem: Could West Germany still attract productive capital, and would others as well as Germans still consider it a competitive place to produce?[19] The debate had a somewhat unreal tone, as West Germany was entering a phase of dramatic export growth, but it still dealt with a serious problem.

No German could deny the statistical evidence, which showed that West Germany consistently had a very high savings rate but that much of that potential capital did not remain in Germany but fueled a strong and continuing outflow of investment capital from West Germany to other countries. Some of that investment capital was short-term oriented, and much of it merely balanced the considerable West German trade surplus. But foreign direct investment in West Germany had fallen behind German direct investment abroad during virtually every year since the early 1970s.[20] During the first nine months of 1989, West German direct and real estate investment abroad rose to a level of DM 15.7 billion, more than four times as high as the corresponding level of foreign investment of DM 3.5 billion in West Germany.[21]

This difference could hardly be described as capital flight, but it represented what one author termed "under-investment."[22] Over time, it could leave the West German and the united German economy locked into an obsolescent configuration.

Some institute analysts thought that the West as a whole, and especially Germany, might well face a new form of international rivalry, "site competition," the struggle to attract enough capital to provide the fixed investment base for modern industries. Without those industries, a state could not hope to compete either in production or in attracting the engineers, technicians, and workers it most wanted. If the investment gap could not be corrected, the institutes warned, West Germany could not hope to overcome its technology lag.

The Westfälische Landesbank in 1989 concluded that the situation could not be summarized on a national basis but had to be analyzed on a factor basis, with some factors attracting investment to the Federal Republic, some being neutral, and others actually discouraging investment.[23]

The bank listed the following factors as attractions:

• The level of training of German workers;
• The travel and telecommunications infrastructure;
• Research and development in certain industries;
• A spirit of competitiveness.

The bank described a number of other factors as neutral:

• The size and dynamism of the German market;
• Comparative financial services;
• Commitment to work;
• The web of regulation;
• Likelihood for profit.

The bank cited three factors as major disadvantages:

• High energy costs;
• High environmental burdens (in terms of regulations as well as unpredictable financial burdens);
• High taxes.

Other studies also concluded that these factors helped inhibit foreign investment from coming to Germany, but a number of them gave much higher weight than the bank study to the burden of high West German wages (the highest in the world) and—in particular—to non-wage labor costs

despite the high qualifications of West German workers. Another study cited
the fact that the German work force was aging and that workers were less
ready to let themselves be trained or to relocate for new positions and new
industries.[24]

Some other studies focused in particular on the web of German taxation
and regulation, insisting that it was inducing capital to leave Germany and
was making foreigners reluctant to invest. They argued that many investors
were afraid to commit themselves to situations where their decisions might
be circumscribed by complex rules that they could not understand and that
might be applied arbitrarily to their disadvantage.[25] Although German companies could work within the rules and could even reduce the taxes that they
actually paid by accumulating reserves and by other similar policies (Chapter
4), foreign investors might not want to do the same and might not be
permitted to do so by their own domestic tax authorities.[26]

The factor analysis made by the institutes and others showed that
Germany's attractiveness as an industrial site could vary from industry to
industry, depending on the importance of any given factor for that industry.
The most successful sectors of West German industry, and the ones that
continued to attract additional investment, have been those that have relied
on such well-known German strengths as a serious, well-trained, and reliable
work force, a sound infrastructure, and a social consensus to work efficiently
and to produce quality goods. Other industries, such as those requiring more
hand labor, a less skilled work force, or more flexible cost structures, would
move elsewhere. Those requiring postal and telecommunications services or
high utility usage also found Germany prohibitively expensive.[27]

With German unity, the issues regarding location in Germany have
assumed a completely different shape but have not yet been studied in the
same detail as in West Germany. But the location of united Germany, not at
the edge of half a continent but in the middle of a whole one, should add an
important location factor as an investment incentive. Service or assembly
firms that want to operate or sell across the whole of Europe might find a
location in Germany highly attractive, but the evidence of this would
probably not be clear until the mid-1990s.

EXCESS SUBSIDIZATION

Despite Germany's commitment to a social market economy, exceptions to
market principles existed in West Germany and risk proliferating in united
Germany. West Germany's prosperity and collegial economic management
have contributed to getting them started and have also made it possible to

finance them. The economic institutes and the Sachverständigenrat have repeatedly pointed out that West German authorities at various levels supported countless economic activities that should long ago have been discontinued or compelled to become competitive.

The West German authorities which have received the institutes' reports have joined in condemning subsidies and have promised to terminate or at least reduce them. Count Otto Lambsdorff, former German Minister of Economics, wrote in 1987 that Germans had become less ready to accept the subsidies.[28] But the level of subsidies has grown even as they have been denounced. Every Federal Chancellor who has denigrated subsidies has found himself unable to end or even to curtail them.[29]

West German subsidies were extensive and costly. The federal government and various states supported a number of industries and services, such as coal, steel, air and space, ship-building, and agriculture, with the federal government supporting many activities across the board and the states supporting locally important and influential industries.

The following table shows the development of West German federal-level subsidies from 1970 to the most recent recorded year, in millions of D-Marks. The agricultural subsidies category includes payments to the European Community Common Agricultural Policy (CAP).[30]

Year	All Subsidies	Agri- culture	Energy, Mining	Manufac- turing	Travel
1970	1.78	5.80	0.64	2.00	2.56
1975	20.39	6.21	1.52	3.49	7.45
1980	30.53	9.13	5.02	5.95	7.62
1985	37.81	12.99	4.49	8.41	8.05
1987	44.78	15.50	9.33	8.90	7.62
1988*	47.67	17.54	8.06	9.04	8.18
1989*	45.41	...	...	...	...

* Preliminary

The statistics demonstrate the difficulty of terminating subsidy programs, even in an economy as powerful and competitive as West Germany's. The level of subsidies rose almost uninterruptedly, and by over 50 per cent between the *Wende* and German unification although the German government had committed itself to reducing them. Some of the categories, like agriculture, are not fully under West German but under EC control, but even the portion specifically designated for German farmers also rose (by 250 per cent since the *Wende*). Other subsidies, such as those for coal, steel, Airbus, or passenger rail travel, have their own constituencies and reasons.

The federal government provided only about one third of total West German subsidies, which during 1988 represented DM 133 billion, or about 6 per cent of West German Gross Domestic Product.[31] The other two thirds came from states and localities.[32] About 60 per cent of the total, or DM 81 billion, took the form of direct financial assistance; the remaining DM 52 billion took the form of preferential treatment on taxes. From year to year, many industries received over DM 1 billion each in subsidies, and one study estimated that the industries in the Ruhr area had obtained a total of about DM 45 billion between the mid-1960s and the mid-1980s.[33]

Despite the concern expressed about West German subsidies, a 1990 OECD review concluded that German subsidies were not unusually high by the standards of the European Community.[34] The OECD has described them as being around the average for OECD countries. Separate IMF and German Finance Ministry studies reached a similar conclusion, indicating that West Germany was actually somewhat below the average among European Community members in the level of subsidies.[35] The Germans have also argued that the United States did not offer a better model. The Deutsches Institut für Wirtschaftsforschung concluded that U.S. government policy was as guilty of subsidies as the Germans and other Europeans.[36]

While such conclusions might offer some comfort as a matter of general policy, it is also true that some West German industries——especially in the traditional coal and steel complex——have become subsidy-dependent to such an extent that they would have to be closed if they no longer benefited from government support of one kind or another.[37] But subsidies are also often paid even to some of the largest and most profitable German concerns, such as Daimler-Benz, Bayer, Volkswagen, or BMW, for special production or research lines, although those companies state that the subsidies cover only a minute part of their research expenditure.[38]

Some of the subsidies have a long history. The coal subsidy originated in the late nineteenth century, in the *Jahrhundertvertrag* ("Accord for a Century")——and may be reduced when the 100-year agreements end during the 1990s. Ship-building subsidies began during the naval and merchant marine competition with Great Britain and France before World War I.[39] More than 30 tax preference systems which had already been in effect before 1945, and which were taken over when the Federal Republic was founded in 1949, added a total cost of DM 6 billion to West German budgets every year. But most of the subsidy arrangements are of more recent origin.

One effect of government intervention through subsidies and other practices was the further strengthening of West Germany's trade and current account surpluses, at least in the near term, because imports could not compete with the subsidized prices. Another effect, strongly denounced by the German economic institutes, was that the subsidized and protected industries were able to expand their fixed plant and equipment as well as to raise wages and prices, thus raising government expenditures instead of reducing them, increasing inflationary pressures, and keeping workers from more profitable sectors. One wag wrote that Germans would still be listening to fiddlers in movie theaters if the silent film industry had possessed a lobby as powerful as that of the coal and steel industries.[40]

West German subsidies for the most part helped to preserve the character of the West German economy and its established allocation of resources. Some of the more modern German industries, such as electronics and information technology, were among the most vocal critics of German structural policies, and they reiterated their complaints even more forcefully after German unification.[41]

Although some subsidy programs, like Airbus or research and development support, created new forms of production and increased West Germany's role in future as well as past or present technologies, the economic institutes asserted that more efficient and genuinely progressive industries could have been formed if private industry had been able to use those same resources on the basis of its evaluation of market needs.

The director of the Kiel Institute, Horst Siebert, complained that the most detrimental impact of subsidies "has been to ward off the location of new industries."[42] As an example of these misplaced allocations, he pointed out that a work place in the West German coal industry in 1986 was subsidized by DM 35,000 per year, an amount that could have been far better spent on research and development in advanced technology.

The subsidies have become a highly visible issue in German-American relations. Carla Hills, the U.S. Trade Representative, denounced them in March 1990 as disruptive factors in German-American trade, complaining inter alia about the Airbus subsidy, the delays in opening the communications industry to foreign competition, as well as complex and allegedly restrictive standards intended to protect medical and diagnostic equipment.[43] The United States made a formal complaint to the GATT about Airbus subsidies, and specifically against the German government's guarantee to Daimler-Benz against losses incurred through adverse exchange rate movements. Washington claimed that Germany had paid out a total of $257 million for

Airbus subsidies between January 1990 and January 1991, for a total of $2.5 million for each aircraft.

The German financial press agreed with the U.S. charge, reporting that the Airbus could not continue without some form of subsidy, especially as the global airframe market weakened in 1990/1991—although Airbus had turned its first profit in 1990.[44] But Airbus Industries in turn announced that it would begin producing and selling jumbo jets by the early 1990s in order to complete its product line. This plan was certain to require large subsidies and also to irritate the United States, which had long held a monopoly in civilian jumbo jets and which is the departure or arrival point for most jumbo flights.

More significantly, the German decision to continue to finance the European Community's CAP and to turn a deaf ear to Washington's insistence on including and reducing agricultural subsidies under GATT rules helped to generate a crisis in European-American relations at the end of 1990 (see Chapter 9). Many Germans also complained about the agricultural subsidies, pointing out that farm income was rising faster than other income in Germany.[45]

The great unknown with respect to future all-German subsidy policy remains the level of support that the new all-German government may find itself compelled to provide in order not to permit an excessive level of structural unemployment in the former East Germany. Official East German statistics suggested that the level of subsidies in the GDR budget before unification had been 30 per cent, but in reality the level may have been much higher because of the generally low level of productivity in the GDR. East German workers who were to be displaced for efficiency reasons complained that the united German government was biased in favor of Western industry because it continued subsidies for Western German firms but not for Eastern.

By early 1991, in response to these complaints, the government of united Germany found itself compelled to subsidize competitive production on both sides of the former inner-German border, with good prospects for continuing subsidy demands well into the future if the government wanted to avoid high structural unemployment in Eastern Germany. The total all-German subsidy bill now threatens to rise significantly above the share of 6 per cent of GNP that it had represented in West Germany. Keeping elements of Eastern German industry alive will almost certainly require a higher proportion in subsidies than it will add to GNP, at least initially.

THE BURDEN OF THE STATE

West German politicians, businessmen, and economists consistently had difficulty calculating the most suitable role for the state in the West German economy. The West German economic institutes and the Sachverständigenrat argued that the role grew too large during the 1970s and had to be reduced, either by cutting subsidies, accelerating privatization, or paring the general activities of the state. The arguments were, like other structural arguments, accepted in principle if not fully implemented in practice, and there was a consistent disagreement in West Germany about the right objectives and levels of state intervention in the economy.

Two main considerations accounted for uncertainty about the best role of the state in the West German economy. The first, and probably most important, was the discontinuity of German political and economic experience. Germany's growth to industrial power during the nineteenth century grew out of intimate collaboration between the Prussian and German governments and the great leaders of German banking and German industry. Germans believed that neither could have succeeded without the active engagement and support of the other. But West Germany's—and especially Ludwig Erhard's—policy after World War II attempted to break with the past, to take the state out of the economy and to curtail the influence of the industrial and financial establishment in government decisions. Although the role of the state in West Germany has since expanded, there are still many German economists who feel uncomfortable with that expansion.

The West German uncertainty about the role of the state also reflected a second factor, more ideological than historical, which was the almost continuous debate between different German political parties about that role. The Free Democrats, the traditional liberals, consistently wanted to limit the role of the state. The Christian Democrats shared the FDP view, although less strongly. The doctrine of Catholic liberalism, to which the CDU and CSU have broadly subscribed, permitted a large state role in postwar France and Italy. But the German Christian Democrats have opposed too much state prominence because of the abuses of German state power under the Nazis and because of the tradition left by Erhard. The Social Democrats, on the other hand, have remained faithful to moderate socialist doctrine, believing that the state has a useful and even essential role to play in economic affairs but should not own, control, or direct all factors of production. The SPD expanded the role of the state in West Germany after it came to power in the late 1960s, but mainly toward larger transfer payments and more direct efforts to manage the economic cycle, not toward government ownership or management of the means of production.[46]

As a share of national income, German government expenditures at all levels were 15 per cent before World War I, 25 per cent during the interwar period, 35 per cent around 1960, 48 per cent in 1975, and about 50 per cent by 1980-1981. Federal government expenditures rose most quickly, largely because of the federal social budget. But Bonn also assumed additional expenditures, including investment costs for urban renewal, transport, hospital construction, subsidized housing, environmental protection, and many other domestic programs.[47] After the *Wende*, the state role began to fall, and the budget deficits declined.

The government's share of spending, while worrisome to the West Germans, still remained lower than that of several other European states, such as Sweden, the Netherlands, Italy, France, and Belgium. In fact, Germany and Great Britain were the only major states to reduce government spending as a share of Gross Domestic Product during the 1980s. But it still remained higher than that of two principal competitors, the United States, at about 37 per cent, and Japan, at about 33 per cent.[48]

Despite the declining deficits of the 1980s, the cumulative public sector debt of various levels of German government has grown during virtually the entire existence of the Federal Republic. During the ten years of the 1960s, the total debt doubled. During the 1970s, it doubled every five years. The growth rate in debt began to slow after the first years of the 1980s but began to pick up speed quickly in the early 1990s.

By the end of 1989, the West German government gave the following statistics on cumulative German public sector debt:[49]

Level of Government	Accumulated Debt (billion DM)
Federal	490.5
State	306.5
Local	110
Bundesbahn	44
Bundespost	69.1
Total	1,020.1

These levels of gross government debt were among the lowest of any industrial nation. An OECD study showed that the West German gross debt ratio at 42.7 per cent of nominal GNP was the second lowest among the members of the G-7 nations. Only Great Britain at 39.6 per cent was lower. Italy, Canada, Japan, the United States, and France were higher, some significantly.[50] Almost all EC states were higher and had their cumulative deficits rising faster. With German budget deficits coming down, there even seemed some prospect for cumulative debt reduction.

The record of diminishing deficits ended, however, with German unification. With the total public sector deficit in united Germany rising significantly during at least the early 1990s, the German cumulative public sector deficit can be expected to rise above DM 1.4 trillion by the end of 1992.

Such a high level of cumulative public sector debt would represent a break-out into a completely new level of debt calculations and effects for Germany, by raising the total up to or above one half of all-German GNP (depending on how Eastern German GNP and earlier GDR debt are then calculated). At that level, interest payments will become a significant economic factor in themselves, rising to between 2.5 and 3 per cent of GDP, and providing yet another source of fiscal stimulus that the Bundesbank may well feel obliged to counteract.

But the cumulative deficit level is not the only element in the state role that might have to be recalculated with unification. The entire function of the state in the economy has to be thought through anew, both on a permanent and on a temporary basis. The all-German economy must reconcile the social market economy of the Federal Republic, in which the state played a significant but not overwhelming part, with the nationalized economy of the former German Democratic Republic, in which the state dominated all economic activity. Private capital could and would take over some former GDR state functions, but many would require public expenditures either temporarily or permanently.

The precise boundaries for the role of the state in a united Germany will require extensive planning, careful calculation, and many concrete decisions that were not made in the first phase of unification. They depend on the amount of industry that the German government will decide to protect, on the types of economic activity that can be preserved in Eastern Germany, and on the degree to which the state may find itself obliged to sustain various elements of the Eastern German economy until they begin to grow.

For those who advocated a smaller state role, the prospects and the potential costs of German unification were particularly worrisome, reversing the effects of the *Wende* and perhaps again bringing into question the prospects for private sector growth until Eastern Germany had been fully absorbed and revitalized.

THE PAST AND THE FUTURE

As the analysis of different elements of the structural dilemma has shown, the attitude of the West German authorities at all levels has consistently been ambivalent.

The Kohl government took steps during the 1980s to solve structural problems as part of its general move toward supply-side policies after the *Wende*. It even made some headway toward a solution of structural problems, although it did not solve them.[51] It also committed itself to continuous action toward modernization.[52] There was a gap between what the government said and what it could or would do, but it was making a genuine effort.

The structural debate, having in part been fueled by the West German growth lag during the mid-1980s, even began to subside in the late 1980s, although an IMF study warned against the persistently high level of German subsidies[53] and the Sachverständigenrat continued to press for further changes and recommended cutting subsidies by at least a third by 1995, a target that it described as ambitious but attainable.[54]. The Economics Ministry in April 1990 wrote a long study which suggested that it would attempt to make further progress toward reform but which did not appear to perceive it in urgent terms.[55]

As 1990 advanced, however, the tone of the argument shifted. As the costs of unification and of aid to Eastern Europe and to whatever followed the Soviet Union became more apparent, the entire structural dilemma appeared in a new and different light. It became increasingly clear that the German government could not at the same time pay old subsidies, add new ones, and pay all the other bills that were coming due. With the growing German world role imposing new burdens on the German economy and financial system, new and different solutions had to be found.

The German federal government tried to make selective subsidy cuts but soon found itself confronted with the usual opposition. Berlin and the former inner-German border regions that had been subsidized because of Germany's division insisted that their burdens would be all the greater because of unification. The traditional industrial and agricultural lobbies protested against any reductions in their benefits. Defense industries even argued that they would now need to be subsidized more than before because they would have to spread their fixed costs over a smaller output.

A new and dramatic element in the debate appeared during early 1991, however, when the new Economics Minister, Jürgen Möllemann, staked his office on subsidy reduction. He proposed an annual across-the-board cut of 10 per cent on all German subsidies. He even suggested a new look at farm subsidies and at the EC agricultural system as well as a termination of the coal subsidy. He threatened to resign if the level of subsidies was not reduced by at least DM 10 billion in 1992, and added that he wanted to cut them by another DM 20 billion in 1993 and 1994.[56] Other politicians had earlier regarded such proposals as suicidal. They posed a genuine challenge, especially because only a third of the level of total West German subsidies was under federal control.

Möllemann's arguments had their intended effect, especially because they mirrored widening German public and political concern about the spread of subsidies. After long meetings of special study commissions, new budget figures were agreed for 1992 through 1994. The figures met Möllemann's target total of DM 30 billion, although there were questions about the accuracy of the projections and about the sustainability of the reductions that the government announced. It was also apparent that the reductions did not address the core of the structural problem. Some of the largest budget cuts were achieved through reducing life insurance premium deductibility, Berlin support, military infrastructure costs, and research costs. The institutes had not listed those items among their concerns regarding the competitiveness of the German economy.[57]

Even before Möllemann's statements, there had been growing discussion in West Germany about scaling down subsidy levels significantly in the 1990s. The West German government had spoken of plans to reduce direct and indirect subsidies when contracts for the steel industry and the electricity-generating industry have to be renegotiated in 1992 and 1995 respectively. It had also argued that earlier subsidies of the steel industry have been repaid in part, that the steel industry was now competitive, and that steel subsidies could and should stop. Moreover, the long-standing contracts that compel German electric utilities and the German steel industry to use high-priced domestic coal are to expire in 1995 and 2000 respectively, and the West German government had said that it would reduce the subsidies. The Airbus support program was also proposed for reduction by 1995 and for termination by the end of the century, although that may prove unrealistic.[58]

But the demands of German unity and of aid to the East, combined with Möllemann's threat to resign, called renewed attention to the German subsidy policy and highlighted once again the full scope of Germany's structural dilemma. Whatever may happen to the current plans for subsidy reduction, especially to the details of the government proposals, the structural debate promises to remain intense and divisive during the 1990s as Germany grapples simultaneously with the costs of unification and the need to remain competitive against those who do not have similar burdens.

NOTES TO CHAPTER FIVE

1. The discussion in this chapter is based largely on the reports that were prepared in 1987 as part of the third round of the dialogue between the West German government and the five West German economic institutes about the structural problems of the West German economy. Those reports reviewed the previous discussions as well as the immediate situation at their time. Summaries of the five institutes' reports are in the following West German government publication: Der Bundesminister für Wirtschaft, *Analysen der strukturellen Entwicklung der deutschen Wirtschaft durch fünf wirtschaftswissenschaftliche Forschungsinstitute, BMWI Dokumentation Nr. 287* (Bonn: Federal Ministry of Economics, February 1988), as follows: Deutsches Institut für Wirtschaftsforschung, Berlin, *Exportgetriebener Strukturwandel bei schwachem Wachstum,* pp. 4-38; HWWA-Institut für Wirtschaftsforschung, Hamburg, *Analyse der Strukturellen Entwicklung der deutschen Wirtschaft,* pp. 39-60; Ifo-Institut für Wirtschaftsforschung, *Analyse der Strukturellen Entwicklung der deutschen Wirtschaft,* pp. 61-86; Institut für Weltwirtschaft an der Universität Kiel, *Mehr Strukturwandel für Wachstum und Beschäftigung,* pp. 87-98; and Rheinisch-Westfälisches Institut für Wirtschaftsforschung, *Analyse der Strukturellen Entwicklung der deutschen Wirtschaft,* pp. 99-129. The government's statement is available in the following publication: Deutscher Bundestag, 11. Wahlperiode, *Stellungnahme der Bundesregierung zu den Berichten der fünf an der Strukturberichterstattung beteiligten Wirtschaftsforschungsinstitute (Strukturberichte 1987), Drucksache 11/3017* (Bonn: Deutscher Bundestag, September 29, 1988), pp. 1-27 (hereinafter cited as *Stellungnahme der Bundesregierung*). To avoid overloading the reader, the author has not here dwelt on many separate reports in what has become a large body of literature, as the institute reports cite them and effectively summarize them. But statistics or particularly noteworthy statements by one or another institute are cited separately.

2. Institut für Weltwirtschaft Kiel, *Zehn Jahre Strukturberichterstattung des Instituts für Weltwirtschaft—Eine Bilanz,* Kiel Discussion Paper #137, (Kiel: Institut für Weltwirtschaft, 1988), (hereinafter cited as *Zehn Jahre*).

3. *Wirtschaftswoche,* September 15, 1989, pp. 146-149.

4. Ardagh, *op. cit.,* pp. 86, 94-98.

5. Leo A. Nefiodow, *Der Fünfte Kondratieff* (Frankfurt: Gabler for the Frankfurter Allgemeine Zeitung, 1990), pp. 148-155; *The Economist*, April 20, 1991, pp. 85-86.

6. Henning Klodt, "Industrial Policy and Repressed Structural Change in West Germany," *Jahrbücher für Nationalökonomie und Statistik*, February, 1990, pp. 25-35.

7. For general reviews of West German innovation and research policy, see Wolfgang Krieger, *Technologiepolitik der Bundesrepublik Deutschland* (Ebenhausen: Stiftung Wissenschaft und Politik, 1989); *"Bundesrepublik Deutschland im Internationalen FuE-Wettbewerb,"* DIW Wochenbericht, No. 37/89, September 14, 1989, pp. 443-450; *New York Times*, March 22, 1991, p. D7.

8. *Der Spiegel*, May 6, 1991, pp. 126-128.

9. *Manager Magazin*, September 1990, p. 166.

10. "Die Deutschen haben noch Nachholbedarf," *Handelsblatt*, December 27, 1990, p. 9.

11. Bruce R. Scott, "National Strategies: Key to International Competition," Scott and George C. Lodge, eds., *U.S. Competitiveness in the World Economy* (Boston: Harvard Business School Press, 1987), pp. 71-143; *Süddeutsche Zeitung*, August 30, 1990, p. 31; Konrad Seitz, *Die Japanisch-Amerikanische Herausforderung* (Bonn: Aktuell, 1990), pp. 309-336.

12. *Business Week*, Innovation 1990, p. 122; *The Economist*, June 30, 1990, p. 76; Speech by Edzard Reuter, New York, October 11, 1988.

13. For a review of West Germany's return to scientific research after the war years, see Wolfgang Krieger, *Technologiepolitik der Bundesrepublik Deutschland* (Ebenhausen: Stiftung Wissenschaft und Politik, 1989).

14. B. R. Inman and Daniel F. Burton, Jr., "Technology and Competitiveness," *Foreign Affairs*, Spring 1990, p. 127; *The Economist*, October 6, 1990, pp. 16-17; *Business Week*, Innovation 1990, p. 121.

15. FRG, *Bulletin*, November 1, 1989, pp. 1013-1017.

16. For some of the Research Ministry's actions and policies as well as a review of the past ten years of government-sponsored research, see FRG, Ministry for Research and Technology, "Fields of Action in Information Technology" and *Facts and Figures 1990* (Bonn: Ministry for Research and Technology, 1990). For current research priorities, see *Handelsblatt*, May 2, 1990.

17. David Marsh, "Balancing the Scales," *Financial Times*, February 1, 1991.

18. Institut für Weltwirtschaft Kiel, *Zehn Jahre*.

19. Among the studies, some of which were commissioned by the West German Economics Ministry from the economic institutes, were the following: Martin Bangemann, ed., *Produktions-Standort Bundesrepublik Deutschland auf dem Prüfstand* (Herford, Germany: Busse-Seewald, 1988); Alfred Boss, Institut für Weltwirtschaft Kiel, *Unternehmensbesteuerung und Standortqualität*, Kieler Diskussionsbeiträge 145/146, November, 1988; Reinhard Büscher and Jochen Homann, *Wandert die deutsche Wirtschaft aus? Standortfrage Bundesrepublik Deutschland* (Zurich: Edition Inter-

form, 1989); _____, "Standortdiskussion: Altes Thema mit neuer Brisanz," *Wirtschaftsdienst*, May 1989, pp. 236-240; Deutsches Institut für Wirtschaftsforschung, *Zur Entwicklung der Totalen Faktorproduktivität in den Wirtschaftszweigen der Bundesrepublik Deutschland*, Wochenbericht 8/89, February 23, 1989; _____, *Die Bundesrepublik Deutschland im internationalen FuE-Wettbewerb*, Wochenbericht 37/89, September 14, 1989; _____, *Unternehmensgrösse und Innovationstätigkeit*, Wochenbericht 42/89, October 19, 1989; Gerhard Fels, "Der Standort Bundesrepublik Deutschland im Internationalen Wettbewerb," Armin Gutowski and Bruno Molitor, *Hamburger Jahrbuch für Wirtschafts-und Gesellschaftspolitik* (Tübingen, Mohr, 1988), pp. 9-25; Bernhard Gahlen, Fritz Rahmeyer, and Manfred Stadler, "Zur internationalen Wettbewerbsfähigkeit der deutschen Wirtschaft," *Konjunkturpolitik*, Drittes Heft, 1986, pp. 130-150; Karl-Heinz Hartwig, "Die Bundesrepublik Deutschland im internationalen Standortswettbewerb," Dieter Cassel, ed., *Wirtschaftssysteme im Umbruch* (Munich: Franz Vahlen, 1990), pp. 307-410; Fides Krause-Brewer, "Hürden für Investoren," *Politische Meinung*, January/February 1988, pp. 45-49; Dieter Murmann, "Industriestandort Bundesrepublik Deutschland im internationalen Vergleich," Klaus Weigelt, ed., *Soziale Marktwirtschaft im Aufwind* (Herford, Germany: Busse-Seewald), 1989, pp. 259-276; Rheinisch-Westfälisches Institut für Wirtschaftsforschung, *Standortqualität der Bundesrepublik Deutschland und Veränderung der Standortfaktoren im sektoralen Strukturwandel*, 1989; Adolf Rosenstock, "Die deutsche Industrie im internationalen Preiswettbewerb," *Wirtschaftsdienst*, July 1989, pp. 352-356; W. Ruppert, "Standort Bundesrepublik im Urteil des verarbeitenden Gewerbes," *Ifo-Schnelldienst*, April 1989; Rudolf Sprung, "Sicherung der weltweiten Wettbewerbsfähigkeit," Weigelt, *op. cit.*, pp. 242-257; Westfälische Landesbank, *Investitionsstandort Bundesrepublik Deutschland* (Düsseldorf: Westfälische Landesbank, 1989); Eckhardt Wohlers, "Internationale Wettbewerbsfähigkeit, Wechselkurse und Aussenhandel - einige Anmerkungen zur gegenwärtigen Diskussion in der Bundesrepublik," Gutowski and Molitor, *op. cit.*, pp. 27-40; Ralf Zeppernick, "Die Diskussion um die Standortqualität der Bundesrepublik Deutschland," FRG, *Aktuelle Beiträge*, Nr. 7, 1990, January 30, 1990, pp. 2-7.

20. Westfälische Landesbank, *op. cit.*, p. 2.
21. Sachverständigenrat, *1989/90 Report*, pp. 302-303.
22. Fels, *op. cit.*, p. 9.
23. Westfälische Landesbank, *op. cit.*, p. 25.
24. Ruppert, *op. cit.*, p. 27; Büscher, *op. cit.*, pp. 77 and 84.
25. See, for example, Fels, *op. cit.*, pp. 16-18.
26. "Steuern & Standort," *Wirtschaftswoche*, October 14, 1988, pp. 54-76; Boss, *op cit.*, pp. 1, 18.
27. Deutsches Institut für Wirtschaftsforschung, *Exportgetriebener Strukturwandel*, p. 13.

28. Otto Graf Lambsdorff, *Frische Luft für Bonn* (Stuttgart: DVA, 1987), p. 47.
29. Peter Christ and Ursula Reinsch, "Die unheimliche Verschwendung," Michael Jungblut, *Wirtschaftsjahrbuch 1985* (Hamburg: Die Zeit, 1986), p. 49; International Monetary Fund, *The Federal Republic of Germany: Adjustment in a Surplus Country*, IMF Occasional Paper 64 (Washington: IMF, 1989), p. 87; Thies Thormählen, "Deutschland: Vize-Europameister bei den Subventionen?", *Wirtschaftsdienst*, May 1989, pp 241-248.
30. Sachverständigenrat, *1990/91 Report*, p. 370.
31. "Umorientierung der Subventionspolitik des Bundes?", Deutsches Institut für Wirtschaftsforschung, *Wochenbericht*, August 31, 1989, p. 417; Bundesministerium der Finanzen, *Bericht der Bundesregierung über die Entwicklung der Finanzhilfen des Bundes und Steuervergünstigungen für die Jahre 1987 bis 1990*, cited in OECD, *Germany, 1989/1990*, p. 43. The statistics on subsidies in Germany (as elsewhere) may vary from source to source because of different definitions as to what may constitute a subsidy.
32. West Germans have long discussed and debated the desirability of *Land* and local subsidies. Two efforts to summarize the debate and point of the advantages and disadvantages of such policies within the broad context of industrial policies are: Otto Graf Lambsdorff and Lothar Späth, *Aktive Industriepolitik* (Bonn: Aktuell, 1988); Paul Klemmer, "Ist regionale Strukturpolitik Sinnvoll?", *Wirtschaftsdienst*, August 1987, pp. 379-388.
33. Jutta Helm, "Structural Change in the Ruhr Valley: What Price Social Peace?"; Peter H. Merkl, *op. cit.*, p. 211.
34. For a review of German subsidy policies on which this summary is based, see OECD, *Progress in Structural Reform*, a supplement to OECD Economic Outlook 47 (Paris: OECD, 1990).
35. IMF, *op. cit.*, p. 86; Thies Thormählen, *op. cit.*, pp. 241-248.; also see Michael Bergus, "Europa sät unvermindert Subventionen," *Handelsblatt*, March 1/2, 1990, p. D1.
36. Frank Stille, "Subventionen in den USA," Deutsches Institut für Wirtschaftsforschung, *Vierteljahresheft zur Wirtschaftsforschung*, Heft 1, 1985 (Berlin: Duncker & Humblot, 1985), pp. 5-20.
37. *Stellungnahme der Bundesregierung*, pp. 23-24.
38. Christ and Reinsch, *op. cit.*, p.54; *Handelsblatt*, May 8, 1991.
39. IMF, *op. cit.*, p. 57.
40. *Frankfurter Allgemeine Zeitung*, June 3, 1991.
41. See, for example, Rudolf Scheid, "Subventionen," *Handelsblatt*, December 14/15, 1990, p. 6.
42. Horst Siebert, *op. cit.*, p. 16.
43. *Frankfurter Allgemeine Zeitung*, April 2, 1990.
44. *Frankfurter Allgemeine Zeitung*, September 10 and November 13, 1990; *Der Spiegel*, November 12, 1990, pp. 152-154; *The Economist*, February 16, 1991, pp. 51-52; *Financial Times*, January 10, February 15, and February 27, 1991; *New York Times*, February 15, 1991.

45. Hermann Priebe, "Übersteigerte Klagen geben ein falsches Bild der Lage," *Handelsblatt*, March 26, 1991, p. 7.
46. A detailed study of the state role in the West German economy is Dieter Grosser, ed., *Der Staat in der Wirtschaft der Bundesrepublik* (Opladen: Leske und Budrich, 1985).
47. Katzenstein, *Policy and Politics in West Germany*, pp. 48-54.
48. OECD, "The Public Sector: Issues for the 1990s," quoted in *The Economist*, March 2, 1991, p. 63; for an extensive German comparison, see *Aktuelle Beiträge*, No. 15, 1991, June 3, 1991.
49. *Handelsblatt*, March 26, 1990.
50. *Wall Street Journal*, August 16, 1990; *Financial Times*, August 27, 1991.
51. For a review of German structural policies on which this summary is based, see OECD, *Progress in Structural Reform*, pp. 21-22.
52. *Stellungnahme der Bundesregierung*, pp. 25-26.
53. IMF, *op. cit.*, pp. 52-54.
54. Sachverständigenrat, *Auf dem Wege zur wirtschaftlichen Einheit Deutschlands*, hereinafter cited as 1990/91 Report, pp. 189-193.
55. "Stellungnahme des Bundeswirtschaftsministeriums zu den 1989 vorgelegten Gutachten der Strukturberichterstattung," FRG, *Aktuelle Beiträge*, No. 21, 1990, April 17, 1990. The report of the Economics Ministry summarizes some of the principal observations of the institutes in making its own observations.
56. *Handelsblatt*, March 7, 1991.
57. Wilfried Herz, "Klotzen statt kleckern," *Die Zeit*, April 26, 1991, p. 37; *Frankfurter Allgemeine Zeitung*, July 10, 1991; *Financial Times*, July 10, 1991.
58. OECD, *Germany, 1989/1990*, pp. 44-45.

Six

Theory and History: Erhard and the German Tradition

Ludwig Erhard's actions in June 1948 may have seemed rash to the Allied occupation authorities. They were perhaps risky, given the political and economic circumstances at the time. But Erhard did not act without premeditation. He had carefully considered every step he took, not only by himself but in long discussions with a small group of German economists who had worked and planned in silence and discretion during the Nazi era and the war years.

The leading figures of the group were Alfred Müller-Armack, Wilhelm Röpke, Alexander Rüstow, Leonhard Miksch, Wilhelm Eucken, and Erhard himself. A number of them had elaborated and refined their theories in the relatively secluded confines of Freiburg University during much of the Nazi period and had come to be known as the "Freiburg School." Others had worked in exile, in Geneva or elsewhere. Erhard himself had been in Nürnberg, in what was to become the American zone, and he therefore came to the attention of the Americans.

Erhard and the theorists of the Freiburg School knew what they wanted to achieve and what they wanted to avoid. They wanted to introduce concepts and methods for an entirely new German economic philosophy. They agreed that the postwar economic system should offer Germans new and radically different opportunities. They wanted a solid currency as the foundation of real value and true prosperity. They wanted freedom for individual initiative. They wanted a system that would combine growth and stability, and that would make a radical departure both from the Weimar and the Nazi era. They rejected inflation, cartelization, and connivance between big business and government.

The German political leaders who slowly emerged from jail, seclusion, or exile shared the hopes and fears of the economists. They also wanted a new economic system. Despite many sharp and fundamental disagreements about economic doctrine between various German political parties and factions before and after the establishment of the Federal Republic, they and all other Germans agreed that the economy of the new Germany had to be different from those of the past.

The political leaders wanted social peace as well as prosperity. Conservatives like Konrad Adenauer agreed with postwar German trade union leaders such as Hans Böckler that neither would provoke the pitched political and physical battles between Left and Right that had divided the democratic forces during the 1920s and early 1930s and had thus opened the door to reaction. Despite their different views about the direction that Germany was to take after the war, they sought consensus and accommodation as worthy objectives in their own right. They wanted an economic system that would give all an equal opportunity in order to avoid creating social groups whose bitter frustration would erupt into revolution and—in turn—repression.

As the German economic and political leaders shaped their plans for the future German economy, they found themselves thinking in political, societal, and human terms as well as economic. They saw in Germany's *Stunde Null* an historic, and perhaps a final, opportunity to take Germany on new and totally different bearings. The economy was to be an instrument for prosperity but it was also to safeguard democracy and to help maintain a stable and peaceful society.

THE ALLIES AND THE BIRTH OF THE "SOCIAL MARKET ECONOMY"

The Germans were not yet, however, in charge of their country. It was the victorious Allies who were directing the German economy, and they fully expected to continue to do so for quite a few years. Most German economists and managers were believed to have worked for the Nazis and to have disappeared or at least been discredited with that regime.[1] The Allies were not disposed to turn Germany over to them.

But the Western Allies did not agree with each other about the type of economy they wanted in the Western occupation zones. They agreed, as did the Germans, about what they wanted to avoid, but they had sharply divergent approaches about what they wanted to create.

The 1945 accession of the Labour government of Prime Minister Clement Attlee in England sharpened Allied differences. The British Labour government saw Germany as a place to introduce some of the same socialist principles that it planned to implement in England, and it was also determined never again to permit in Germany the combination of German industry, banking, and reaction that the Nazi era had represented. But London also did not wish to burden the German economy excessively, as had been done after World War I. British leaders, like other Western leaders, read John Maynard Keynes' *The Economic Consequences of the Peace* far more attentively after World War II than after World War I.

Paris above all else feared Germany's potential power. French leaders expected the Americans to retreat again across the Atlantic and the British to retreat again across the Channel, leaving the French once again to face the Germans alone. The French government was far less ready than the Americans or the British to permit, much less support, a German recovery. Paris feared the industrial might of Germany as much as it feared German military force.

The U.S. government began to differ with its friends in the first years of the occupation. Washington became more and more disturbed by the prospect of Soviet domination over all of Europe after the anticipated American withdrawal. The American occupation commander, General Lucius Clay, increasingly saw Germany as a potential bulwark against the Soviet Union. Clay also wanted to prevent Germany from becoming a permanent liability for the United States and others, and he repeatedly blocked Russian and even French efforts to exact reparations from the Western zones. Nor did Clay endorse or support London's efforts to establish a socialist system in Germany.

Allied uncertainties and disagreements served not only to delay and finally to block the originally planned dismantling of the German economy. More important, they gave the Germans themselves the unexpected opportunity to define their own economic destiny, and Erhard took full advantage of that opportunity to establish a system based on his own thinking and on that of the Freiburg School.

THE DOCTRINE OF THE "SOCIAL MARKET ECONOMY"

It was Alfred Müller-Armack who coined the name "*Soziale Marktwirtschaft*," or "Social Market Economy," after considerable debate. He chose it to indicate that the system was based upon the market but that it also had a social—or human—side. He and others stressed the term "market" because they wanted an economy that would be free of state intervention and domination, with the only state role being to protect the competitive environment from monopolistic or oligopolistic tendencies—including its own.

Whatever one might choose to call the system, its single most important principle was that it raised economic freedom for the first time to an honored place in the shrine of German economic doctrine. The principle of free competition in open markets was at the core of the system, and that principle formed the basis of the social market economy even as different theorists propounded variations on how the elements surrounding that principle were to function.

One area of disagreement, which began to emerge over time within the Freiburg School itself and among postwar German economists, was whether the word "*Soziale*" in "*Soziale Marktwirtschaft*" meant that the state could actually be given a useful role as the guardian of social welfare in a competitive system in which, as in all economic systems, there would be losers as well as winners.

Müller-Armack believed that the state could serve such a function without overstepping the bounds of intervention. He argued that the purpose of the social market economy was not only to make competition socially productive but to provide the means needed "to correct inequalities of income." Nonetheless, he also insisted that such expenditures and policies should conform to the principles of the free market, for only the free market would or could create the prosperity needed to finance social programs, and the social programs should not prevent prosperity.[2]

But Müller-Armack, despite his belief in a social system, did not believe in a major state role in management of the economy. He warned that the state's penchant to impose regulation and guidance, even with the best of intentions, could easily "overstep the threshold" of excessive intervention in the market system. He especially warned of "excessive tax rates."[3]

Erhard believed that any state involvement, no matter how well intentioned, would corrupt the system and dilute its blessings. He believed that the market itself was the best social program. He feared the state's good intentions even more than Müller-Armack did, and he warned that even the most well-meaning social measures could condemn the market mechanism to destruction. He had no objection to what he termed "complementary social service measures," but stressed that those had to be introduced and managed in such a manner that they would not destroy the private system that made them possible.

Erhard stated that "economic freedom and obligatory insurance are like fire and water," and warned that a welfare system would reduce persons to subservience and would cripple economic progress. Denouncing the welfare state as "the modern madness," he asserted that true social security could only come about through a person's own efforts and own achievements.[4]

Despite these differences, the theorists of the social market economy generally agreed on a number of common elements. Walter Eucken, a leader of the Freiburg School, drew up the following list of principles that the social market economy needed to respect in order to function effectively:

1) A system of free prices to guide decisions;
2) Currency stability;
3) Open markets;
4) The right to private property;
5) Freedom of contract;
6) Liability for actions and decisions;
7) Consistency of economic policy;
8) Control of tendencies to monopoly.

Beyond these principles of the social market economy, but linked to them and to it, came a more traditional German concept, that of *Ordnung*, which can be directly translated to mean "order" but which really means much more.

Order in the wider German sense is not limited to neat or precisely shaped and proper arrangements. Nor does it mean the paralysis created by an omnipotent administrative structure or by a dictatorship. It does not mean the imposed order of the Nazis. Instead, it expresses a systemic and almost heuristic concept: All things are part of a whole, and must be evaluated in terms of their effects on that whole. All elements shape the whole, and are in turn shaped by it. All depend on it, as it depends on them. This is what *Ordnung* expresses and preserves.

The founders of the social market economy insisted that *Denken in Ordnungen*—to think in terms of systems of order—was essential, and they also spoke of "*Ordo-Liberalismus*."[5] They established what they termed *Rahmenbedingungen*, a framework of conditions within which the system and its components were to function and interact. But the essence of the concept is that this must be a chosen order, not a command order.

Ordnung and *Rahmenbedingungen* were, therefore, not intended to restrict the individual initiative of the participants but to free them, to frame their actions and to emerge from them. The system interacts with the individual in ways that each influences, affecting the other and in turn being affected. The system of order protects freedom, and vice versa. The government's function is to preserve the system, against abuse by the participants but mainly against itself.

GERMAN ECONOMIC HISTORY AND TRADITION

Medieval Germany, lying on the open Central European plain, was divided into hundreds of contending aristocratic, clerical, or burgher sovereignties, whether kingdoms, principalities, dukedoms, bishoprics, or free cities, with their crafts, their trades, their local industries, and with their sense of separation from others. Economic survival in that environment, like political or even physical survival, did not mean expanding across uninhabited terrain, as in the United States. It meant a constant struggle in which there would have to be collaboration with some, competition with others, and an intimate understanding between government, commerce, and production.

Even under these difficult conditions, Germany had already developed a strong economy.[6] It was based on guild and craft production but with elements of merchant capitalism and mercantilism. The trade conducted by its cities ranged far and wide throughout Europe in all directions, and Germany as a whole often had trade surpluses with neighboring states. It also had a tradition of local, regional, or national monopolies going back to the fifteenth and sixteenth centuries, a tradition that was not unique in continental Europe.

The historian Fernand Braudel, commenting on the influence of the German economy in medieval times, observed: "It was as if Germany was constantly pulling after her a Europe which both surrounded and adapted to the German experience—and as if Germany was also changing to conform to her new destiny."[7]

As the European economic system advanced and as the Industrial Revolution began on the Continent itself, Prussia emerged as the strongest German state not only because of its military successes but also because of its dominant economic role. Berlin became an industrial and commercial center, in part because of its position between East and West astride the North German plain and in part because of conscious Prussian efforts to encourage industry. Prussia also came into possession of a portion of the German Rhineland, including what was to become the Ruhr coal and steel basin.

The industrial revolution reached Germany long after it had flowered in England, and the governments of the German states supported local industry because they did not want to be left behind. Many enterprises were government-initiated, government-financed, government-managed, and government-subsidized. As industry grew and prospered in the nineteenth century, the Prussian and other German states consciously supported all economic development and especially transport and industry.[8]

Foreign workers played major roles in German agriculture and industry during the nineteenth century. Many German farm laborers migrated to the cities and to the industrial regions during the century, and they were replaced by workers from Poland or from Galicia. There were almost 300,000 Polish seasonal workers in Germany during the early 1900s, and their numbers continued to rise. A few years later, 62 per cent of the seasonal workers in Mecklenburg were foreigners, largely Poles.[9]

The Northern German states were for the most part richer in natural resources than the Southern states. They had vast agricultural tracts from Schleswig-Holstein in the West through Prussia in the East. They also had coal and iron in the Ruhr Valley. Through the doctrine of primogeniture, widely followed in Northern Germany, large estates and fortunes grew, as did close relations between their owners and the local as well as national governments.

The Southern German states were relatively poor in natural resources except for their people, and those Germans therefore engaged more often in small economic enterprises. They also had no primogeniture rule but subdivided the land between several offspring, leading those offspring to remain in their native towns but not fully able to support themselves from their small parcels of land. The Southern German states, therefore, fostered cottage industries, crafts, and a more independent and self-reliant spirit less closely linked to government.[10]

The German determination to create products known for quality and durability was born in the guilds of the Middle Ages, in which a craftsman was not permitted to pursue a trade until he could demonstrate the ability to make high-quality products. Out of that same tradition came an equally strong passion for education, for no craftsman was recognized until he had thoroughly learned a trade, passed a test, and been certified. The desire to save was born in the German experience of political, military, and economic uncertainty. The desire to export, the subconscious but pervasive mercantilism of the German system, arose out of the sheer necessity for the small states to sell everything they could in order to buy the many things that they still needed.

German banks provided the financing for German industrialization, becoming the essential engines of the German advance to economic power. Many major banks were in Prussia but there were many in other states. The largest six banks included the so-called four "D" banks, the Deutsche Bank (the largest), the Dresdner Bank, the Disconto-Gesellschaft, and the

Darmstadt Bank, as well as the Schaffhausen Bank and the Handelsgesellschaft.[11]

The banks issued stock in new companies, holding some and selling the remainder. They used their holdings to gain seats on the boards of many new companies, beginning to exercise control over those companies and sometimes over whole industries. The Germans called this "finance capitalism." The banks also led the drive for vertical and horizontal integration of German industry, while making certain that the banks would be in a position to guide or at least monitor the functioning of the integrated companies.[12]

Banks also played important and even central roles in shaping industry-wide arrangements for coordinating and directing production and distribution. Different banks formed different arrangements in different industries, especially in coal and steel. Contracts for those arrangements, which came to be known as cartels, were accepted as legal and binding by German courts although they were held to be illegal in England and the United States.[13]

The first German cartel was a salt cartel, the Neckar Salt Union of 1828, formed in Württemberg and Baden. The process of cartelization took hold slowly at first, with six cartels formed by 1870. It was only after 1873, in the slump and depression that followed the post-unification speculative bubble, that the movement took hold. It began in heavy industry and spread throughout other industries. By 1900, there were 275 cartels in operation; by 1908, there were over 500. The major ones were in heavy industry.

The cartels followed different practices, depending on what their members wanted to achieve. Some firms agreed to divide the market in fixed proportions; others, to set prices; others, to limit production; still others, to share profits. Many attempted to reach several of those objectives simultaneously. Many made arrangements under which, with the agreement of government authorities, they would charge high prices on the domestic market while dumping in export markets. By some estimates, different cartel arrangements may have numbered in the thousands at different times.

Relations within the cartels themselves were often bitterly disputatious as members argued about how to coordinate their actions and share the cartel's benefits. Many firms left the cartels because they disagreed about organization and operations. Renegotiation of cartel arrangements when they expired often generated significant defections, and most German companies stayed outside the cartels because they did not welcome the restrictions that membership imposed.[14]

The German Empire, like earlier German principalities, supported crafts and trades, not only for sentimental reasons but also because it wanted to maintain prosperity in all parts of the Empire.[15] Even where it did not act, the highly autonomous regional and local governments would support local industry. They feared centralization and did not want to suffer from its effects. Each state tried to keep as much local industry and other forms of production going to be as economically independent as possible.

Despite several ups and downs of prosperity and depression that marked the first decades of the German Empire, the ultimate wealth and power of the Empire proved immense. German aristocrats, landowners, bankers, and producers put aside their quarrels and worked together to overcome the centrifugal forces that had split the German nation for centuries. They created what might be termed the first German "economic miracle," the turn of the century surge in German industry and commerce in which the bankers, the General Staff, the industrialists, the mercantilists, and the Hohenzollerns joined forces. But many Germans, seeing the war and chaos into which the Imperial establishment had led them, firmly believed after the war that military, diplomatic, and industrial policy had become too closely intertwined.

The German Empire also established, under Chancellor Otto von Bismarck, the social compact under which the German laboring class supported the national ambitions of the newly united German state in exchange for a system of social welfare that would make them, if not full participants in the system, at least its beneficiaries and pensioners. Bismarck was not a socialist, but he believed that it was necessary to accept parts of the socialist platform to sustain prosperity and social cohesion.

From the prosperity of the Wilhelminian Empire, Germany plunged into World War I, a war it was to lose and which was followed by a wide range of economic sanctions, including heavy reparations payments, that Keynes denounced as destructive to world prosperity. The war and its bitter aftermath were in turn followed by that element of their historical experience that has most profoundly marked German economic attitudes, the Great Inflation that wreaked havoc on Germany's social structure and political stability.

It remains difficult, even 70 years after the event, to find a German family, especially in the middle class, that does not have either a direct or a family recollection of the destruction wrought upon them by that inflation. They speak of lost jobs, lost homes, lost savings, of heirlooms that they sold in a desperate attempt to recoup only to find that the money they had received had lost its worth within days. They speak of a life's work wrecked in a single hour.

The record of the inflation can best be conveyed in the following table, the exchange rate for the German Mark against the U.S. Dollar:[16]

U.S. dollar Quotations for the Mark
(monthly averages)

July 1914	4.2
Jan. 1919	8.9
July 1919	14.0
Jan. 1920	64.8
July 1920	39.5
Jan. 1921	64.9
July 1921	76.7
Jan. 1922	191.8
July 1922	493.2
Jan. 1923	17,972.0
July 1923	353,412.0
Aug.1923	4,620,455.0
Sep. 1923	98,860,000.0
Oct. 1923	25,260,308,000.0
Nov. 15, 1923	4,200,000,000,000.0

The fragility of value, the risk of total loss that can shatter lives and demolish families, still remain deeply ingrained in the German psyche even to this day. And with those sentiments came—and remains—a profound determination to reduce the effect of chance and to preserve what one may have achieved, to the point where it is both a doctrine and a mandate.

It would be a mistake, however, to attribute the German odium toward inflation only to the 1923 experience. Serious German economists, like others, recognize that the situation after World War I was unique and is not likely to be repeated. But they, like most other Germans, oppose inflation for reasons that also reflect Germany's current situation.

The single most important reason is the mercantilism, conscious or unconscious, that has been a constant in German thinking since the Middle Ages. In an inflationary world, the country that can maintain stable production prices will be more competitive than the one that cannot, even if the latter periodically devalues. Over the long run, whether through domestic cost pressures or international terms of trade, others will be forced into higher production costs, especially if they have to import many raw materials (as the Germans do). For the stable country, capital and labor costs also remain lower because lower inflation expectations make lower interest rates and stable wages acceptable.

The Germans thus believe that, over the same long run, stable prices promote real growth. They know that this theory runs counter to many notions regarding the stimulative effect of reflationary monetary or fiscal policy, and they might even be prepared to accept stimulation for the short run and particularly during a slowdown. The German government even tried it on several occasions between 1966 and 1982 (Chapter 2). But it was in many ways antithetical to the German way of thinking. When it also failed to produce satisfactory results, it was abandoned.

Beyond theory, German demographic realities have added further reasons for anti-inflationary policies. As the population ages and as more Germans live on pension or on fixed investment incomes, the importance of price stability has become a powerful consideration for a growing sector of the electorate.

The doctrine is deceptively simplistic yet demonstrably successful: Take care of the free market and take care of the value of money, and growth will take care of itself.

THESIS, ANTITHESIS, SYNTHESIS

The review of German postwar economic doctrine and of German economic history and tradition points to a sharp and seemingly irreconcilable contradiction between some elements of the doctrine and some elements of the tradition.

On the one hand, Germans believe firmly that they want and have a doctrine of social market economy, a doctrine that stresses freedom, competition, efficiency, and the open interplay of market forces. German economic texts, including some written by persons who have functioned within the system and understand how it may on occasion deviate from market principles, constantly stress that the economy is based on a free and pure price mechanism.

On the other hand, Germans are not only creatures of their theory but also of their history and their tradition, not only because they may have subconsciously assimilated them but because some elements—like the role of the banks—are part of the present as of the past. Although the situation of present-day Germany is very different from that of the earlier Germany, a powerful tradition remains in place, and it can come to life in a united Germany perhaps even more than in a divided Germany.

Germany throughout its history did not produce any internationally or even nationally influential schools of economic philosophers or even any individual economic philosophers as well known and as influential as those produced in England or France, although a number of Germans wrote about economic theory.[17] Therefore, German economic tradition has at least as powerful an influence on German economic behavior as German economic philosophy does, and that tradition is in many ways antithetical to Erhard's doctrine. It has always included a strong and very direct state role, consistent and determined protectionism, and private collaborative agreements very often linked to the state as well.

But the German tradition also includes the excesses that the Nazis committed in the name of tradition. The Hitler regime carried dictatorial centralism to such an extreme that it not only encouraged but legitimized radical shifts in the opposite direction. It discredited any elements of the German tradition that it embraced.

The German economic philosophy that exists today in practice is based on the reconciliation of opposites. It is, in a very real sense, under a constant tension between the Erhard principles, the German tradition, the Nazi excesses, and the historical recollection of panics and collapses. Germans operate at different levels in different ways, carrying within them both the entrepreneurial spirit and the cooperativist tradition, sometimes confusing others but usually not themselves.

For the Germans, an equally important element in the tradition is not in economic, but in almost metaphysical, thought, in the dialectic of Georg Wilhelm Friedrich Hegel. Hegel, the German philosopher of history who formulated the notion of the dialectic, believed that thesis and antithesis resolve themselves in synthesis. He saw the shaping of synthesis not as a compromise between opposites but as their combination at a higher level. That combination contains elements of both the thesis and the antithesis but brings them together in a new entity that does not derogate either but supersedes both.

Hegel's doctrines have always been controversial, especially in Anglo-Saxon nations, with both Marxism and Nazism being attributed to them, and the notion of the dialectic has not been widely accepted in Anglo-Saxon philosophy. But, however one may evaluate his teachings, they have left in German thinking a readiness to accept the notion of constructive coexistence of opposites. Germans see no internal contradiction in the term "social market economy," but only a synthesis, just as Müller-Armack saw the competitive market and social protection as mutually reinforcing.[18] They see and appreciate the possibility for combinations that outsiders would find illogical and even suspect.[19]

From the German standpoint, each element of the system serves the other. Only free competition can produce the efficiencies that create prosperity.

Only a framework accepted and established by the competitors can make certain that the struggle turns neither to anarchy nor to hierarchy. And it is acceptable for firms within that framework to maintain relations that soften the edge of the competitive struggle without, however, eliminating it. The system represents the belief that separate persons and organizations cannot be fully free except as parts of an overarching structure, and that the structure in turn cannot survive if the components are not truly free.

Systems, be they political or economic, fit those who believe in them and can operate comfortably within them. Every nation may, and perhaps must, have its own system, and the differences between them reflect the differences in doctrine and in the readiness of a nation to accept that doctrine because it fits its own experience or its broad structure of belief. For Germans, the social market economy as it evolved in West Germany represents the synthesis that fitted and the synthesis that worked.

THE EVOLUTION OF DOCTRINE AND PRACTICE

West German thinking about some aspects of economic doctrine evolved significantly throughout the 40 years before unification, going through at least two different phases before coming to rest in a third.

The original doctrines of Ludwig Erhard and the Freiburg School, with their almost Schumpeterian thrust toward venture capitalism and toward rapid if perhaps irregular growth, were mainly followed during the first decade and a half of the West German state. Erhard's firm personal aversion to state intervention or to collusion in the economy held sway, especially because he was Economics Minister but also because it represented a consensus. His revulsion to state intervention and to monopoly or oligopoly were all the more accepted because they represented a reaction to the Nazi state and to its industrial collaborators. New and small German enterprises were formed at a rapid rate that was not to lag significantly until the 1960s.[20] Foreign investors, many of them American, helped to fuel the boom, as did the influx of refugees. As fate would have it, the strong growth philosophy of the Erhard years gave Germany precisely what it needed at a crucial time.

Erhard's success was not as sweet as it might have been because his principles were not followed as perfectly as he would have preferred. The philosophical divisions within the Freiburg School itself, especially about the meaning and implications of the term "social," helped to sow some uncertainty. So did Konrad Adenauer's own reservations. The Chancellor was much more inclined than Erhard to work with the major figures of German industry and labor. For political reasons, he periodically—and increasingly—took actions that disturbed Erhard and disrupted the application of Erhard's ideas.

Over time, the Federal Republic also moved further toward Müller-Armack's than Erhard's interpretation of the social market economy. The word "social" began to take on a life of its own and a different meaning than Erhard had originally intended, moving away from the principles that he had advanced and espoused toward social welfare systems that some of Erhard's supporters still believe to have jeopardized Germany's long-term growth.[21]

But there were other pressures that were even more troubling to Erhard. He was disturbed to see the industrial associations and the chambers of commerce reestablishing themselves as factors in economic decision-making, to the degree to which some spoke of the "self-administration" of business.[22] Although the poisonous link between industry and government that dominated the German Empire and the Nazi era did not return (and has not returned), Erhard feared the growing strength of lobbies and he even came to feel it. He was deeply disappointed in the final version of the *Kartellgesetz*, the cartel law, which had been drafted in his ministry in 1950 and which was then the subject of bitter disputes that made it one of the most controversial bills of the 1950s. Industry opposed the draft vigorously and Adenauer did not fully support it. When the law was finally passed in 1957, it specified eight major exceptions to its application whereas Erhard's draft had contained none.[23]

By the late 1960s, the original doctrine of the Freiburg School had suffered dilution from the right and the left. The competitive environment was less rigorous than Erhard and his followers would have wished. Social welfare legislation had advanced further than Erhard wanted although it remained well within the bounds of what some members of the Freiburg School found acceptable. Government had become a more prominent player in the social field than Erhard wanted, and it was no longer as firm in maintaining competition as he would have wished. Growth had slowed somewhat. But the foundations of Erhard's doctrines were still widely accepted and supported.

After the 1967 election and Erhard's fall, Karl Schiller's Keynesianism became the dominant doctrine of German economic management, at least at the Bonn level. The principles and practices of "*Globalsteuerung*" and the "*Konzertierte Aktion*," which particularly offended Erhard, had their day. Fiscal policy and government direction (by influence, if not by decree) of broad economic activity became the dominant theme, and the SPD's concept of the social market economy combined with the party's desire for fiscal stimulus to produce a large social welfare program.

Although Schiller fell when the German system proved to be unresponsive to his guidance, the Keynesian interlude continued for some time after his resignation in moderated form. The Social Democrats remained in power, continuing to expand the social welfare system and adding to state subsidies. Schiller's successor at the Finance Ministry, Helmut Schmidt, also practiced what could be termed Keynesianism, although his pragmatic instincts modified it in some ways.

As growth slowed and competitive pressures on occasion shifted against West Germany, the German tradition began increasingly to assert itself. The definition of a social market economy began to give ever less weight to the word "market." The federal system and the states began to compensate for irregularities in economic cycles and for shifts in world production by beginning to support some sectors and industries while sheltering others. In an even greater departure from the Erhard tradition, the government became an instrument for the preservation of existing structures rather than a force for renewal. It stepped into the arena ever more frequently to favor one or another established player or groups of players.

By the late 1970s and early 1980s, however, German public and political opinion increasingly turned away from experiments in coordination, fiscal stimulus or restraint, and demand manipulation. One economic analyst observed that the West German economy had performed more successfully when it had been managed on the basis of the rather "primitive" doctrine of the pure Freiburg School than when more "sophisticated" economic theory came to be applied.[24]

Helmut Kohl's *Wende* represented a turn away from Keynesianism but not a full turn back to a pure market economy. Too much had changed since the 1960s to make a complete turn feasible or desirable. Nonetheless, there was in Kohl's thinking a clear conviction that the state had become too powerful and that its activities needed to be curtailed and their costs reduced. He, too, had come to fear the destabilizing ratchet effect created by the combination of Keynesian economic doctrine and the temptations of political budget manipulation. Kohl thus qualified as a supply-sider and also as a supporter of a more traditional definition of the social market economy.

With the *Wende*, German economic philosophy tried to find a balance that could represent its true resting point. It sought a synthesis that combined the economic dynamism of Erhard's and the Freiburg School's original concepts with the German tradition of cooperation among different elements of the economy. The *Wende* also had strong streaks of pragmatism and of Bundesbank policy. It represented an effort to combine the many strands that were part of German economic theory, history, and tradition into one common policy.

By 1989, the doctrines of the *Wende* had combined with European integration and relative global stability to offer solutions to the problems that had beset the German economy during the late 1960s and 1970s, but unification has posed new problems and may again arouse questions of doctrine.

THE SOCIAL MARKET ECONOMY AS THE "THIRD WAY"

The discussion about German economic doctrine came alive during 1990 as the prospect of German unification drew near and as it also became clear that the West German economy would essentially take over the East German. Several East German political parties and a number of intellectuals insisted that they did not wish to replace the failures and shortcomings of the Communist system with a capitalist system that they perceived as excessively materialistic and potentially exploitative. A number of East Germans said that they preferred to look for what they termed the "Third Way," a system that would combine the dynamism and growth of the capitalist system with some of the leavening and protective effect that a socialist system offered—at least as originally conceived by such democratic German socialist thinkers as Eduard Bernstein.

To reply to these concerns, the Ludwig Erhard Foundation published a book by Willy Kraus which described the social market economy itself as the "third way."[25] The book argued that the social market economy represented an original and correct path beyond capitalism on the one hand and central direction on the other. It added that the social market economy combined the great historical theories of liberalism and the goals of socialism, with competition as the crucial link. It assured East Germans that the social elements of the system would compensate for the potential inequities of the market.

Otto Schlecht, then state secretary in the Economics Ministry, added the official imprimatur of the West German government to the "third way" thesis. He said that the social market economy could claim to represent the true third way because it not only maximized prosperity and opportunity but also the social well-being of individuals.[26] Schlecht added, as the Freiburg School had believed, that only a free economic existence could guarantee a free political existence. The social market economy was, therefore, not only the foundation of prosperity but also the prerequisite for democracy. For East

Germany, it represented not only a prospect for a decent life but even an essential prerequisite for the liberty that its people had long sought.

Schlecht's arguments, like those of the Erhard Foundation, were accepted by the East German government that came to power in 1990 and that negotiated the treaty for unification with Kohl and West Germany. The GDR, through the treaty and subsequent regulations, essentially agreed that it would adopt the social market economy of West Germany.

What remains more difficult to determine, however, is the effect that German unification will have on the German economic style and—perhaps—even on the German economic philosophy as they have been articulated and practiced in West Germany. For the real challenge to the German doctrine will come over the decade of the 1990s, and German unity will become the crucial test.

With unification, West Germans are joined by a population that will represent about one fifth of the total population of united Germany but that has had a very different experience. It has already demonstrated that it wants both the free market and the social element of the social market economy. Many East Germans appear to want economic freedom perhaps even more than West Germans want it, because they feel that they need to catch up. But many others want the state protection and a measure of state guidance, also perhaps more than the West Germans want it because they are accustomed to it and because they are uncertain what unity will bring.

The main test that the Eastern Germans will add is the determination to ask questions. Having come to unity with highly exaggerated expectations, they will measure their achievements against standards that may be impossible to meet. But each major shortfall may well raise questions not only of performance but of doctrine, asking not how policy may have failed but whether the philosophy on which that policy was based is fundamentally correct. This will prove to be one of the major challenges of the German system throughout the decade of the 1990s, and it is not yet clear whether the decade will pass without some new shift in the doctrine that brought West Germany from defeat to prosperity.

CONSERVATIVE DYNAMISM

The West German structure, based on the combination of doctrine and tradition, makes for conservatism, for a policy of small rather than giant steps, for slow evolution rather than revolution. This was evident in the discussion of the German style and of German thinking.

This conservative economy has, however, been dramatically productive, prosperous, and even dynamic. It has also been remarkably successful, although the reasons for that success are not all to be found within itself. It has not been as innovative as the American or the Asian economies, but it has been at the core of what is arguably the strongest and longest period of expansion in European history since the age of discovery.

Like the West German style, West German economic philosophy was most successful because it represented a consensus. Even the Bundesbank, for all its power and prestige, could not act without that consensus. The consensus was shaken during the downturns of the 1960s and 1970s and also by the effects of the two previous oil shocks, but it was reinforced by the growth of the latter 1980s.

The very simplicity of the basic concepts behind the German consensus probably reinforces it, especially because the concepts grow out of German experience and German needs. Germans will respond positively to such words as "stability," "constancy," "caution," or "predictability," and they will respond not only as economic but also as political beings. Most of all, perhaps, the concepts offer assurance that the values of the economic and political system will not again be permitted to deteriorate or to collapse. The object of the doctrine remains, as Erhard himself wrote, *Wohlstand für Alle*, or prosperity for all.

Some German economists say privately that their theory of the social market economy, as well as the way it is applied, may not bear profound analysis in comparison with the great structures of economic thought that have been created in Great Britain or the United States during the twentieth century. The social market theory does not even bear critical comparison to the Austrian School, the major school to which it is perhaps most closely related. Unlike a number of major economic concepts, the social market economy has not generated an extensive body of writing or even a structured and disciplined school, although there are regular publications—such as those of the Ludwig Erhard Stiftung—that continue to analyze the theory and to point out its relevance to the solution of current problems. It will probably never win a major international prize in economic theory. But it cannot be dismissed as inconsequential in its effects. Germans shrug their shoulders and say, "Others may have the better economists, but we have the better economy."

NOTES TO CHAPTER SIX

1. In addition to separate citations in this chapter, some of the general information on German economic philosophy has been drawn from the following sources: Bernhard Keller, *Wirtschaftstheorie und Wirtschaftspolitik in der Bundesrepublik Deutschland* (Frankfurt: Verlag Moritz Diesterweg, 1984), pp. 1-44; Graham Hallett, *The Social Economy of West Germany* (London: MacMillan, 1973), pp. 13-24; Lampert, *op. cit.*, pp. 76-104.
2. Alfred Müller-Armack, "Soziale Marktwirtschaft," quoted in Keller, *op. cit.*, pp. 31-32.
3. *Ibid.*
4. Ludwig Erhard, *Wohlstand für Alle*, pp. 245-263.
5. Siebert, *op. cit.*, p. 6.
6. The material on medieval Germany is based on Fernand Braudel, *The Wheels of Commerce* (New York: Harper & Row, 1982), pp. 188-191, 207, 320-321, 332, 377, and 418.
7. *Ibid.*, p. 321.
8. W.O. Henderson, *The Rise of German Industrial Power, 1834-1914* (London: Temple Smith, 1975), pp. 71-79.
9. Hajo Holborn, *A History of Modern Germany, 1840-1945* (New York: Knopf, 1969), pp. 373-374.
10. Norbert Walter, *West Germany's Economy* (Washington: The American Institute for Contemporary German Studies, 1987), p. 5.
11. W.O. Henderson, *op. cit.*, p. 183.
12. Holborn, *op. cit.*, pp. 382-383.
13. Henderson, *op. cit.*, p. 184; Holborn, *op. cit.*, pp. 384-385.
14. Henderson, *op. cit.*, pp. 178-181; Holborn, *op. cit.*, p. 384; Frank B. Tipton and Robert Aldrich, *An Economic and Social History of Europe, 1890-1939* (Baltimore: Johns Hopkins University Press, 1987), pp. 20-21.
15. Holborn, *op. cit.*, pp. 385-387.
16. Gordon A. Craig, *Germany, 1866-1945* (Oxford: Clarendon Press, 1978), p. 450.
17. For a summary review of German economic writing and thinking, see Joseph Schumpeter, *History of Economic Analysis* (New York: Oxford University Press, 1955), pp. 501-511, 801-807, 843-855, 877-885, and 1155-1157.
18. Comment by Horst Wünsche, Ludwig Erhard Stiftung, Bonn, September 5, 1990. For greater detail on this reconciliation and synthesis, including Müller-Armack's and other German discussion of the double content of social market doctrine, see Alan Peacock and Hans Willgerodt, eds., *Germany's Social Market Economy: Origins and Evolution* (New York: St.

Martin's Press, 1989), and Peacock and Willgerodt, eds., *German Neo-Liberals and the Social Market Economy* (New York: St. Martin's Press, 1989).

19. It is, therefore, possible to find in Germany the most ardent advocates of the Erhard doctrine even among those who may try to influence government import lists, obtain subsidies for excess agricultural production, or try to shape legislation on behalf of their associations. They will not accept any suggestion that their actions lack logical consistency (of course, for that matter, neither would lobbyists in other countries).

20. Hardach, *op. cit.*, pp. 141-143.

21. For an analysis of Erhard's concepts and the way they became distorted in the evolution of the West German economy, see Norbert Walter, "Das Phänomen Ludwig Erhard" and "Wettbewerbspolitik—eine Aufgabe von Gestern?" in Norbert Walter, ed., *Was würde Erhard heute tun?* (Stuttgart: Horst Poller Verlag, 1986), pp. 7-19 and 47-68.

22. Katzenstein, *Policy and Politics in West Germany*, p. 87.

23. Katzenstein, *loc. cit.*, p. 88.

24. Hallett, *op. cit.*, pp. 66-67.

25. Willy Kraus, *Soziale Marktwirtschaft* (Bonn: Ludwig Erhard Stiftung, 1990).

26. Otto Schlecht, "Ein Modell macht Karriere," *Frankfurter Allgemeine Zeitung*, March 3, 1990.

Seven

Uniting Germany: Where did the "Economic Miracle" Go?

East and West Germany used to be both the closest and the most distant European states in economic substance and style. The economies were very similar. Both concentrated on industrial production, especially machine tools, chemicals, automobiles, and precision manufactures. Both had a well-trained labor force and an important foreign trade sector although their trade went largely in opposite directions. But the East German economy was under highly centralized direction, with virtually no private property, guided by a detailed and purportedly precise planning system, and with no separate room for decision or initiative.

On July 1, 1990, the two Germanies became one economy in law and on paper, but not yet in reality. Much more will be needed to create a truly united economy. The main adjustment burden in this process falls on Eastern Germany. It is that economy that will have to be reshaped and restructured. The main cost burden falls on West Germany. Once the Wall came down on October 9, 1989, the choice for West Germany was either to absorb East Germany where it was or to have East Germany come West. The West German government chose the former.

The economic aspects are the most demanding but also the most important aspects of German unification. East Germany had 43 per cent of West Germany's area, 26 per cent of its population, and an optimistically estimated 12 to 14 per cent of West Germany's economy. Merging that relatively small economy into the larger one has led to major economic, social, psychological, and political problems on both sides, and it will also change both.

The basic paperwork of unification was accomplished quickly and relatively smoothly in 1990 despite some arguments about specific issues. West

German economic and financial laws and regulations now apply in all of Germany. The D-Mark is the common currency. The business practices of Eastern Germany are now supposed to match those of Western Germany.

The hard part of unification, however, was yet to follow. For there was from the beginning a pernicious link between the earlier and later phases of the East German transition to a free market economy. Policies calculated to make the initial adjustment as painless as possible would almost certainly hamper long-run growth and prosperity. Permanent economic efficiency could only be achieved by permitting and even by forcing some immediate dislocations, whereas temporary compromises could lead to permanent structural burdens. But excessively severe disruptions might jeopardize the economic and political stability required for a smooth unification process. The German government has had to find a policy that navigated between the horns of that dilemma, and it has had difficulty finding such a policy.

THE EAST GERMAN ECONOMY

The East German economy, 40 years after the founding of the German Democratic Republic (GDR) and almost 20 years after the building of the Wall, presented a shabby picture at the time of the merger. Few firms could compete internationally. Consumer goods were of such low quality that many persons refused to buy them even when they were available. The infrastructure was in disrepair. Building walls and plumbing were in decay. Environmental damage was so great that children throughout the Southern GDR suffered massively from bronchial disorders and the water throughout much of the region was unsafe to drink.

The picture was all the more lamentable because East Germany covered what had been a highly prosperous area. The Berlin-Leipzig-Dresden triangle contained Germany's most advanced industries from the nineteenth century until 1945. The headquarters of many distinguished German firms, including Zeiss, Leuna, and Schott, had been there. Even during the GDR period, more of Saxony's *Land* product came from industry than that of any *Land* in West Germany. Before World War II, the per capita GDP in Eastern Germany exceeded that in Western Germany. Mecklenburg and Brandenburg were prime agricultural areas. East Germany's combination of industry and agriculture should have produced a powerful and wealthy economy, one of the most successful in Europe and even in the world.

Some of the weaknesses of the GDR economy could be traced to its slow revival after World War II. The Soviet army dismantled, shipped, and often carelessly destroyed countless factories for reparations. Until 1953, East Germany also had to send considerable production to the Soviet Union for the same reason. But East Germany suffered not as much from its slow start as from the directions that it chose in the 1950s and that it never abandoned despite several half-hearted efforts to introduce market incentives and practices.

The principal internal thrust was toward centralized planning, centralized direction, centralized production, and centralized distribution, intended to produce economies of scale and to put the entire economy under the control of the state. Only 2 per cent of the officially calculated East German GDP was privately produced, and that was mainly in handicrafts and small shops. Most economic activity was directed by the appropriate ministries (industry, agriculture, etc.) and managed through cartels termed *Kombinate*, or combines.

The *Kombinate*, introduced and expanded in the 1970s and early 1980s, controlled and coordinated all productive forces in any sector, usually by industry and area. The number of nationwide *Kombinate* grew to 126 and of regional *Kombinate* to 95. Together, they managed virtually all East German production and export.[1] Although a thriving black market was often reported in East Germany, productive resources could officially be allocated only in accordance with plans developed by the appropriate ministries and carried out by state enterprises under *Kombinat* control.

Exports, like production, were centrally controlled. The trade ministry negotiated export agreements. The *Kombinate* carried them out. Almost three-quarters of all exports went to the Soviet Union and to other members of the CMEA (the Council for Mutual Economic Assistance), mainly in Eastern Europe. Only one quarter went to the West, and half of that to the Federal Republic.[2] This proved to be a special problem in unification, because the East European and Soviet markets for East German goods collapsed during 1990.

The centralized direction of the economy and the lack of such Western concepts as credit or depreciation produced the rigidities of monopoly as well as a slow and inadequate pace of investment. East German capital development lagged far behind the West's, leaving an aging and inefficient production base.[3] The managed trade agreements with CMEA countries reinforced those inefficiencies, as East German producers did not have to compete either domestically or internationally and as they had no reason to develop or defend markets.[4] Finally, even trade between the Germanies slowed because of low East German quality.[5]

As the East and West German economies increasingly diverged during the last several decades, the largest single gap appeared in productivity. A 1990 Deutsche Bank survey showed that productivity in East Germany averaged less than half that in West Germany on a sector basis,[6] but the economists who wrote the survey later explained that they had been unrealistically optimistic and that East German productivity more probably averaged only a third of West German.

By the same token, labor costs and wages in East Germany before unification were well below those in West Germany. The average industrial wage in East Germany during 1988 was 1,292 East marks; that in West Germany was 3,657 DM, and per capita currency assets in East Germany were 11,022 marks as opposed to 40,747 DM in West Germany.[7] On the other hand, such average wage figures for East Germany did not include special premium wages, child allowances, or other designated benefits that might have amounted to an average of 300 marks per month.[8] Therefore, East German wages were not nominally out of line with productivity.

Low wages in East Germany could be tolerated because of the considerably lower cost of necessities. Basic foodstuffs, such as potatoes, cabbage, and bread, when available, cost only one sixth as much in East as in West Germany. So did children's shoes, a bus ticket, or home heating and electricity. Housing—although often decrepit and substandard—cost only about one fifth as much. On the other hand, such consumer durables as washing machines, refrigerators, or color television sets cost three or four times as much in the East as in the West, if one could find them.[9] The GDR over time constructed a tangled system of subsidies, funded by tax revenues and by profits from state enterprises, to allocate incentives and disincentives while maintaining political stability. Perhaps a third of the GDR state budget was spent on some form of subsidy.[10]

It would be misleading, however, to conclude from this recital of East German economic problems that the economy did not function at all. Although it lagged badly during the 1980s and increasingly failed to meet plan objectives even in officially released statistics, it did gradually increase productivity and it undertook steps intended to stimulate individual inventiveness. It maintained traditional German vocational schooling, steadily increasing the percentage of trained employees, including those with advanced education.

The East German leadership also did make some efforts to modernize the economy. GDR indices of gross industrial production between 1970 and 1988 rose dramatically in three important modern industries. With 100 as the 1970 base, the 1988 production index of the electrotechnical industry reached 872, that of data processing and office machinery reached 684, and that of precision mechanics and optics reached 520.[11] These statistics showed that East Germany had actually made greater efforts than West Germany to concentrate investment in areas of growing importance. One third of all new GDR investments during the 1980s concentrated in microelectronics, a higher proportion than in any West European state and a reflection of the GDR's assigned responsibilities within the CMEA system.[12] Much of the investment was dissipated by mismanagement and by a wish for autarky which led the GDR to spread its limited resources too thin. No single technology became internationally competitive.[13] But the high-technology trainees and workers, as well as some facilities, existed when the Wall came down and went West at unification.

The East German economy also grew. Its GDP (by its own statistics) would have ranked it seventh in the European Community in 1983, and its production per capita would have ranked it eighth.[14]

The economy of the GDR was not, therefore, the total failure often portrayed. But its production had not been shaped by a competitive market system. When the Wall fell the economy was grossly inefficient and paralyzingly centralized. It could be characterized as having a strong but ill-shaped body, a large but slow head, failing circulation, and a severely impaired nervous system.

The East German economy's principal failure, however, was not mechanical or statistical but human. The GDR could produce, but it could not produce what its people wanted. It left them dispirited, indifferent to their work, impoverished in the midst of their labor, and after a life's effort owning nothing except some crumply paper bills and chipped coins that were worthless outside their borders and scorned within. East German workers said derisively and bitterly: "We pretend to work, and they pretend to pay us."

UNIFICATION PLANNING AND ACTIONS

Many studies about the prospects and problems of German economic union appeared soon after the collapse of the Wall. The West German government asked the five economic institutes and the Sachverständigenrat to evaluate the state of the East German economy and to recommend improvements, which they did. The major West German banks produced analyses, as did many official and private economists.

The studies of the German economic institutes and of the Sachverständigenrat all agreed that the transition to a smoothly functioning and fully integrated German economy would take a long time and would require some substantial structural adjustment in Eastern Germany. The Sachverständigenrat insisted that the best way to accomplish this was through private investment and private initiative, and that it was better to have a brutal but short transition that would quickly weed out inefficient producers and production lines rather than to begin a program of subsidization in order to save jobs. Like the other estimates, it expressed confidence that German unity would stimulate growth over the long run. Studies done by staff members of the U.S. Federal Reserve and the IMF agreed.[15]

Rapid actions toward economic and political unity followed on both sides during 1990:

- On March 18, general elections established a new East German government under the leadership of the East German CDU. That government renounced a "third way" and decided to adopt the political and economic system of West Germany by unification.
- On July 1, monetary union followed and the Bundesbank became the central bank for East as well as West Germany. This, more than any other economic measure, could be regarded as the basic and irreversible step toward German unity, for it had been the creation of separate monetary regimes in 1948 that had put the two Germanies on separate paths.
- On that same date, East German marks were converted into West German D-Marks at a ratio of one to one for many transactions and for modest personal accounts. The Bundesbank had favored a more widespread two-to-one ratio, which would have come closer to expressing the real purchasing-power ratio of the two currencies, but the government chose parity for political reasons and mainly to prevent large-scale East-West migration. This exchange rate revalued the East German mark by 300 to 400 per cent, far more than the East German economy could bear.
- On October 3, 1990, political union followed, and East Germany not only joined West Germany but adopted major elements of West German law and regulation. The law governing economic unification, which listed only the titles of the laws and regulations to be adopted in East Germany, ran to over 500 closely spaced pages.[16]
- In December 1990, the Minister-Presidents of the 16 German states met for the first time since 1947, in a meeting that was distinguished by mutual assurances of cooperation but very sobering disputes about how to finance unification.

- On January 1, 1991, a united German tax code came into force. In addition, a number of measures were introduced to support business and investment in Eastern Germany.[17]

The West German government also moved on the microeconomic side. On June 17, 1990, it took over a trust agency, the Treuhandanstalt, which had been established by the GDR to assume control over East German firms and to turn them over to new management through privatization. The agency had also been given the authority to reorganize and reconstruct (*sanieren*) the companies. It assumed the assets and liabilities of about 8,000 East German enterprises, valued officially (and highly optimistically) at DM 600 billion, in order to sell them to German and other bidders. Almost one fourth of those enterprises, however, were involved in public functions (utilities, etc.) that were not to be privatized.

The Treuhandanstalt became the focal point for the modernization of East German industry. After a bitter dispute about which major government entity, if any, would supervise it, the Finance Ministry was finally given the task because the Treuhandanstalt's mandate was to handle government property, a financial responsibility. This gave the Ministry considerable power over the future of Eastern Germany and, indirectly, over the future of German economic policy for at least a decade.

The Treuhandanstalt began excruciatingly slowly, delaying rather than speeding the movement of investment funds to Eastern Germany. By late 1991, it had sold only about 3,500 firms for several hundred million DM, with about 20 per cent of the purchases being management buy-outs.[18] It was moving very carefully, expecting to be in business for a long time. Even as it sold some firms, it created others, as West German investors often wanted to buy only a core East German company and not those firms that had been tied to it by East German planners. The unbought firms had to be sold or restructured separately, creating a virtually interminable task.

To support the process further, the West German federal and state governments in May 1990 established a special "Fund for German Unity" of DM 122 billion to support East German public expenditures until 1994. A condition for establishing the fund had been that the new Eastern German states would not immediately benefit from the normal division of federally collected tax revenues, or from the burden-sharing allocations that had been used to transfer funds from the richer to the poorer West German states. These exceptions have proven to be costly for Eastern German states, and they have protested them.

The European Community began taking steps to bring East German territory into the Community. Even before German unification, the EC Commission issued a statement welcoming the anticipated development and pointing to the growth potential of East Germany despite transition problems. It stated that the East German states would be eligible for certain forms of Community assistance.[19]

After some negotiation, the EC and Germany agreed that the former GDR territories would be brought into the Community in phases, with the full application of EC law to be postponed until an undetermined date linked to the 1992 Single Market process but allowing for special temporary exceptions on such particularly sensitive and difficult problems as environmental standards until 1996.[20]

The Community also permitted some funds to be used in Eastern Germany as part of its common structural policy framework, but the EC Commission—and the Federal Republic itself—made certain that the amount of support that Eastern Germany was getting from the EC did not divert significant resources from European areas that were considered more needy and that did not have the benefit of a wealthy brother.[21]

The EC role in German integration also posed problems, however. It could be good for investors in Eastern Germany, as their production would be marketable across most of Europe, but it also meant that Eastern Germany would be subject to the growing body of EC regulation. EC agricultural rules began to be applied in Eastern Germany even before the others, leading already before the end of 1990 to familiar arguments about EC quotas, prices, and agricultural subsidies. The EC rules also led to farming cutbacks, costing large numbers of jobs. The Sachverständigenrat complained that East German agriculture would be hobbled by the EC system. It urged that East German agriculture be freed, not put under yet another bureaucracy.[22]

East German firms as well as individuals began taking steps to prepare for unity long before that unity came about. The West German business newspaper *Handelsblatt* introduced a classified column in which East German firms could advertise either for Western partners or for information about establishing ties. The column was popular and effective. It carried hundreds of notices within a few weeks and sometimes covered a half or even an entire page of the newspaper. Many relations were established. In addition, West German firms sent salesmen, managers, or buyers into East Germany, trying to establish new contacts or—in many cases—to renew old ones. As investors, speculators, or curiosity-seekers flooded into East Germany, many observers complained that the new arrivals had a carpetbagger mentality and would exploit the situation and the people in Eastern Germany.

Many West German firms did indeed go into Eastern Germany. Volkswagen, Daimler-Benz, BASF, Siemens, and others made major investments. General Motors Opel began production at Eisenach. Allianz insurance and other large service firms opened offices. The most important Western firms to go to the former GDR were the West German banks, especially Deutsche Bank, Dresdner Bank, and Commerzbank. The banks not only published a great deal of information about Eastern Germany,[23] but tried to establish links with potential purchasers of Eastern German firms in order to get a share in financing and perhaps in directing the new companies.

The very presence of the Western banks, some of which took over the accounts from the former East German Staatsbank, proved the dilemma of operating in Eastern Germany. By early 1991, the Deutsche Bank announced that it had opened 500,000 accounts with more than DM 12 billion in East German deposits, and that it had made loans totaling DM 6.8 billion. This meant that the bank, whatever its intentions, had actually drained capital from Eastern Germany and had, in combination with the Treuhandanstalt, helped create a liquidity crisis.

Unification also demonstrated the difficulties of operating in a new territory under the West German infrastructure. The West German postal and telephone monopoly was expanded to cover Eastern Germany as the German government rejected competitive offers from foreign utilities, but it was not geared to emergency operations. Even as late as mid-1991, Eastern Germany could hardly be reached by telephone from the West except at night, and it was even difficult to call from West to East Berlin. It became a standard joke among West German managers that when they went to Eastern Germany they were harder to contact than when they were in Africa, Latin America, Australia, or Moscow. Non-German companies, especially American, complained that they could have provided better and cheaper service. The poor telephone service, even to the Treuhandanstalt, helped deter potential investors.

A special problem arose out of the almost universal East German preference for Western consumer goods. Eastern German factories closed for lack of customers while Western German firms established retail sales points, new stores, and every kind of outlet including street kiosks—all things that had not been seen in Western Germany for years. West German mail order houses thrived. All this, however, also added to the drain on Eastern German liquidity and deepened the post-unification slump.

Surveys also showed that many West German *Mittelstand* firms were looking for potential areas to produce and firms to buy. Some firms wanted to use facilities in Eastern Germany to produce for the Soviet Union and

Eastern Europe.[24] In many instances, the firms also wanted to keep their market share in united Germany, acting perhaps more defensively than venturously. Sometimes they only wanted to buy in order to forestall potential competitors. They often could not find Western German managers who were ready to live in Eastern Germany except for high incentive pay.

Nonetheless, many persons were ready to move into a free market system. Over 300,000 new firms registered to do business in Eastern Germany during 1990 and early 1991, mostly in the southern and southwestern industrial areas. Although many of those registrations were for small-scale operations, such as shops, restaurants, and other services, and although many of the new firms were to go bankrupt, their number did show that there was widespread interest in Eastern Germany.

Despite these and other investments, the Eastern German economy went into a deep and precipitous slump immediately after unification. The liquidity crisis helped bring industry to a halt. In addition, exports collapsed by mid-1990, as orders from Eastern Europe, the Soviet Union, and the West were cancelled. The number of unemployed rose to nearly a million by mid-1991. Well over a million East Germans registered as "part-time workers," which became a euphemism for unemployment under which companies could hold personnel in reserve and the unemployed could get somewhat higher income. The number continued to rise and escalated when the former East German army began dismissing soldiers and the various administrations in Eastern Germany released their employees. Within a year after unification, the number who were to all intents and purposes unemployed had risen to 3 million, although many of them may have been working in the underground economy, in construction, or at odd jobs. No statistics were reliable.

Industrial production in Eastern Germany fell to less than half of the previous rate and the total regional product fell precipitously through much of 1990 and 1991 (Chapter 2), although exact calculations were impossible because there was no agreed basis for comparison. One estimate was that by 1991 the entire Gross Regional Product of Eastern Germany amounted to less than 8 per cent of Western German production.[25]

Prices began rising in areas that were politically very sensitive and that had been subsidized in the GDR. By early 1991, housing costs had climbed by 58 per cent, health costs by 28 per cent, and food by 15 per cent. Consumer goods prices, which had been artificially sustained in the GDR to restrain demand, fell between 10 and 30 per cent.[26] The potential political resentment resulting from these price changes alarmed the German upper house, the Bundesrat, which voted to delay any further rent increases in Eastern Germany for at least several months.

Although many economists had originally expected the Eastern German economy to bottom out by mid-1991, that date was clearly unrealistic. There were some modest signs of an upturn in some sectors in 1991, but most economists began warning privately that no real recovery would begin until 1992. They also feared that the recovery, when it finally came, would originate from such a deep base that production and employment levels would not return to 1988/89 levels for several years. Macroeconomic statistics could not show the true picture, as firms were rising, stumbling, falling, and picking up again, and as investors were trying to determine what to do with their new assets. The true upturn could probably be discerned only after it had taken place.

One reason for concern was that many of the best East German workers were moving to the West, either as commuters or permanently. The West German boom, fueled in part by sales in Eastern Germany, drew hundreds of thousands from Eastern Germany. Most East German workers could qualify to work in Western Germany with some retraining. They could function under West German methods with a minimum of adjustment and they preferred that to remaining unemployed in East Germany. Over 10,000 a month were moving permanently to Western Germany in early 1991.

The German government, anxious to avoid a total collapse in Eastern Germany, began sending more state funds to the East. Given the increases in German taxes, government funds going to Eastern Germany under various programs began to reach over DM 150 billion during 1991. A high rate of disbursement was expected to continue for some years, even if not at that level. As 1991 advanced, however, German authorities increasingly realized that it was not only important to send public funds to Eastern Germany but that it was also important that those funds should remain there and be invested there. Otherwise, the funds would only return to Western Germany and would add to the capacity pressures that were disturbing the Bundesbank. About DM 25 billion in private investment funds had gone to Eastern Germany, and there was also some concern about inflation pressures in the new states.

THE TRANSITION: SPECIAL PROBLEMS

The full extent of the mismanagement and misallocation of resources of the GDR regime only became apparent during 1990 and 1991 after the first wave of unity euphoria had waned and the hard realities had begun to sink in. The most important of those hard realities was that some industries in the GDR had no economic justification and could perhaps not be preserved at all, while others would need extensive restructuring and considerable investment before they could have any hope of becoming viable.

Two examples of potential mass dislocations were the East German steel industry and the Rostock port and ship-building facilities on the Baltic. There was little historic or economic reason to have iron and steel production in the GDR, but the GDR leadership wanted to be fully independent of West Germany and also believed that steel and iron were required features of a Marxist model. The GDR built large steel mills and iron foundries, including a giant showcase complex at Eisenhüttenstadt, and by the end of the 1980s produced 8 million tons of highly subsidized steel every year with 80,000 workers.[27]

By the same token, there was no economic reason for the GDR to have a major port at Rostock. The ports that historically served Berlin and what became the GDR were the ports of Hamburg, Lübeck, and Stettin (now Szczcin in Poland), which enjoy easy access by river and canal to the heartland of Eastern Germany as well as into Poland and Czechoslovakia. Rostock was designated as principal port for the GDR to reduce East German dependence on West German ports, but Hamburg began voicing its interest in East German traffic within weeks after November 1989 and began shipping large quantities of East German production by 1990.

Even when industries survive, many firms will not. Some will have to be closed. Others will change roles. A number of West German firms taking over East German facilities want to use them for producing specific components or selected lines rather than the full range of goods they were making. Whatever role they may ultimately play, East German facilities either have been or will almost certainly be scaled back. Some of this will be unfortunate because the Eastern German potential will not be fully used. Thus, the great Zeiss complex at Jena, one of the original sites of Germany's optical industry, was not offered to international bidding but was turned over to the Western German Zeiss as a subsidiary despite protests from its management and work force, and it is scheduled to make components rather than to develop a full range of production.

Not all firms would close or risk closing, however. Some might expand. There are good individual firms, including some in such traditional German specialties as printing-press production. Many such firms were quickly bought by West Germans and others. The service and trade sectors, long neglected in the East German economy, began expanding dramatically after unification. Moreover, despite the mismanagement of East German high-technology efforts, the very existence of the appropriate equipment could provide the foundations for united Germany to enter a sector where West

Germany itself has not been as successful as it might have been. Electronics, optics, and high technology have been traditional Saxon and Thuringian industries, opening the possibility for robotics, computers, and even software production if West German managers and investors would be prepared to place such production in Eastern Germany.

The most important economic difficulties were caused by potentially conflicting property claims, by the risk of almost unlimited environmental damage liability, and by the problems of adjusting East German attitudes to West German production methods.

Property claims in former GDR territory could arise out of the three different waves of expropriations that took place there from the 1930s through the 1980s:

- The Nazis were the first to confiscate private property, some under an "Aryanization" program directed at Jews and some under programs aimed at political opponents or exiles. They seized homes, industrial properties, and land.
- After 1945, the Soviet occupation authorities confiscated millions of acres of agricultural land, either in large or small estates and properties, from alleged "*Junkers*." They also seized some industrial property and real estate.
- After 1949, when the GDR was established, expropriations of private property continued in waves. Even some of the properties that had been granted to East German individuals after 1945 were seized by the state to form large agricultural cooperatives. Private firms were nationalized. Homes, lands, and accounts left by refugees were confiscated, as were other properties.

Claims for restitution began almost as soon as German unity became a real prospect. More than a million claims had been filed by an initial deadline at the end of 1990, but more might yet be expected because of subsidiary deadlines. At least one out of every four properties in the territory of the former GDR appeared to be subject to a claim. Many of the challenges and claims have been placed by heirs.[28]

Before unification, the East and West German governments tried to find ways to limit the liabilities of potential investors. They agreed that claims for property seized by the Third Reich and the Soviets before 1949 would be disallowed, in part because some restitution had already been made to victims of Nazism and in part because Bonn and East Berlin wanted to minimize potential Soviet opposition to the unification process. The Soviets insisted that they would not agree to a German peace treaty if their expro-priations were to be challenged.[29]

The German Constitutional Court upheld the Soviet view, deciding not to accept claims made against Soviet expropriations between 1945 and 1949. It decided that those expropriations were legal under the occupation authority at a time when the occupiers exercised sovereignty over Germany, but it allowed compensation. The German government established a special fund to provide such compensation.[30]

To make certain that other claims would not retard investment, the German government decided that previous owners should be able to claim and receive their properties if they were prepared to initiate or to continue production. If they were not, they would be compensated, and the new investor would be entitled to develop the property. The decision was intended to stimulate investment and to reduce the potential property barrier, although it was promptly protested by a group representing earlier owners.[31]

The government and court decisions did not fully resolve the property questions, as they left many claimants uncertain and frustrated and perhaps determined to try other avenues. They also raised delicate questions about who would determine the best use to be made of a property, and who should have the final authority to deny a claim and to determine the value of a property. The decisions did, however, at least begin to clarify the property muddle in such a way that decisions about privatization could be more easily made.

The massive environmental pollution throughout the GDR faced potential investors with another deterrent. The full extent of environmental degrada-tion under the Communist regime had not been understood or reported in the West. The GDR in 1982 had declared that data on pollution constituted a state secret, and persons who usually protested environmental degradation in the West were not able or prepared to do so in East Germany. But the damage done to the environment became starkly evident within weeks after the Wall collapsed.[32]

The environment in parts of the GDR had been almost life-threatening, with many cities in Saxony, Saxony-Anhalt, and Thuringia having an air pollution level 50 times higher than what the West has regarded as safe. In Bitterfeld, at the center of the East German brown coal district, nine out of every ten children were suffering from respiratory diseases during the last years of the GDR.[33] In addition, the Elbe River carried tens of thousands of metal pollutants every year from Czechoslovak and East German industry, poisoning the water throughout Eastern Germany and past Hamburg into the North Sea.

West Germany had first became concerned about its own environment during the 1970s, when reports of massive forest damage and river pollution led to a series of laws to limit further damage. The situation during the 1980s had improved considerably throughout West Germany as throughout the EC as a whole, but the environmental issue remains important in West German politics. West German industry has spent heavily to reduce pollution, with almost DM 25 billion being invested by West German electric utilities between 1983 and 1988 alone.[34] A number of problems persist in Western Germany, especially because carbon dioxide emissions remain high and because of waste disposal problems, but they are not comparable to the problems left by the GDR regime. Some estimates for the cost of pollution clean-up in Eastern Germany have ranged in the hundreds of billions, with one fifth of that required to clean up the brown coal wastes alone.

West German businessmen learned during the 1980s that environmental rules need not jeopardize profits. They also learned that compensatory and punitive judgments could severely damage firms that did not protect themselves from liability. Under West German law, the buyer of a plant can be held responsible for environmental damage that might have been caused by a predecessor.[35] Once potential investors began to appreciate the full extent of the East German ecological disaster, they hesitated. The chairman of the BDI, Tyll Necker, asked the German government to assume the liability if it wanted early investment, and the government has been reviewing what can best be done.

The quality, the work habits, and the potential cost of Eastern German labor have represented other reasons for hesitation. Many investors feared that Eastern German workers might not be able to make the transition from the slow-paced work habits of the GDR to the intensely demanding atmosphere of a modern Western industrial plant. They also noted that under West German law the buyer of a company has to abide by existing employee contracts, obliging investors to keep the excess employees hired under the GDR or compelling them to pay massive severance benefits.[36] But some of those fears seemed misplaced. As workers in Eastern Germany realize that they will be properly paid for their work, and as they get good tools, Eastern German workers should be every bit as efficient and hard-working as a Western one, and perhaps even more so because of a desire to catch up.[37]

A more complex question arose over managers. East German managers had a simple and one-sided obligation, which was to comply with a numerical production plan or to exceed it. Such considerations as cost, marketability, depreciation rates, or efficiency did not enter into consideration. Persons who have worked in Eastern Germany since unification have been shocked by the sclerotic management techniques that they have found everywhere, especially at the *Kombinat* level, with many managers owing their places to political connections rather than ability or willingness to work. A number of firms have decided to bring West German managers to Eastern Germany, as they found some who were willing to come, creating a potential for later resentment.

Eastern Germany lacked other essential elements of a capitalist system, such as an entrepreneurial class or a credit structure. Although a number of small firms might be opened by East Germans in the process of unification, and some management buy-outs by Eastern Germans have been accepted by the Treuhandanstalt, large-scale capital has to come from West Germany or abroad, as do the capitalists. There are no resources in Eastern Germany to start large firms, and no East German capitalists to place funds. Moreover, many East German firms found themselves saddled with enormous debts that had earlier represented administrative and paper obligations which could not be depreciated but which suddenly were counted as real. Both these factors compounded the political and social as well as economic problems brought on by unification, as there might soon appear to be only Western capitalists and managers directing Eastern workers, and as Eastern firms that might have been viable found themselves burdened with overwhelming debts that should long ago have been depreciated but that now had to be paid in real money to Western banks.

THE TRANSITION: WEST GERMANY'S ROLE AND POLICY

As Eastern Germany tries to catch up after 40 years of mismanagement, Western Germany will heavily influence whether the effort will succeed or fail. Western Germany is the brother, the banker, the manager, perhaps the builder, and in some ways the competitor. When the German government decides what funds to send to its Eastern portion, it is Western German money that will go. Thus Western Germany is in a position to play a decisive role for good or ill, and to shape the future of the all-German economy by determining the future of the East.[38] Eastern Germany benefits from Western cash but it must also take Western direction. Western Germany's role has also become more politically as well as economically sensitive, because the government's decision to use official or semi-official agencies to conduct the transition rather than to rely on market forces has subjected the government to the political as well as the economic risks of unification.

The government in Bonn, the banks in Frankfurt, and the Treuhandanstalt in Berlin are making the decisions that govern the transition of Eastern

Germany into the modern and Western world. The trade unions as well as other associations are West German in background, structure, and orientation. West German politicians and economists, and other persons who have made their careers in the West rather than in the East, are shaping Eastern Germany much more than the natives.

The most basic impact of Western Germany on Eastern Germany arises from the very presence of Western Germany itself. For Western Germany competes with Eastern Germany for some resources even as it provides others. East Germans can now work in the West, and estimates on the number of East German workers who may finally choose to go to the West range up to 1.2 million. There has been steady Western recruiting for trained Eastern industrial workers.[39] A Western German firm can remain where it is and still serve the Eastern German market. Eastern Germans can and do put their savings into Western Germany.

There is, however, a basic conflict of interests and even needs. Eastern Germany wants and needs rapid growth. But Western Germany, and thus the institutions that govern all of Germany, had their rapid growth during the 1950s and 1960s. They are now committed to stability, or at most to slow growth. When Western German decisions about Eastern Germany are made, they are made on the basis of many interacting considerations in which economic development will be a primary but not a controlling motive. Other objectives, such as smoothing adjustment, preventing migration, reassuring East and West of German steadfastness in its political and economic obligations, and balancing the needs and objectives of every part of united Germany, may prevail. Eastern Germany will be fitted into the Western German system, with its advantages and disadvantages, and will not be governed as a separate economic entity.

Even as the all-German government has transferred billions of D-Marks of investment funds to the Eastern states in order to stimulate growth, the Bundesbank has kept interest rates high—mainly because of the rapid West German growth which had, ironically, been stimulated by the Eastern German market, and also to counter the fiscal stimulus of a German budget deficit that results largely from German programs for the East. Although there is no necessary correlation between the short-term rates controlled by the Bundesbank and the long-term rates determined by the capital markets, long-term rates are not likely to fall very far while short-term rates remain high. Potential investors in Eastern Germany frequently complain about the high cost of capital. This is one reason why large-scale funds have been coming more from state than private sources. Moreover, as West German banks seem more ready to lend money to their traditional Western clients than to Easterners, Eastern Germans may find it especially hard and costly to obtain investment funds.

Western Germans also control the Eastern German economy in micro-economic as well as macroeconomic terms. The Treuhandanstalt, staffed by Germans from the West, has been deciding who may or may not buy East German firms or services, and at what price, and those decisions have had a political and social as well as economic content. There have been no open auctions, but all bidders have been and apparently will continue to be carefully screened and evaluated. The shape of the Eastern German economy during the early 1990s depends not only or perhaps not even primarily on market forces, and certainly not on Eastern German decisions, but on the trustee agency. This is a responsibility of considerable consequence.

Some voices have called for a less centralized approach, and for policies like those that created the West German economic miracle. Shortly after the Wall collapsed, the Ludwig Erhard Foundation published a book by a prominent economist, Willy Kraus, arguing for a return to the thinking behind the economic miracle.[40] Kraus said that East Germany needed free economic conditions, exposure to global competition, and the total abolition of subsidies and other non-market incentives. He allowed for short-term measures to ease social unrest, but warned that they had to be strictly limited and should not detract from the rapid introduction of a fully market-oriented system. The Sachverständigenrat has commented in the same terms.[41] Karl Schiller came out of retirement to complain that too many funds were going into Eastern German community, social, and welfare programs instead of going into investment; he also suggested very generous tax benefits for investors in Eastern Germany instead of more government programs—thus leaving more decisions to individual investors.[42]

The Treuhandanstalt was also accused of giving preference to West German investment. Reports persisted throughout 1990 and 1991 that foreign investors were being screened more carefully and more skeptically than West German firms and that they were being given second priority, even as they were being invited to invest and as the agency opened offices in New York and Tokyo in mid-1991 to attract foreign capital.[43] Until mid-1991, less than 5 per cent of all investment in Eastern Germany had been non-German, and most of that was from companies with subsidiaries in Western Germany who were expanding to the East along with other West German firms. The Treuhandanstalt had forestalled foreign investment in some important areas, like communications and utilities, to the point that foreigners became intensely suspicious of German intentions and—with the possible exception of the French—did not carry their potential weight.

West German trade unions have played an important role. They have tried hard to organize Eastern German workers, often by offering promises of high pay. The unions hope that this will prevent Easterners from migrating West. Agreements have been negotiated that would bring Eastern German wages to Western standards by about 1994 or 1995 (although the greater readiness of Eastern Germans to work long hours and to shorten their holidays may keep labor costs reasonably competitive), but raising wage rates in the East has actually pushed more workers into the West because firms have not wanted to invest in the East.

The handling of the former GDR airline, Interflug, showed the many issues that German policy has felt compelled to keep in mind. Originally, Lufthansa had wanted to buy Interflug in order to create one large German airline. The Bundeskartellamt raised objections and other bidders were invited. Those bidders included a British firm, British Airways, and at least one American firm, United Airlines, as well as several other non-German firms. After months of screening and negotiations with the foreign firms, the Treuhandanstalt concluded that Interflug should go to Lufthansa, especially as 800 Interflug employees had already applied for jobs at, and been hired by, the West German airline.[44] Whatever the merits of that decision, it again left foreigners convinced that they were not being given an equal chance. But by then, Interflug was so near collapse that Lufthansa decided it no longer wanted to buy the airline. When the collapse finally came, Lufthansa simply began flying many of its former routes.

If Western Germany has posed problems for Eastern Germany, it also offers considerable assets. The German government and Western German investors will send hundreds of billions of D-Marks to Eastern Germany during the 1990s, about half of it for investment and infrastructure construction and the other half for consumption and social expenditures.[45] The German government has pledged that it will not construct second-rate facilities but will put into place an infrastructure that will be the most modern in Europe and even the world. No East European country will receive such Western support.

Despite these considerable immediate and planned expenditures, Eastern German managers and politicians began complaining soon after unification that the German government was applying a double standard. It was insisting on market principles in Eastern Germany when it had ignored them for decades in Western Germany. Instead, they argued, the German government should either equalize subsidies throughout all of Germany or should subsidize only the Eastern firms because they needed it more than the Western firms. The Sachverständigenrat tried to counter the argument by returning to its insistence on universal application of market principles,[46] but the DGB trade union denounced this proposal even as the BDI supported it.[47]

As the debate about unification heated up, and as unemployment in Eastern Germany rose, the German government began to listen more attentively to the trade unions than to the experts. The government did not assert, as it might have, that a certain level of structural unemployment in Eastern Germany might be necessary and even desirable in order to revitalize the economy and to make it competitive over the long run. Instead, the Treuhandanstalt began looking for places to restructure in order to avoid their collapse. It also began selling companies not on a price basis but on the basis of the job maintenance plans of the purchaser. Potential buyers had to submit proposals which would include a pledge to preserve a fixed number of jobs. They would be fined if they did not preserve those jobs but they would be granted a concessionary price (as low as DM 1) if they would offer a good plan which included considerable job maintenance and investment.[48]

The Treuhandanstalt policy encouraged further wage increases in Eastern Germany and raised the costs of unification by reducing the prices that investors might be willing to pay. It also marked a further step toward stressing the *Sanierung* rather than the *Privatisierung* side of the Treuhandanstalt's task. It piled the structural burdens of Eastern Germany on top of those long carried by West Germany. It added further to the responsibility of the West for the future of the East. Most important, it meant that the German budget would have to be used to help the Eastern German economy for much longer than had been expected at the time of unification. For the Treuhandanstalt increasingly found itself forced to turn from a liquidation agency to a management and subsidy enterprise, larger than any of the *Kombinate* had ever been.

ANOTHER ECONOMIC MIRACLE?

Any effort to compare the conditions that led to the legendary West German "economic miracle" to those that prevailed in the Eastern parts of Germany after unification could find many similarities and differences, some of which were more important than others.

By way of similarities, many East Germans became unemployed after 1990, like West Germans after 1945. In the 1990s, as in the 1940s, there have been ample needs and countless opportunities for investment, although complicated by non-economic considerations. After the 1990 elections, as after 1949, there was a four-year period before the next national election (scheduled for 1994) during which potentially painful measures could be carried out. Most important, there was in the 1990s, as there had been during the 1940s, a talented and energetic labor force.

But the differences became increasingly important. During the economic miracle, West German labor and social costs were low and were rising more slowly than productivity. After 1990, Eastern German labor costs began rising quickly, much faster than productivity, and the costly West German social net spread over the East. Moreover, during the economic miracle the opportunities for investment were regulated by the Allies, whose rules were being consistently reduced in number and effect. During the 1990s, the regulations have been German, and have been mainly designed for West Germany. They have been difficult to ignore but have not always been appropriate to growth needs. Soon, additional EC regulations will be added, all perhaps good in themselves but also based on the needs and capabilities of the developed economies of Western Europe instead of those of Eastern Germany. Although exceptions to some of the rules have been made, the overall burden has remained considerable.

The cost of short-term and long-term capital was lower during the economic miracle. From 1949 through the early 1950s, the German discount rate was never over 6 per cent and was often well below that, even at 3 or 4 per cent. Long-term rates were low to match.[49] After unification, the discount rate remained at 6 per cent at first and rose to over 7 per cent by 1991, with little immediate prospect of dropping below that level or of permitting long-term rates to fall very far. Although investment incentives could compensate for higher capital costs to some degree, they could not compensate completely.

The force of personality could not be ignored. The economic miracle was centered about one man, Ludwig Erhard, who acted uncompromisingly on the basis of superficially simple but quite sophisticated market principles that, like him, became important economic factors in their own right. No political figure on the scene in Eastern or Western Germany during the 1990s was prepared to follow the same principles in the same rigorous, confident, and persuasive way.

Against this background, there will be no economic miracle like the last. There should be steady improvement after the bottom is touched, probably in late 1991 or 1992, although that would depend to some extent on the state of the global economy. There could be dramatic growth rates in total Eastern German output at some point. Services and construction should do well, and other sectors should gradually follow. As time goes on, many inefficient producers should be weeded out.

By the end of the 1990s, Eastern Germans should have acquired a standard of living well above that which they had in the 1980s, but still years behind that of Western Germany. The policies followed to date suggest that the transition will most probably last longer than originally expected, that a great deal of productive capacity will be shifted to Western Germany, and that a number of inefficient operations will be preserved for some time. The true economic miracle of German unification, therefore, has occurred in the West.

Many Germans began worrying that the Eastern states might long remain an underdeveloped region—like the South Italian *Mezzogiorno*, the English Midlands, or the American South after the Civil War. But there are many reasons why the prospects for Eastern Germany are better than those. It has an industrial tradition and labor force. It will be at the center of Europe, not at the edge like the *Mezzogiorno*. It has several important municipal centers, including Berlin, Dresden, Leipzig, and others, to draw investment and services. The development of Berlin as the capital of united Germany will create a wide ring of prosperity around the entire city, whose suburbs may be at the Oder by 2000 and across it by 2010.

East Germany also brings some considerable real and potential assets. It has a somewhat higher percentage of young people than West Germany. Re-equipment of the East German production base could provide united Germany with state-of-the-art industrial technology. The resurrection of the Berlin-Leipzig-Dresden triangle should help bring all of Germany into the information age of the twenty-first century, if Western German firms are prepared to introduce their latest production techniques into the East and to permit their Eastern subsidiaries to develop along their own lines.

Western Germany can and will remake Eastern Germany in its own prosperous image. It will be a long process, delayed by some policies and advanced by others. But the development of the Eastern German economy will be a success. One day, the merger of East and West Germany will have produced more than the sum of its parts. Growth will come, despite the difficulties of the transition. But it will be the stuff of progress, not of legend.

The transition will change Western as well as Eastern Germany. It has already reversed the policies of the *Wende*. It will enlarge the German state sector and compel a shift the policies of the Bundesbank. Most important, it will widen the framework and the potential impact of German economic policy and will make the German government and its bankers and managers think in new and different terms. In conjunction with the openings toward the East, it creates a new German economic perimeter whose dimensions can not yet be predicted or analyzed but which are certain to be different from those that preceded unification.

THE FUTURE: THE RICH AND THE POOR GERMANS?

Beyond and yet within the logic of economics, however, lies the logic of human attitudes. And it is in this area that the greatest differences can be found between the economic miracle and German unification.

Between 1945 and 1948, the mood in Germany was a mixture of desperation and determination, but mainly a sense of common destiny. They were in the same boat, before and after the economic miracle, and most of them believed that they would have equal opportunities in a free land.

The greatest danger for German unification may be that the Eastern Germans may be left with the conviction that the Western Germans have been the winners but that they themselves have lost three separate times: First, in the Soviet occupation; second, in the GDR; and third, in unification. If, when economic unification is finished, the Westerners are the owners and the Easterners the workers, unification will have failed even if statistics proclaim it a success. The main issue confronting the Westerners who are directing unification may, therefore, not be structural but societal, the need to bring along not the East German economy alone but also the persons that must live in it.

The unification of Germany is only superficially a merger between a capitalist and a socialist economy. It is really a merger between rich and poor. Fifty years after World War II, most Western Germans are prosperous or at least financially secure. Most Eastern Germans own little of value. Despite the common nationhood, it remains a union between two groups whom fate has treated so very differently that their unification cannot be treated or evaluated as only an economic task.

It was this cruel dilemma that German policy had to resolve. It would have been difficult enough in itself, but it became even more complex when seen in conjunction with the structural dilemmas of Western Germany and with the issues facing Germany in the world and in Europe.

NOTES TO CHAPTER SEVEN

1. Basic statistics on the *Kombinate* are in GDR, *Statistical Pocketbook, 1989,* p. 45.
2. East German trade statistics showed trade between East and West Germany as "foreign trade"; West German statistics showed it in a separate category from foreign trade, as "intra-German trade."
3. Dieter Lösch and Peter Plötz, *Soziale Marktwirtschaft - Jetzt* (Hamburg: HWWA/Institut für Wirtschaftsforschung, 1990), p. 2.

4. Deutsches Institut für Wirtschaftsforschung, *DDR-Wirtschaft im Umbruch* (Berlin: Deutsches Institut, 1990), pp. 29-31.

5. Lösch and Plötz, *op. cit.*, p.5.

6. Deutsche Bank, *Special: East Germany* (Frankfurt: Deutsche Bank, 1990), pp. 7-11.

7. Sachverständigenrat, *Zur Unterstützung der Wirtschaftsreform in the DDR: Voraussetzungen und Möglichkeiten, Sondergutachten vom 20. Januar 1990* (Wiesbaden: Sachverständigenrat, 1990), pp. 52-53. In making the distinction between the West German currency and the former East German currency, I follow the customary practice of describing the former by its abbreviations, D-Mark or DM, and the latter by its full name, the mark.

8. *Handelsblatt*, April 26, 1990.

9. Sachverständigenrat, *op. cit.*, p. 54.

10. Deutsche Bank, *loc. cit.*, p. 4; Deutsches Institut für Wirtschaftsforschung, *loc. cit.*, pp. 18-21.

11. GDR, *Statistical Pocketbook, 1989*, p. 47.

12. Christine Kulke-Fiedler, "Die Integration des Wirtschaftsgebietes der ehemaligen DDR in den EG-Binnenmarkt," *Deutschland-Archiv*, December 1990, p. 1874.

13. Interview with Dr. Jürgen Klose, fellow at the American Institute for Contemporary German Studies, January 22, 1991.

14. Deutsches Institut für Wirtschaftsforschung, *loc. cit.*, p. 10.

15. Lewis Alexander and Joseph Gagnon, *The Global Economic Implications of German Unification*, International Finance Discussion Papers, No. 379 (Washington: Federal Reserve, 1990); Leslie Lipschitz and Donogh McDonald, eds., *German Unification: Economic Issues*, Occasional Paper #75 (Washington: International Monetary Fund, December, 1990), pp. 78-92.

16. For a 400-page compilation of West German legislation to be taken over, see Deutscher Bundestag, 11. Wahlperiode, *Entwurf eines Gesetzes zu dem Vertrag vom 31. August 1990 zwischen der Bundesrepublik Deutschland und der Deutschen Demokratischen Republik über die Herstellung der Einheit Deutschlands - Einigungsvertragsgesetz*, August 8, 1990.

17. For a summary of various forms of legislation and the respective dates of coming into force, see FRG, *Aktuelle Beiträge*, No. 44/1990, November 5, 1990, and No. 49/1990, December 18, 1990.

18. Hans Moock, director of operations at the Dresden Treuhandanstalt, briefing at Transatlantic Futures, Washington, D.C., May 9, 1991.

19. For the text of the European Community statement, see Commission of the European Communities, "The Community and German Unification," Brussels, April 20, 1990.

20. For a review of the principles governing East Germany's entry into the EC regulatory system, see Kulke-Fiedler, *op. cit.*, pp. 1873-1880.

21. Roland Schönfeld, "Unification and the Future of German Trade," Gary L. Geipel, *The Future of Germany* (Indianapolis: Hudson Institute, 1990), p. 91.

22. Sachverständigenrat, *1990/91 Report*, p. 483.

23. For example, Deutsche Bank, "The New German Federal States," 1990.

24. Ifo study reported in *Handelsblatt*, October 1, 1990, p. 4.

25. *Süddeutsche Zeitung*, April 24, 1991; *Handelsblatt*, April 24, 1991.

26. *Süddeutsche Zeitung*, April 25, 1991.

27. The West German economic institute in Essen, the Rheinisch-Westfälisches Institut für Wirtschaftsforschung, produced a series of studies on the nature and prospects of East German steel; see *RWI-Pressemitteilung*, April 27 and May 3, 1990.

28. *Handelsblatt*, December 27, 1990, p. 4.

29. *Handelsblatt*, January 23, 1991.

30. *Handelsblatt*, April 24, 1991.

31. *Frankfurter Allgemeine Zeitung* and *Süddeutsche Zeitung*, March 12, 1991.

32. *Frankfurter Allgemeine Zeitung*, February 24, 1990, p. 4.

33. *U.S. News and World Report*, April 30, 1990, p. 27.

34. *Handelsblatt*, January 10, 1991.

35. Sven Oehme, "Eastern Germany - The Next Economic Miracle," occasional paper 1991/#2, the American Council on Germany, January 1991, p. 4.

36. *Ibid.*

37. *Handelsblatt*, November 15, 1990, p. 5.

38. Forms of economic support that the united Germany will provide to its Eastern portion, and how individual firms can use that aid, was summarized in a paper on *Economic Assistance for the former GDR* published by the FRG Ministry of Economics on October 3, 1990, but plans for support expanded and shifted after that date and could best be followed in periodic German regulations.

39. *Financial Times*, January 8, 1991.

40. Willy Kraus, *op. cit.*

41. Sachverständigenrat, *1990/1991 Report*, pp. 299-300 and 501-506.

42. *Frankfurter Allgemeine Zeitung*, April 23, 1991.

43. For example, *The Economist*, August 10, 1990, pp. 12-13.

44. *Süddeutsche Zeitung*, January 16, 1991, p. 21.

45. Hans Willgerodt, *Vorteile der wirtschaftlichen Einheit Deutschlands* (Köln: Institut für Wirtschaftspolitik, 1990), p. 10.

46. Sachverständigenrat, *Marktwirtshaftlichen Kurs Halten: zur Wirtschaftspolitik für die neuen Bundesländer*, Special Report of April 13, 1991.

47. *Frankfurter Allgemeine Zeitung*, April 18, 1991.

48. Moock, *loc. cit.*

49. Wallich, *op. cit.*, pp. 74-103.

Eight

Germany in the World: Money and Trade

When the Interim Committee of the International Monetary Fund (IMF) met in Washington during May 1990, it had on its agenda a delicate issue that had required three years of discreet negotiations: the relative positions of the senior states in the IMF. There were few shifts, and those were barely noticed outside a small club of international financiers. But, to those in the system and especially to those who shifted, they were of considerable symbolic and some real importance.

Great Britain, which had been second only to the United States since the formation of the IMF, moved down to the same level as France. Japan, which had been number five, moved up to number two. And West Germany, which had been number three, joined Japan at the level immediately below the United States.

Like so many other steps in the long process of Germany's climb to greater global influence, this step was replete with ambiguities. West Germany was moved up not so much because it wanted to be, but due to the maneuvers of others. A number of IMF members wanted to move Germany up because they did not want Japan alone at number two. Great Britain wanted Germany and Japan at the same level so that London could say that it still remained at third rank, not fourth, and France wanted to be able to say the same.

West German reactions were mixed. Many German bankers and economists found the promotion uncomfortable. They expect Japan to grow faster than even a united Germany, and they were uneasy about sharing a position that they might not be able to hold. But they could not decline the "promotion" because it was an essential part of the total package. Therefore, when the new IMF ranking was introduced, Germany had a somewhat higher IMF quota and voting power, and a modest although not entirely welcome boost in its prestige.[1]

There was also, of course, some genuine German pride in the promotion. One German commentator in the normally understated *Börsen-Zeitung* wrote enthusiastically that "if there was one delegation that could leave Washington triumphantly, it was the German."[2] To the many who might be inclined to accept former Chancellor Helmut Schmidt's assertion that "monetary policy *is* foreign policy,"[3] the IMF meeting, and the German elevation, represented proof positive of the rightness of German policy for many decades.

The IMF meeting specifically confirmed and recognized one important aspect of West Germany's international role, its financial and monetary strength and especially the stability and attractiveness of the D-Mark. The D-Mark will be the most sought-after currency of united Europe, and united Germany will also have immense influence in Europe and in global economic matters. An important effect of West Germany's domestic economic policy had been the contribution it made to the country's international standing. The Interim Committee plainly had these factors in mind, whatever role may have been played by internal IMF maneuvering.

But if some West German bankers and economists are troubled about Germany's growing role and responsibility, it is because Germany's international position remains imbalanced.

Germany has a global currency but it does not yet have a global economy. It has the D-Mark, carefully managed to maintain its value and attraction. This gives it a powerful role in international financial and monetary affairs. West Germany has also been a successful trading state, and united Germany will be. But the German economy remains essentially a continental economy, with many of its activities concentrated in Europe and limited to the EC. It has lacked the size necessary to deal with the effects of truly massive currency flows, and West Germany has always needed to look for partners.

On the international monetary scene, the West German government and the Bundesbank have therefore been active members of the formal and informal international institutions and arrangements that try to solve global problems and to coordinate global policy. West Germany has also helped make European economic cooperation a success, from its early days in the European Coal and Steel Community to its present position as a leader in the European Community, the European Monetary System (EMS), and the European Exchange Rate Mechanism (ERM). But it has not forgotten its domestic politics, and where there has been a conflict between international and home interests it has—like others—acted most often on the basis of its domestic interests and of highly developed and generally predictable instincts and attitudes.

The promotion of Germany and Japan to the second rank of the IMF recognized not only German and Japanese economic reality, but also the broader reality that there are now three states and three central banks that dominate the global economy as the big three, the United States, Germany, and Japan. Of the three, Germany remains the smallest, the most vulnerable, and the one that can least well afford to be isolated.

THE DEUTSCHE MARK

At the core of Germany's success and influence lies its currency. That currency, the D-Mark, gave concrete expression to West Germany's international financial and economic success and has also contributed to it.

The success of the D-Mark was in turn anchored in the success of German exports, in the Bundesbank's judicious and solicitous management of the currency's value, and in the confidence generated by West Germany's prosperity.

The D-Mark has been a model of stability since it became fully convertible at the end of 1958. No major currency, except for the Japanese yen and the Swiss franc, has been as consistently strong or stronger. Even the U.S. dollar, the cornerstone of the global system, has lost about two thirds of its value compared to the D-Mark since 1958.

The D-Mark has become the second-largest currency component of global monetary reserves, second only to the U.S. dollar and well ahead of the yen, the British pound, or the French franc. Central banks have turned to the German currency at remarkable speed. Less than 10 per cent of the world's monetary reserves were held in D-Marks throughout most of the 1970s, but the amount had risen to 15 per cent by the end of 1987 and the percentage has continued to climb steadily. By the end of 1989, D-Marks constituted around 20 per cent, or one fifth, of all global monetary reserves (including certain official and private Ecu reserves), and the level remained constant during 1990.[4] The rise from the level of $87.8 billion at the end of 1987 to $130.3 billion at the end of 1989 represents an increase of 50 per cent over a period when the U.S. dollar was declining as an element of monetary reserves and the yen was only rising 25 per cent.[5]

The D-Mark's position in global monetary reserves in part reflects the extensive D-Mark holdings in European foreign-exchange reserve accounts, with three quarters of all D-Mark reserve holdings being in Western industrial state treasuries or central banks, and to a lesser degree the holdings of the rapidly industrializing Southeast Asian states. It also reflects the wish of industrial state treasuries and central banks to hold a stable currency. IMF statistics showed that 19.3 per cent of all global non-metallic reserves were in D-Marks at the end of 1989, with 22.9 per cent of the reserves of industrial states held in D-Marks but only 11.4 per cent of the reserves of the developing states.[6] The Bundesbank gave a somewhat higher figure, reporting that D-Mark holdings in September 1989 were about 21 per cent of world reserves, and also noting that this was higher than even before World War I, when the former German currency was also one of the leading global reserve currencies.[7]

The D-Mark is not as widely used as a transactions currency. Global commodity prices are still denominated in U.S. dollars. Whatever the D-Mark's strengths may be, it does not offer the kind of global liquidity that the dollar does. The German government does not wish it to do so. Invoicing in D-Marks is concentrated around Germany's own trade, but almost 15 per cent of world trade is conducted on a D-Mark basis. The D-Mark is also much less important than the dollar in international credits or in debt servicing. But a growing quantity of international bond issues—including some being floated in the United States—are denominated in D-Marks. Major U.S. banks offer D-Mark accounts for Americans who want to hedge some of their assets against a fall in the dollar.[8] The World Bank has floated Euro-D-Mark bonds, as have U.S. corporations. The D-Mark has also become increasingly important as an intervention currency, both on a global level and in the ERM. In Europe, the D-Mark has virtually become a parallel currency, with prices in Western and Eastern Europe increasingly quoted in D-Marks as well as in local currencies.

The Bundesbank worries constantly that the increasingly widespread circulation of the D-Mark makes it difficult to control the supply of its own currency. A total of about one trillion D-Marks held abroad, circulating abroad, and even used for currency intervention abroad, are part of the total stock of German money. Sudden and large flows could have undesirable impacts on German interest rates or German prices, materially complicating the execution of German monetary policy.[9] The bank is afraid that any decline in the D-Mark's value or in the German current account surplus could set off a selling wave that would force it to intervene massively and perhaps unsuccessfully.

The Bundesbank has complained that its room for maneuver was being reduced. Hans Tietmeyer, vice president of the Bundesbank, has warned that the high D-Mark holdings abroad placed a particular stability burden on the Bundesbank because any loss of faith in German currency could provoke large-scale selling.[10] Tietmeyer stressed that states had to consult carefully to avoid undercutting each other's policies, and reported that such consultations already took place regularly inside the European Monetary System when any state planned D-Mark sales. They also take place between the Bundesbank and the U.S. Federal Reserve acting on behalf of the U.S. Treasury.

The D-Mark has thus become a burden for Germany as well as a blessing. The Bundesbank stated in May of 1991 that one reason it had to maintain high interest rates was to avoid the kind of decline and subsequent market effects that Tietmeyer had cited.[11] The German currency risks being on a treadmill, where the stronger it gets the stronger it must remain until the German monetary authorities no longer dare to reduce interest rates at all. This could represent a potentially dangerous inflexibility at a time when the German government and central bank must simultaneously weigh many conflicting responsibilities and obligations. It is almost a poisoned chalice, which obviously fascinates but which can bind German policy when it may need to be free.

GERMANY AND THE WORLD ECONOMY

The global economy, as it has developed since World War II under the leadership of the United States, was virtually made to order for West Germany and for German economic predilections. Most of the basic elements that have characterized the global economy favor the kind of international trading state that West Germany represented and that united Germany should become, although they also pose problems.

The most important element from the German standpoint has been the gradual development of an almost worldwide openness from which fewer and fewer states exclude themselves. The Western world created a virtually universal trade structure, the General Agreement on Tariffs and Trade (GATT), which has gradually expanded across much of the globe. It also established the International Monetary Fund (IMF). The combination of open trading and financial structures has helped promote continuous and even dramatic trade expansion since World War II, with the level of world trade still growing at about 6 to 7 per cent during 1989 and 1990.[12] The open trading system, and especially the European elements like the European Community, have contributed to West Germany's growth and wealth.

Global trade, global markets, and global transportation systems have generated remarkable factor mobility, especially for capital. Global financial institutions, such as the IMF, the World Bank, and the Bank for International Settlements (BIS), function on an almost universal basis, and will do so even more if the Soviet Union and other former socialist states are able to join.

Capital is the factor that can be shifted most easily. It flows almost uninterruptedly from market to market and from country to country, and it often moves independent of trade. In fact, the reverse of the classic fixed exchange-rate system is now true: interest and exchange rates do not follow trade flows but help determine them. Even labor, long a relatively stable factor, has become fluid as well, although not to the same degree as capital. Millions of workers move from state to state and from continent to continent, either temporarily or permanently, coming from Asia to the Middle East and Europe, from Africa to Europe and America, and from Latin America to North America. There are continental markets for unskilled and migrant labor, and there is a global market for technicians and engineers as well as for managers. Germany is part of that market and benefits from it, although it remains reluctant to recognize foreign labor as a long-term reality.

Many economists have concluded that there are no longer any independent national economies and that only global economic issues and policies are important. That is not fully correct. National governments still make the basic decisions. What is more correct is that national states have to consider the international effect of any actions that they take, and that they also have to take into consideration the effect of others' policies on them. The global economy is one vast financial and monetary transmission system, constantly reverberating in response to the actions taken by governments and central banks and in turn passing those responses to other governments and central banks. A national government and its central bank can select the international impact that they choose to make by adjusting their domestic policies. Otherwise, they may decide what domestic policy adjustments will compensate for international developments. In both cases, there is an intimate link between domestic action and international reaction, and vice versa.

The open system will respond to different policies in different but normally predictable ways. States that are widely regarded as sensible and stable will—theoretically—in the long run be rewarded if other factors remain equal. The open system, therefore, actually puts a greater premium on correct national policies than a closed system in which each state could move immediately to protect itself from the effects of its own or another's actions.

The open system creates another type of incentive: to coordinate. If states can no longer protect themselves against the effects of another's actions, they want to be able to influence those actions or at least to have time either to adjust their policies or to limit whatever negative effects they and their markets may suffer. Governments and central banks must be highly sensitive to the impact their decisions will have on others and on those markets, and to the way in which states and traders are likely to react. Coordination and consultation have, therefore, become virtual necessities. The West Germans quickly recognized this new reality, adjusted to it, and helped make coordination a norm rather than an exception. They also recognized its potential importance for German interests, as they needed coordination more than others did.

In this open environment, and despite a number of problems and short-comings within the system, the states in the Organization for Economic Development and Cooperation (OECD) enjoyed almost a decade of prosperity after the 1980-1982 recession. That prosperity in turn helped encourage further openness in trade and capital flows during most of the 1980s. Growth rates held relatively steady between 2 per cent and 5 per cent. The terms of trade improved for the industrialized world, with global commodity prices falling relative to industrial prices and with petroleum and food prices gradually declining during much of the decade except for a spike triggered by the Persian Gulf crisis in 1990-1991. Compared to the 1970s, the 1980s have seen a broadly disinflationary trend, although there was some fear (especially in Germany) and even some evidence that inflation might return.

West Germany in particular has thrived in the liberal global economic environment, and a united Germany could also expect to do so once the integration of East Germany is complete. West Germany's productive capacity far exceeded the absorptive capacity of its domestic market. This helped fuel the German export drive and helped generate German investment capital.

GERMANY'S ROLE IN THE EVOLUTION OF THE GLOBAL MONETARY SYSTEM

The global monetary system has passed through a number of phases since World War II. West Germany played a key role in each phase, either in beginning it, managing it, or ending it.

The first phase was the Bretton Woods era, named after the New Hampshire resort in which the Allied monetary conference of July 1944 created the IMF and shaped the global postwar order. The dollar was pegged to gold at a fixed rate of $35 per troy ounce, constituting the official backing of the global monetary system, and other currencies were linked to the system through their own fixed exchange rates to the dollar. The exchange rates of other currencies to the dollar could be adjusted as necessary to take account of the effects of national policies and of divergences in trade and payments balances. Countries could devalue or revalue with respect to the dollar, and the dollar price of gold could thus—at least theoretically—remain constant even as the rates of exchange between separate currencies could fluctuate.

The Bretton Woods system of fixed exchange rates helped promote postwar prosperity. Fixed exchange rates facilitated the resumption of trade because they permitted producers, exporters, and importers to calculate costs and market prices without the risk of currency fluctuation. Although some hedging was always wise, it was normally not as costly as it would have been in a less stable environment. Although the system at first appeared to offer other countries no chance to compete against America's productive efficiency and many economists feared what they termed a permanent "dollar gap," European economies recovered by the late 1950s and became competitive again.

American policy and the U.S. dollar needed to achieve two objectives. First, to offer a fixed and stable value. Second, to provide liquidity for world trade by making dollars available through aid, investments, or imports. But the two roles contained the seeds of contradiction, because stability could be best served by limiting money growth whereas liquidity could be best served by expanding it. Other countries also had responsibilities, the main one being to keep the fixed exchange rate to the dollar at a realistic level.

By the late 1960s, the dollar gap had turned into a dollar glut. The United States, largely for domestic reasons, had put far more emphasis on expanding dollar liquidity than on maintaining dollar value. A combination of U.S. fiscal, trade, and monetary policies had put many more dollars into circulation than the trading system needed. Growing fear of U.S. inflation had made those dollars less desirable, and many central banks held more dollars than they wanted. The United States was not prepared to pursue the kinds of fiscal or monetary policies that might curtail the dollar supply. Instead, the United States proposed that other countries revalue their currencies as provided under the Bretton Woods agreement. But those other countries, and West Germany in particular, were not prepared to revalue. The dollar weakened sharply on global markets, especially in the late 1960s and early 1970s, despite repeated interventions by the United States and by others, including West Germany.

The D-Mark constituted a major part of the problem. Money poured into the D-Mark, sometimes to buy German goods but more often to hedge against the dollar or to make a profit when—as was widely expected—the D-Mark would have to be revalued. West German foreign exchange reserves rose from $2.7 billion in December 1969 to $12.6 billion by December 1971 and later to $28.1 billion by September 1973.[13] Germany tried to ease the pressure by imposing controls on capital inflows, but that did not solve the problem. The persistent flow of foreign money into D-Marks threatened to import inflation into Germany by raising the German money supply.

Although some countries, such as France, began heavy purchases of gold from the U.S. reserve, West Germany tried to help support the dollar during the late 1960s and early 1970s. The president of the Bundesbank, Karl Blessing, sent a letter to the chairman of the U.S. Federal Reserve pledging not to purchase U.S. gold but to maintain German reserves in dollars. Chancellor Ludwig Erhard agreed to make large purchases of U.S. dollar instruments and to make "offset" payments to reduce U.S. Congressional demands for a reduction in U.S. forces stationed in Germany. These commitments and others hurt Erhard domestically, but many of them were still carried out by his successors as a sign that the German government wished to support the United States.

The Germans were worried about more than the D-Mark strength itself. They feared the growing tendency of other states—including third world countries—to place reserves into non-traditional assets such as Eurodollars which further complicated German efforts to keep its currency under control. They saw the Bretton Woods system as increasingly inflation-prone and wanted reform, but the main reform they wanted, which was in U.S. policy, they were not in a position to impose.[14]

The markets did not regard West German policies as adequate substitutes for currency revaluation. The rush into D-Marks continued. The United States and several other states pressed Germany to revalue in order to compensate for the dollar glut. Although the Bundesbank would have favored revaluation to reduce the risk of inflation, the German government was afraid that a revaluation would cut into Germany's global competitiveness and would curtail exports.[15]

Finally, in August 1971, after intensifying waves of speculation, the Bretton Woods system collapsed. The United States closed the "gold window" when it became clear that there was no longer enough gold to satisfy all potential claims at the $35 price, and it thus removed the fixed link between the dollar and gold. With that step, the system lost its anchor.

The next phase of the postwar monetary system was a confused and relatively brief period of about 18 months during which many futile proposals for other fixed-rate systems were made. A conference at the Smithsonian Institution in Washington agreed to set new exchange rates that would reflect market realities. The West German government tried to make it a success by pledging to revalue as part of the new alignment, but the results of the conference proved short-lived.[16]

The D-Mark remained under strain throughout the post-Bretton Woods period. It was alternately used for interventions to support the dollar or to hedge against it. Other currencies again flooded into D-Marks. Economics Minister Karl Schiller resigned in part because he believed that fixed rates could not be sustained except at great risk to the freedom of the markets and because he believed that logic dictated D-Mark revaluation—a step still firmly opposed by German industry.[17]

To ease pressure within Europe, however, the Germans and other European states agreed to a special system of relatively narrow exchange rate bands in what was formally entitled the "European narrow margins agreement" but was informally known as the "snake." But the snake also failed to hold. The domestic policies and even the economic philosophies of its leading member states—West Germany, France, and Italy—diverged too widely. The latter two could not remain in the system with West Germany.

Because the dollar and the D-Mark were at the core of the problem, the United States and West Germany played key roles in trying to arrange a new system. But they had opposite objectives:

- The Americans were absolutely determined not to have the dollar again overvalued under an international arrangement, at great cost to American exports and to stability. Washington believed that surplus countries were as much responsible for exchange rate crises as deficit countries, and it insisted on advance agreement for sanctions against any persistent surplus countries, such as West Germany, that refused to revalue. U.S. officials said that countries that claimed to be virtuous in their monetary policies were really practicing mercantilism, curtailing domestic demand while taking advantage of their undervalued currency to maximize exports. They also argued that American strategic responsibilities, like the defense of Europe and Germany, helped strain the dollar, and that countries protected by U.S. policies should help to make the system work.
- West Germany, despite its readiness to make minor exchange rate adjustments for the sake of new currency alignments, refused to

commit itself to any arrangement that would oblige it to revalue in the future. Like other Europeans, it saw the United States as the main culprit and thought that the United States should carry the burden of adjustment. It criticized U.S. domestic policies, insisting that persistent U.S. fiscal deficits brought about inflation, and that Germany had to protect itself to avoid falling into the same pattern.[18]

In March of 1973, the United States and other governments and central banks gave up trying to set new fixed exchange rates. With that decision, the next phase of the postwar international system, "floating," began.

Floating was first perceived as a temporary arrangement that would permit currencies to find their way freely toward a new alignment of fixed rates. But exchange rates fluctuated so widely that no stable new alignment appeared. The first oil shock in 1974 finally put an end to whatever hopes for a new fixed system might have remained. For better or worse, and for lack of agreement on anything that might have been better, floating became the new system.

With floating, the relationship between the U.S. dollar and the D-Mark became subject to market forces rather than official negotiations. The United States welcomed floating because it was no longer obliged to maintain any particular relationship between the dollar and gold and—more important—because countries like West Germany could no longer operate under what Washington regarded as self-serving exchange rate relationships. Germany was less certain whether floating would serve its needs, but was not prepared to pursue any alternative.

Floating brought about some changes in the global economy but not others. The main change was that gold and major currencies were no longer traded at an officially fixed rate but at a free market price. On the other hand, the size and influence of the American economy remained so great that the dollar remained the world's most important currency, the one in which commodities were denominated as well as the most widespread monetary reserve asset. The American economy was to remain the *économie dominante* of the world, at least for the foreseeable future.

Floating did not insulate domestic economies from international events and global economic forces, and was not expected to do so. While the floating era may have ended the period of fixed links to the dollar and to gold, it did not give countries complete freedom. It only meant that adjustments would be made by the markets, not by government decree or agreement.[19] And those adjustments would, at least theoretically, reflect trade and payments imbalances and correct them over time.

The situation did not, however, work out as expected or planned. The increasingly important role played by capital flows, speculative or not, undercut the theoretically self-regulating mechanism of trade flows as the basis of currency values. Investment capital or speculative funds could fix the value of a country's currency at a level very different from that which might be dictated by its trade balance, and also at a level very different from that which that country's government or central bank might have preferred. This left governments where they had been before, obliged to carry out appropriate domestic policies to create the international relationships that they wanted.

The economic consequences of floating for Germany were not uniformly beneficial. The Bundesbank welcomed floating because it gave the bank more flexibility.[20] The bank could, in fact, virtually control the D-Mark's exchange rate if it was prepared to manipulate interest rates to that end. But German industry, and especially German exporters, always disturbed by any change in the system under which they had prospered, did not welcome the unpredictability that flexible exchange rates introduced into commercial arrangements and production plans.

Germany exporters also faced a particular problem, which still remains. The Bundesbank's favorite instrument for fighting inflation, a high real domestic interest rate, is also the instrument that attracts capital to the D-Mark and keeps the currency high. Many German businessmen feared then, as ever since, that the Bundesbank's anti-inflationary policy would always keep the D-Mark stronger than most other currencies, jeopardizing exports. A new element of uncertainty, with the potential for almost uninterrupted domestic controversy, had entered German economic and industrial planning, and different elements of West Germany's domestic and international economic policies were to remain in conflict even more than under the fixed system.

Because of these conflicts, and because West Germany's government as well as its bankers and industrialists recognized German limitations and vulnerabilities, all were anxious to establish the highest possible level of international predictability. They were ready to participate actively in meetings and consultations that might try to coordinate policy in order to guide exchange rate fluctuations and stabilize rates as much as possible. The Germans not only joined in all the consultations that developed, often at summits of heads of state or heads of government, but they encouraged them at every opportunity.

West Germany was thus to play a prominent part in the next phase of the international monetary system, the era of virtually uninterrupted consultations. Just as the head of the German central bank had come to New York to join his American, British, and French colleagues in 1927 for the first intercontinental discussions on monetary affairs, the heads of the Bundesbank as well as German Chancellors and Finance Ministers became global commuters in order to participate in the post-1971 efforts at coordination.

GERMANY IN THE GROUPS AND AT THE SUMMITS

Global economic coordination after the end of the Bretton Woods system has developed a number of coordinating institutions. One, first known informally as the Group of Five (or the G-5), included the United States, West Germany, Japan, Great Britain, and France. After Canada and Italy joined, it has become known as the G-7. That group includes the finance ministers and central bankers of the principal economic powers, which meet periodically and consult regularly between meetings.

The other institution is the economic summit format, a framework for gatherings at which the heads of state or government of the same seven countries meet to coordinate economic policy or at least to understand each other better. The director of the IMF also attends. The summits have been held annually since 1975 on a rotating basis in the capitals of the summit states. Two summits, those of 1978 and 1985, took place in Bonn, and both have been significant although for different reasons. The 1992 summit is also to be held in Germany, probably Munich although there has been some talk of Berlin.

The G-5 and G-7 non-summit meetings have not been scheduled on a regular basis, as the ministers meet when they believe it is necessary. At least two meetings—at the Plaza in New York and the Louvre in Paris—have been highly significant and even more important than most of the summits.

Helmut Schmidt was among those who launched the summits, in part because he had found international consultations useful when he had been Finance Minister under Willy Brandt and in part because he believed that he could use the summits to influence the thinking of other government principals. In 1974 and 1975, when he and Valéry Giscard d'Estaing first proposed the summit format, Schmidt particularly believed that he could influence Gerald Ford, then the U.S. President. He may have had some success doing this. But it did not continue with Ford's successors, as Schmidt came to realize to his disappointment and frustration.

Schmidt and Giscard based their summit proposal largely on their experience with the institution that became known as the "Library Group" because it first met in the White House library. That group included Schmidt and Giscard, George Shultz, then U.S. Secretary of the Treasury, Anthony Barber, then British Chancellor of the Exchequer, and Takeo Fukuda, then Japanese Finance Minister. Paul Volcker, then Shultz's deputy, served as the roving messenger between the five to help prepare meetings. Karl Otto Pöhl, then Schmidt's state secretary, was Schmidt's emissary.[21] The Library Group could meet quietly and thoughtfully, giving the major financial powers of the world an opportunity to resolve many of the problems that arose during the years of financial uncertainty after the end of the fixed exchange rate system. It helped arrange for floating and helped prepare the atmosphere of mutual understanding that led to the summits.

Nothing could have been better than the Library Group from the German standpoint, and especially from Schmidt's. The discreet format did not isolate or pressure Germany. It caused no speculation for or against the D-Mark. It gave the participants a chance to keep each other informed about their respective policies and it provided at least a measure of stability because of their mutual understanding. The very name "Library Group" appealed to Schmidt's conviction that an atmosphere of rational discussion in a calm setting would enable others better to appreciate the merits of the German standpoint.

The summits have, however, provided a setting very different from that of the Library Group. Heads of government and heads of state cannot meet as discreetly as finance ministers can (and sometimes must). Although the Germans hosted their 1978 and 1985 meetings in the relatively businesslike atmosphere of Bonn, many of the summits have been convened in pictur-esque and dramatic settings—such as Venice or Versailles—that conveyed an atmosphere of theater more than of serious and thoughtful reflection or of informal discussion. The agendas have become burdened with non-eco-nomic topics and with separate bilateral meetings that have dealt with many topics other than economic coordination. They have had to include foreign ministers as well as finance ministers, substantially changing the character of the discussion. The 1991 London summit, by including Soviet President Mikhail Gorbachev, departed even more substantially from the original purpose of the meetings.

Nonetheless, even the circus setting of the summits has still offered opportunities for conversation if not for thought. German financiers and officials, attempting to evaluate the summits after a dozen years of experi-ence, concluded that the meetings at least obliged the senior statesmen of the world once a year to concentrate on global economic and financial matters and to become sensitive to each other's views.[22] Hans Tietmeyer, who had been Kohl's Sherpa, wrote that Germany had found the summits useful for addressing common problems such as protectionism, the third-world debt problem, the energy crises, agricultural issues, and environmental consider- ations, even if the summits did not produce agreement and if their full effect was very difficult to measure.[23]

The two Bonn summits have been important. In 1978, Schmidt committed Germany to a more reflationary policy, although he later regretted it.[24] Schmidt wrote later that he had been prepared to reflate the German economy in exchange for Carter's agreement to decontrol domestic oil prices, but that Carter did not keep his promise but did just the opposite by subsidizing U.S. oil prices. This spurred worldwide inflation instead of balancing German and American policy.[25]

Seven years later, Kohl and other summit principals made commitments toward supply-side policies which most agreed were then necessary and which both Kohl and Reagan wanted to use to reduce the government role in their national economies. Kohl was happy to be able to please Reagan while doing what he wished to do for domestic reasons.[26]

More broadly, the West Germans found the summits useful as opportu- nities to influence others, and they have especially tried to influence Amer- ican thinking. German Chancellors rarely get the chance to talk to American Presidents about economics, and the summits do provide a setting for that purpose even if it is far from ideal. Senior Germans have long since given up any illusion that true coordination will follow, but they believe that the summits have improved the chances for cooperation and, most of all, for mutual understanding.

The Germans have, however, complained that the pressures for adjust- ment in such a public atmosphere are all too often focused upon the surplus countries because they are usually in a minority. From that standpoint, at least, the Bretton Woods era may have been better for Germany.[27] To avoid being put under excess pressure at the summits, German leaders and minis- ters have during the 1980s usually not attempted to draw particular attention to themselves at those summits, preferring to let media attention fall on the Americans, the Japanese, or the British. Even when they are hosts, they try not to project themselves too far into the limelight. One of the reasons Germany has been interested in greater European monetary coordination is to have more friends at the summits.

Whatever West German Chancellors and Ministers may have thought, West German bankers and financial officials have usually spoken quite skeptically about the summits, making abundantly clear that the summits do not change their views although they may adjust specific policies. In his review of the summits, Tietmeyer insisted that West Germany saw the summits as occasions for "cooperation," not "coordination."[28] Helmut Schlesinger, when Pöhl's deputy at the Bundesbank, seemed totally uncompromising in his assessment. He warned in 1987 that "participation in cooperative international strategies . . . should be expected of us only if preservation of the stability of the purchasing power of money continues to be regarded as the principal contribution which monetary policy can make to the maintenance of favorable global growth conditions."[29]

Beyond the summits, the Germans played rather different roles in the two crucial meetings of finance ministers, the Plaza meeting of the G-5 in September 1985 and the Louvre meeting of the G-6 in December 1986.[30] The Plaza meeting was called to counter the high dollar (although the dollar had actually peaked seven months before the meeting) and the Louvre meeting was called to stabilize the dollar after its subsequent decline.

West German financial and banking officials welcomed the Plaza meeting because they agreed that the dollar was too high. They feared the potential inflationary consequences of having the D-Mark remain too weak. They were even more fearful, however, that the dollar might tumble so violently from its overvaluation that it could destabilize the global financial system. The ERM was still being tested at the time and the Germans were not certain that it could survive that kind of instability. Pöhl remained very restrained throughout the Plaza meeting, but he must have been pleased with the outcome because no instability resulted. The EMS realignments that followed the Plaza and Louvre meetings remained within ranges acceptable to the Germans, although the realignment in January 1987 was particularly acrimonious when French officials spoke of a "D-Mark problem" and insisted that it was West Germany's failure to lower its own interest rates that was causing a run on the franc.[31] The Bundesbank did subsequently lower rates, but must have been embarrassed to hear the French make arguments that they normally heard from the Americans.

After the Plaza meetings, some of the familiar German-American disputes did indeed surface again. Just as President Carter had wanted Germany to act as a "locomotive" in the latter 1970s, Treasury Secretary James Baker wanted the Germans to stimulate their economy during the mid-1980s. He and Paul Volcker, then chairman of the Federal Reserve, met frequently with senior Germans during 1986 and 1987, sometimes in very informal settings (as at Pöhl's home in Frankfurt or at Finance Minister Gerhard Stoltenberg's home in Kiel). To show the Americans that he was not the sole or main opponent of stimulation, Pöhl invited Schlesinger to the Frankfurt meeting, a move that must have made the Americans appreciate the difficulty of persuading West Germany to act as any kind of "locomotive" and that may have contributed to Baker's later criticism of Schlesinger's attitudes and policies.

The Americans attempted another tactic against the Germans: They began frequent bilateral consultations with Japanese officials and central bankers, attempting to convey the impression that they might begin to pursue a G-2 strategy if the Germans proved too recalcitrant. The tactic did not succeed, in part because the Japanese and Germans had their own direct contacts and in part because the Germans believed that their situation was fundamentally different from Japan's. Only 10 per cent of West Germany's trade is with the United States, as against one third of Japan's. Therefore, the Japanese would be prepared to support a strong dollar more than the Germans.

Despite the many arguments, the Germans and the Americans reached an understanding of sorts in the mid-1980s. The Germans agreed to stimulate demand in exchange for an American commitment to stop encouraging the fall in the dollar. The United States took steps to prevent a further decline of the dollar after the German discount rate cut in January 1987. The Louvre G-6 meeting succeeded on that basis, with the Germans having been much more involved than at the Plaza. But the agreement collapsed only nine months later with even more bitter mutual recrimination when the Bundesbank raised its repurchase rate and global stock markets crashed. Baker was particularly critical of Schlesinger, who had strongly urged the increase in the repurchase rate. The Germans vehemently rejected American charges that the Bundesbank's action had triggered the crash, but in the G-7 statement of December 1987 the Bundesbank specifically cited its several interest rate reductions after the crash as evidence that it did not want to depress global markets for the sake of its anti-inflationary policies at home. As a sign that it would not be pushed around, the Bundesbank before the end of 1987 renewed Schlesinger's contract as vice president for five years.[32]

As the 1990s dawned, the entire process of the G-7 and of international economic coordination had changed its focus and direction. States were making less of an effort than before to coordinate their policies or to pretend to be coordinating them. They had become sufficiently comfortable with floating, and sufficiently confident that they could influence exchange rates when they really wanted to do so, that they believed they could accept the effects of divergent policies and whatever risks there might be to domestic stability.

The New York meeting of the G-7 in January 1991, like the later IMF meeting in early May, illustrated this trend. The G-7 agreed to coordinate fiscal and monetary policies "to create conditions favorable to lower global interest rates," adding that the G-7 members believed exchange rates were at proper levels. But the Bundesbank raised interest rates within a week after the meeting. When the U.S. Federal Reserve almost simultaneously lowered U.S. interest rates, the dollar began to fall. The G-7 central banks intervened strongly in foreign exchange markets to limit the rise in the D-Mark and to slow the decline in the dollar, but the dollar still fell to a postwar low against the D-Mark before recovering. The dollar subsequently rose off the floor, as the problems attendant upon German unification weakened confidence in the D-Mark. But the process of international coordination had clearly not functioned, although the Bundesbank and the Federal Reserve let it be known that they had informed each other before their respective actions.

The New York and Washington meetings, and the subsequent actions of the G-7 members, showed that the world's leading financial powers had given up their efforts to coordinate policies and even to plan joint actions except at the tactical level of coordinated interventions. With many economists in the G-7 countries remaining unconvinced that market interventions even served a useful purpose, the functions of the G-7 had really become quite limited in that respect. It remained possible, however, that the G-7 might return to the original purpose of the Library Group and of the summits if global economic conditions made it necessary.[33]

Whatever value interventions might or might not have had, the Bundesbank continues to use them, if for no other reason than its long-held preference for smooth and steady market movements. Pöhl occasionally suggested that the bank might stop intervening in the markets, but to date it has not stopped. Neither German exporters nor the Bundesbank can thrive with instability any better in the 1990s than in the 1970s or 1980s. The exporters must still fear for their markets. The Bundesbank must fear massive sales of D-Marks held by foreign central banks even more than before. The Germans, like others, learned from the crash of 1987 and the mini-crash of 1989 that markets sometimes panic when they believe that the central banks are not acting in a coordinated manner, and that even limited coordination—or at least the appearance of such coordination—may be better than none.

Another clear trend as the 1990s arrived was that the G-5, by becoming the G-7, have really become the G-3. Although such strong personalities as François Mitterrand of France and Margaret Thatcher of Great Britain could carry considerable weight through the sheer force of their presence, decisions have been made primarily by Americans, Japanese, and Germans. Even as the others attend the meetings, it is the three major financial powers that can act. France, Italy, and increasingly even Great Britain, have often tended to follow the German lead. Canada's economy is tied to that of the United

States. Japan has stood alone, but has been more and more perceived to be representing broad Asian interests as well.

Germany and the D-Mark, as the most important member and the most important currency of the EMS and of the ERM, serve as the link between the dollar and the other European currencies. When the D-Mark has been strong against the dollar, other ERM currencies have been forced to rise with it. When the D-Mark has been weak, the other ERM currencies might have some more room for maneuver but not very much. They also tend to fall unless they take special steps to prevent it.[34]

For Bonn and Frankfurt, the meetings at the beginning of 1991 marked an important point. They showed that German policy would not be swung by others, and they confirmed that Germany did not even have to be limited by ERM considerations. After the Bundesbank had raised the German discount rate and Lombard rate on January 31, 1991, Pöhl said that the bank knew they would meet with no applause but that others (in the ERM) could not have their cake and eat it too. He added that the Bundesbank, unlike the central banks of other countries, did not have to put political considerations ahead of its economic and financial judgment.[35]

THE GERMAN RECORD IN GLOBAL MONETARY MATTERS

The West German role in the development of the global financial and monetary system has been replete with ironies. No state consistently had a greater interest in developing a stable system and in cooperating in such a system. During the Bretton Woods era, German support for the U.S. dollar represented a significant sacrifice. Had the Federal Republic and the Bundesbank chosen to use their reserves for massive gold purchases, as the French did, they could have profited significantly. Later, it was West Germany that helped establish every successor system to that of Bretton Woods, and Germany that played a significant role in every effort at coordination and cooperation. The German search for stability led Bonn and Frankfurt constantly toward new and sometimes imaginative arrangements for international financial and monetary coordination.

Nonetheless, West German policy helped undermine and even destroy some of the arrangements that Germany wanted to maintain. During Bretton Woods, pressures against the dollar almost always expressed themselves in massive purchases of German currency. Moreover, the Bundesbank's efforts to protect the value of that currency always made the D-Mark an attractive and safe alternative for investors and speculators. Thus the strength of the D-Mark became a self-fulfilling prophecy, and any currency—including the dollar—could be under attack if it did not benefit from a similar care. The constant availability of the German option put all other currencies under pressure and even at risk if they were less persistently defended and preserved. The only currencies and systems that survived this pressure were those that determined from the beginning that they would accept and follow a discipline similar to that of the D-Mark and—therefore—of the Bundesbank.

Thus West Germany helped to bring down the Bretton Woods system even though it wished to support it, because the only way to sustain the system would have been to abandon its basic economic and monetary philosophy. But, although Germany was the agent of change, it was not its beneficiary. Both the government and the Bundesbank would have preferred the maintenance of the stable rate system. Neither system, however, spared Germany the problem of dealing with its own contradictory attitudes with respect to the most desirable value of the D-Mark.[36]

German exchange rate policy has constantly struggled with those two alternatives. When a decision absolutely needed to be made, however, German governments and the Bundesbank have almost always during the floating era chosen the path that would fight inflation, preferring a strong currency that might adversely affect trade to a weak one that would jeopardize the stability of the German system. With that choice, they set policy for others as well as for themselves.

That remained true in 1990 and 1991, even as Germany took on the additional burdens of unification. So long as the D-Mark was strong, and so long as German interest rates remained high, even the United States could diverge from German policy only at the risk of seeing its own currency fall.

GERMANY AS A TRADING NATION

West Germany was consistently one of the world's major trading nations, almost from the early days of the economic miracle. It also had high trade and current account surpluses during most of these years and especially during the latter half of the 1980s. It was the world's largest exporter in 1988, being second-largest after the United States during 1989, and again led in 1990 when one included East German exports before monetary unification. Japan was in third place each of the three years. West Germany was also consistently one of the world's largest importers.

Ludwig Erhard himself set the tone when he was Economics Minister. He made his own sentiments very clear, saying in 1953 that "foreign trade is not a specialized activity for a few who might engage in it, but it is the very core and even the precondition of our economic and social order."[37] Commentators and authors on the German economy have spoken of a German "export mystique," of deliberate domestic underconsumption to facilitate exports and increase competitiveness, and of an "almost unconscious" German mercantilism.[38] The export sector had a powerful voice in West German economic and commercial policy-making, including a special Foreign Trade Advisory Council located in the Ministry of Economics. Senior West German political figures rarely made visits abroad without including select German businessmen in their official delegations.

This export mystique is not new, but has a strong tradition in German history with the exception of the autarkic Nazi period. The old German Empire in 1910 had a higher share of world trade than the United States.[39] The following statistics show the share that German exports had in German (and, as appropriate, West German) GNP for selected periods:[40]

Period	Export Share of GNP
1910-1913	17.8%
1925-1929	14.9%
1930-1934	12.0%
1935-1938	6.0%
1950	9.3%
1960	17.2%
1970	23.8%
1980	26.7%

By the end of the 1980s, largely because of high West German exports to the European Community, the level had reached more than 30 per cent. This meant that at least one third of all jobs in West Germany depended directly on exports, and many more depended indirectly. During the entire postwar period, and despite the widespread belief that Japan has been the world's premier exporter, West Germany had a higher share of world exports than Japan.

Several sectors of West German industry contributed most heavily to the West German trade surplus, although West Germany was competitive across a wide range of goods. The following statistics reflect performance of several different sectors during 1989 (in millions of D-Marks):[41]

Sector	Exports	Imports	Balance
Agriculture and Forestry	7,056	30,734	- 23,678
Processed Foods & Tobacco	27,106	30,227	- 3,121
Minerals	3,934	27,921	- 23,987
Basic Industry	157,310	138,804	+ 18,406
Investment Goods	358,011	181,892	+176,119
Consumer Goods	78,139	83,114	- 4,975

Within those broad categories, a number of West German industries participated especially in exports, with significant per cent shares of their total production being destined abroad:[42]

Industry	Export Share of Production
Shipbuilding	62
Air and Space	59
Office Equipment	53
Automobiles	48
Machine Tools	45
Chemicals	44
Iron and Steel	37
Precision Mechanics, Optics	36
Electronics	31

Several of the industries with a high export share, like shipbuilding or airframes, were heavily subsidized in West Germany and have been at least initially subsidized in united Germany. They are competitive in world markets on the basis of those subsidies.[43] The subsidies demonstrate the extent of the German export commitment, for West Germany would have had a substantial trade surplus even without the subsidized products of those industries.

Trade in services did not contribute to the West German export surplus, largely because West German tourists every year spent about DM 25 billion more than foreign tourists in Germany.[44]

The largest proportional rise in West Germany's trade and payments balance occurred during the years between 1983 and 1986, principally because the U.S. dollar was highly overvalued, but there were steady increases in the trade and current account surplus during the entire decade. The dollar-DM relationship had its most direct effect on the West German trade balance with the United States itself, with the German surplus rising dramatically between 1981 and 1986 as the dollar rose in strength, to an annual level of DM 15 billion in 1986, and then declining gradually during the remainder of the decade as the dollar weakened, to a surplus of only DM 5 billion by 1989.[45]

With the West European currencies remaining much more closely tied to the D-Mark during the 1980s through the ERM, the West German trade surplus with those states rose during most of the decade, from a surplus of DM 15 billion in 1982 to a high point of almost DM 50 billion in both 1988 and 1989. It began declining (to DM 25 billion) only in 1990, in part because of unification and in part because of the slowdowns in France and Italy.[46]

Although the true competitiveness of East German production could not be measured in the period following unification, the former GDR also had a consistent trade surplus in machinery, equipment, transport, industrial consumer goods, and chemicals. It had a trade deficit in fuels, raw materials, metals, ores, semi-manufactures, agricultural products, and processed foods.[47]

In 1989, West Germany had the following trade balances with other states (in millions of D-Marks):[48]

Trade Partner	Exports	Imports	Balance
European Community	352,668	258,660	+ 94,008
Other Europe	117,872	79,357	+ 38,515
Socialist States	29,306	25,143	+ 4,163
Non-European	78,421	80,694	- 2,273
United States	46,624	38,265	+ 8,359
Developing States	61,761	62,285	- 524
OPEC States	16,402	12,360	+ 4,042

German trade did not, however, go exclusively to the West. Both the former GDR and the former West Germany were important trading partners for Eastern Europe. One half of all GDR trade was with the Soviet Union, and one quarter was with Eastern Europe outside the Soviet Union. The GDR enjoyed a small trade surplus although CMEA policy favored maintaining the closest possible balances. The Soviet Union subsidized its East European trading partners, including the GDR, by offering oil and gas at prices well below world market levels, and Soviet trading partners were often believed to have offered balancing price concessions on finished goods in return.

West Germany, in turn, was the CMEA's main trading partner in the West. It had 30 per cent of the OECD's exports to European CMEA states in 1989, for a total of DM 13 billion. The share of total West German trade that went to European CMEA states was 3.8 per cent, the highest except for Finland and Austria.[49] (West German statistics did not include the GDR in its foreign trade, so that the CMEA statistics reflected trade with other CMEA states than East Germany.) West Germany also had the highest percentage of high-technology exports to the CMEA states, including computers. The United States periodically expressed concern that West German technology might be helping the Soviet military effort, a charge that the West Germans consistently rejected.[50]

With Germany now united, and with new and even dramatic prospects for greater openings in Eastern Europe and in whatever system may ultimately succeed the Soviet Union, the German government expects trade toward the East to increase not only above the levels of former West German trade but also above the levels that West and East Germany together had traded with Eastern Europe and the Soviet Union before unification. German businessmen have been visiting Russia, the Baltic states, the Soviet Union and Eastern Europe in large numbers to establish or reestablish trade connections and to inspect potential investment sites or joint ventures. They have reported that their contacts with the office of Russian President Boris Yeltsin have been particularly impressive and promising.

Germany will probably become the largest single Western trading partner for those states. The total trade and investment credits insured by the German government, as well as the planned outlays, already amounted to DM 75.3 billion by mid-1991 before the coup against Gorbachev. Bank credits not secured by the German government amounted to DM 26.3 billion. Prospects were for rapid increases to help the new states that had either declared their independence from Moscow or had succeeded the Soviet Union. In addition, about DM 24.5 billion in credits was to go to Poland, Hungary, Czechoslovakia, Yugoslavia, Romania, and Bulgaria.[51] German exporters had complained in the past that Soviet orders had been slow in coming even when credits were available, and that the bureaucracy they had to deal with had been slow and inefficient, but this may change.[52]

The German credits are not free of risk. Soviet and East European debt has been accumulating for several decades and by 1990 already had reached almost $130 billion according to an estimate made by the Deutsche Bank.[53]

Poland had its debts frequently rescheduled during the 1980s and will probably prove unable to service the outstanding debt in the 1990s. The Paris Club, with full German agreement and in recognition of the Polish effort to reform its economy, agreed to write off at least 50 per cent of Poland's debt. Investment and lending to Bulgaria was curtailed after it suspended debt service payments in March of 1990. Hungary's high level of debt was considered less troubling in part because of its success in avoiding rescheduling and its determination to continue to do so. Yugoslavia, being beset with political problems and probable dismemberment, and with a record of unilateral—and some thought unnecessary—moratoriums during the 1980s, also presented very considerable risks.[54]

These many obstacles and objections apparently weighed less heavily on the minds of German officials, exporters, and investors than on other Europeans or on Americans and Japanese. The German determination to move East undoubtedly reflected an old tradition as well as a political interest, and it intensified even further after mid-1991. Moreover, Germany was better located than any other West European state to trade with Eastern Europe, especially as Berlin remains one of the most attractive potential production, assembly, service, or transportation centers for East European trade. A united Germany has given every sign that it will want to trade and invest heavily in the East. Germany has particularly investigated the possibilities for improving oil and gas production in order to enable Russia and other Eastern states to have a highly marketable product to sell in exchange for German and other Western industrial imports.[55]

GERMAN INVESTMENT ABROAD

West German foreign investment compensated to some extent for its trade and current account surplus with other states, but the nature of Germany's foreign investment was different from the investment of other states in Germany. About one quarter to one third, and sometimes as much as one half, of West German investment abroad during the 1970s and 1980s represented direct investment in productive facilities, the remainder being investment in various forms of long-term credits such as equities, bonds, or long-term bank deposits. In the other direction, relatively little foreign investment in Germany during that period was for productive facilities, with the annual share ranging from about one twentieth to one sixth of all foreign investment. During most of the years between 1960 and 1989, and especially during the 1980s, the amount of German investment abroad exceeded that of foreign investment in Germany, thus helping to balance the trade surplus.

During 1990, German investment abroad had amounted to DM 30 billion, with foreign investment in West Germany coming to only DM 3 billion.[56]

Bundesbank analyses showed that West German investment, like the German trade and current account surplus, went largely to Western Europe. They also showed a major increase in net West German investment abroad from 1981 to 1989:[57]

FRG Foreign Investment Pattern, by Region
(in billions of D-Marks)

Region	FRG Assets Abroad		Foreign Assets in FRG		Balance	
	1981	1989	1981	1989	1981	1989
EC States	204	705	227	519	-23	186
Other Indus-trial States	193	474	150	340	43	134
Others*	168	278	122	155	45	123
Totals	**564**	**1,457**	**498**	**1,014**	**66**	**443**

*OPEC states, developing states, CMEA states, etc.

The statistics confirm the very high degree of integration among the West German and other West European economies, with almost half of West German foreign investment abroad being in other EC states and half of foreign investment in West Germany being from other EC states. They also illustrate the growth in West German investment within the EC, amounting to one half trillion D-Marks during the years between 1981 to 1989 alone.

Such statistics inevitably helped fuel long-standing German questions, reflected in the *Standort* discussion and in the planning for the European Single Market, whether West Germany and perhaps all of Germany was not a competitive place to produce, at least for foreign investors. They also showed, however, that foreigners were prepared to invest in German securities and in German obligations. According to Bundesbank statistics, one fifth of all German securities at the end of 1990 belonged to foreigners, and one half of all German publicly offered obligations between 1986 and 1990 had been bought by foreigners. In both cases, foreign purchases had risen strongly during the latter part of the 1980s over all earlier periods.[58]

Because of the large amount of German direct investment abroad, German income from foreign investments exceeds that of foreigners investing in Germany. Bundesbank statistics showed that the net return on German capital abroad had risen to almost DM 25 billion by 1989. If Germans were going abroad to invest, they were drawing a significant return income.[59] The favorite sites for German foreign investment were France and Great Britain. Relatively small amounts went to Japan or to developing countries, but a fast-growing amount (one half billion D-Marks during 1989) went to Eastern Europe.[60]

Any review of German foreign investment and foreign trade patterns, when compared with the German role in global monetary affairs, reveals that West German trade and investment were much more confined to Europe than Germany's global monetary role might have suggested. Although Germany may have an immensely influential position in world economic affairs, the German economy in many ways remains tied to its European roots. Few German firms are as large and as globally oriented in their activities as the giant American and Japanese firms. Only four German companies, Allianz, Daimler-Benz, Siemens, and Deutsche Bank, ranked among the hundred most highly capitalized industrial and banking concerns in summer 1991.[61]

Although some of the rankings of Japanese banks were undoubtedly inflated by the speculative values of their Japanese real estate holdings, the list accurately reflected the fact that German firms have not expanded internationally as Japanese, American, or British companies have done over the past few decades. It also reflected German losses of the two world wars, Germany's absence from the major international oil cartels dominated by America and Great Britain, and the generally cautious German attitude toward expansion abroad.

Europe is, however, a different story. A listing of the 100 European industrial firms with the largest turnover includes 25 West German, 24 British, 19 French, and 8 Italian firms.[62] The West Germans have a particular advantage in large industrial manufacturing companies and can presumably be expected to rise further in the rankings as they purchase operating arms of East German firms and raise them to profitability.

West German investment abroad was also concentrated in Europe. In 1988, over half of it, or 52 per cent, was in Europe (41 per cent in the European Community); 40 per cent was in the Americas (28 per cent in the United States), and only 6 per cent was in Asia (2 per cent in Japan).[63]

EUROPE, FOR GOOD OR ILL

Germans have themselves begun to question the wisdom of Germany's trade and investment concentration in Europe. One German diplomat and planner, Konrad Seitz, warned that the global economic system was rapidly being taken over by a *Duadenmacht*, or dual power, the United States and Japan, and that Germany was falling behind not only in technology (Chapter 5) but in its global presence. He warned that Germany and the European Community as a whole were not holding their own. He described this as the "Japanese-American Challenge."[64] While his study was written before German unification, none of the unfavorable trends that he noted would be reversed by the unification process. They were, in fact, likely to be exacerbated, although a united Germany might be able to correct them over time.

Seitz showed a vast disparity opening between the truly global states and corporations on one hand and the remainder of the world on the other. The truly global states and corporations were investing everywhere in the tradition of the multinational corporation but on a scale that dwarfed anything that had happened in the past. U.S. investments in Japan were three times as high as those of the European Community. Japanese investment in the United States in 1989 reached a cumulative total of $70 billion, three times as high as West Germany's $28 billion, although in 1982 they had both been below $10 billion. While some of the difference might have reflected Japan's more aggressive inroads into American markets and its fears that it would be excluded from importing into the United States, it also appeared to reflect a completely different attitude about international operations.

Seitz also showed some striking discrepancies between the global activities of various states and corporations, such as a ratio of 15 to 1 between Japanese investment in the European Community as against Community investment in Japan. Although the Japanese-German mutual investment ratio was less unfavorable, being only 5 to 1, that might merely underline Germany's disadvantages as a production site—especially as Japanese production facilities in other EC countries might be able to compete better against German goods than Japanese products made within Germany itself. As for banking, the capitalization controlled by Japanese banks in the United States was $363 billion; that controlled by German banks was $13.5 billion.[65]

Seitz noted that only a few major German firms, including the large pharmaceutical firms (BASF, Bayer, Höchst) and Siemens were even trying to swim against the tide by making foreign production investments and by establishing strategic alliances with firms in Japan, the United States, and elsewhere. He also cited some smaller German firms, such as Bosch and

Trump, that were attempting to operate internationally. But the proportions of what he showed indicated that West German firms were not going to play the dominant international role that the American and Japanese firms would play.

Seitz was not the only German to be disturbed by the German and European lag. The German Economics Ministry in 1990 commissioned the Ifo Institute to conduct a study of Japanese investment in Europe and of European investment in Japan.[66] The conclusions of the report could not have been reassuring to the Germans, either in terms of Japanese investment in Germany or of German investment in Japan, for the study indicated that Japanese investment in Europe had increased consistently throughout the 1980s, not only in absolute but in relative terms, and that the cumulative levels of investment had reached $45 billion by 1989, representing 17.7 per cent of Japan's foreign investment (as against 41.1 per cent to the United States and 15.8 per cent to Southeast Asia). The largest amounts went to Great Britain, the Netherlands, and Luxembourg, with West Germany being fourth with $3.5 billion or about 7.5 per cent.

Almost half of Japanese investment in Germany during 1989 was in wholesale and retail trade outlets, and only one fifth was in production facilities. These totals suggested that Japan regarded Germany more as a place to sell than as a place to produce, although the Japanese community in Germany was concentrated around one of the traditional centers of German production, Düsseldorf. German investment in Japan, on the other hand, was concentrated in production sectors and especially in chemical production. It was, however, relatively low, representing only 2.2 per cent of all West German investment abroad at the end of 1988, although it had gradually risen each year between 1985 and 1988 and had reached a cumulative total of $690 million (one fifth of Japan's investment in West Germany). As one half of all foreign investment in Japan was from the United States, it was clear that Europe as a whole, and not only Germany, was lagging in its efforts to invest in Japan.

The Ifo study concluded that Japanese barriers to foreign investment had been eased since the 1970s and no longer represented the main hurdle to foreign investment in Japan. Instead, it argued, German investment had most recently lagged because the Germans thought primarily in European terms and had become accustomed to investing and selling in Europe more than in Asia. A subsequent study, done by another Ifo analyst, pointed to the same problems but said that the Germans were making some headway.[67]

The dilemma that Seitz and others posed, and that the Germans had to think about as they were concentrating on their national unity and on unifying

Europe as well, was how Germany could actually benefit from its concentration in Europe. In this respect, the collapse of the Wall and the changes in the Soviet Union and Eastern Europe offer new and perhaps historic opportunities. For the Europe of today and tomorrow is not the Europe of yesterday. And a Germany that can help to set the policy of the new Europe to the East as well as of the older Europe to the West can gain much more influence across the world. Germany might be called upon to play on a continental scale the role that the United States played after 1945 on a global scale.

As the 1990s arrive, united Germany thus finds itself increasingly confronted with the dilemma of choosing a coherent global monetary and trade policy and of deciding how to balance the world and Europe within that policy.

For political as well as economic reasons, Germany must expand its trade, aid, and investment toward the East, and it must do so largely by offering credits to states that can ill afford to service the credits they have already been granted and that will want to pay off at least some of those credits with farm exports. Germany must achieve all those potentially conflicting objectives while keeping the D-Mark strong and financing unification, and it cannot abandon its West European and European Community base.

Germany has different weights at different levels. The D-Mark is a global currency, one of the strongest and most important, and long one of the most stable. In the monetary realm, Germany is a global player. In Europe, its monetary policy sets the tone for the entire continent. But if its influence and its interests go well beyond Europe, and if it helps to set the policy options for many other states as well, it does not dominate any particular group with sufficient power to compel that group to go against the perceived interests of other members.

The Japanese, the Americans, and several smaller states are increasingly operating on a global basis, taking advantage of the open global financial environment to position themselves everywhere. If the global trading environment suffers from a failure to resolve trade disputes between the United States, the European Community, and others, it may well be the Americans and the Japanese rather than the Europeans that will be able to function effectively within each separate trading area. Japan and the United States can indeed look upon a regionalized and a managed global trading system with greater equanimity than the Germans and other Europeans, especially if the Europeans continue to lag in *Spitzentechnologie*. They have production facilities everywhere, including in the European Community. They can still negotiate special arrangements with each other, and the American position would be strong because it has the principal national market although the EC is a larger international one.

It is in this context that Germany in Europe now itself deserves a closer look.

NOTES TO CHAPTER EIGHT

1. IMF quotas are only proximate, as they vary whenever new members are added or other shifts take place, but the shift from 6 to 6.10 per cent represents the general amount of the increase in the German quota.
2. Karl Grün, "Deutschland in Washington," *Börsen-Zeitung*, May 10, 1990.
3. Helmut Schmidt, *Men and Powers*, p. 158.
4. Bayerische Landesbank, *Money and Capital Markets*, February 1990, p. 1; Hans Tietmeyer, "Die D-Mark als Währungsreserve," *WISU-Magazin*, May 1990, cited in *Auszüge*, May 29, 1990, pp. 5-6; the 1990 statistics, reported in the Bundesbank's *Monatsbericht* for May 1991, were summarized in *Handelsblatt*, May 22, 1991.
5. *Report of the Deutsche Bundesbank for the Year 1989* (Frankfurt: Deutsche Bundesbank, 1990), pp. 57-58.
6. International Monetary Fund, *1990 Annual Report* (Washington: IMF, 1990), pp. 67-68.
7. "Longer-Term Trends in Global Monetary Reserves," *Monthly Report of the German Bundesbank*, January 1990, p. 40.
8. Maxwell Watson, Russell Kincaid, Caroline Atkinson, Eliot Kalter, and David Folkerts-Landau, *International Capital Markets: Developments and Prospects* (Washington: IMF, 1986), p. 29.
9. *Ibid.*
10. Tietmeyer, *loc. cit.*
11. *Handelsblatt, loc. cit.*
12. International Monetary Fund, *World Economic Outlook*, May 1990, p. 22.
13. Brian Tew, *The Evolution of the International Monetary System, 1945-1973* (London: Hutchinson, 1977), p. 180.
14. A description of German attitudes and policies during this period is in John Williamson, *The Failure of World Monetary Reform, 1971-74* (Sunbury-on-Thames, England: Nelson, 1977), pp. 85-88.
15. Robert Solomon, *The International Monetary System, 1945-1976*, pp. 159-160.
16. *Ibid.*, p. 207.
17. *Ibid.*, pp. 221-222.
18. Tew, *op. cit.*, p. 192; see Williamson, *op. cit.*, for a detailed review of the entire post-Bretton Woods crisis.
19. Günther Grosche, "The United States, Germany, and the International Monetary Fund: Lessons in International Cooperation," a speech made at

the invitation of the Program in German Public and International Affairs of Georgetown University, December 8, 1988, p. 3.

20. Yoichi Funabashi, *Managing the Dollar* (Washington: Institute for International Economics, 1988), p. 115.

21. Helmut Schmidt, *op. cit.*, pp. 156-157.

22. The viewpoints of several Germans are presented in Wilfried Guth, *Economic Policy Coordination* (Washington: IMF, 1988).

23. Hans Tietmeyer, "Comment," Guth, *op. cit.*, p. 139.

24. Randolph Henning and Günter Grosser, "Empirical Evidence of Effects of Policy Coordination among Major Industrial Countries since the Rambouillet Summit of 1975," Guth, *op. cit.*, pp. 117-121.

25. Helmut Schmidt, *op. cit.*, p. 264.

26. Tietmeyer, *loc. cit.*, p. 137.

27. Guth, "Summary and Conclusions," Guth, *op. cit.*, p. 212.

28. Tietmeyer, *loc. cit.*

29. Helmut Schlesinger, "Comment," Guth, *op. cit.*, p. 33.

30. Material regarding these meetings and the arrangements preceding and surrounding them is drawn from Funabashi, *op. cit.*, pp. 109-127 and 151-176. The Louvre meeting was a G-6, not G-7 meeting, although Canada and Italy had joined the G-5 at the Tokyo summit, because Italy did not attend.

31. When a French official was asked about the "franc problem," he replied: "There is no franc problem. There is a D-Mark problem."

32. Schmidt, *op. cit.*, p. 293.

33. For comments on that meeting, see *Washington Post*, February 10, 1991, p. H4; *Financial Times*, January 23, 1991; *Handelsblatt*, January 24, 1991.

34. Hugo M. Kaufmann, *Germany's International Monetary Policy and the European Monetary System* (New York: Brooklyn College Press, 1985), pp. 110-111.

35. *Handelsblatt*, February 2, 1991.

36. For a full analysis of this problem, see Patrick M. Boarman, *Germany's Economic Dilemma* (New Haven: Yale University Press, 1964).

37. Ludwig Erhard, "Deutschland's Rückkehr zum Weltmarkt," speech given in Düsseldorf, 1953, cited in Helga Haftendorn, Lothar Wilker, and Claudia Wörmann, *Die Aussenpolitik der Bundesrepublik Deutschland* (Berlin: Wissenschaftlicher Autoren Verlag, 1982), p. 403. Translated by the author.

38. Kreile, *op. cit.*, pp. 196-197; Wolfgang Hager, cited by Elke Thiel in "West Germany's Role in the International Economy," *Journal of International Affairs*, Fall 1988, p. 63.

39. Rainer Vollmer, "The Structure of West German Foreign Trade," Rudolf Richter and Wolfgang Stolper, *Economic Reconstruction in Europe: The Reintegration of Western Germany*, a symposium reported in *Zeitschrift für die gesamte Staatswissenschaft*, September 1981, p. 576.

40. Werner Abelshauser, *Wirtschaftsgeschichte der Bundesrepublik Deutschland, 1945-1980* (Frankfurt: Suhrkamp, 1983), p. 148.

41. *Ibid.*, Table 60.

42. Statistisches Bundesamt, cited in *Die Zeit*, November 17, 1989.

43. See the earlier cited reports of the German economic institutes for specific citations on West German subsidies for individual industries.

44. Sachverständigenrat, *1990/91 report*, Table 57. For more detailed statistics on German foreign trade and financial statistics, see Series 3 of the Bundesbank monthly reports, entitled *Statistische Beihefte zu den Monatsberichten der Deutschen Bundesbank, Reihe 3.*

45. Bundesbank, "Die längerfristige Entwicklung der deutschen Zahlungsbilanz nach Regionen," *Monatsberichte der Deutschen Bundesbank*, January 1991, p. 24.

46. *Ibid.*

47. GDR, *Statistical Pocketbook, 1989*, p. 101.

48. *Ibid.*, Table 63.

49. Deutsche Bank, "Perspektiven des Osthandels," *Deutsche Bank Bulletin*, December 1990, pp. 8-14; _____ *Rebuilding Eastern Europe*, April 1991, p. 99; greater details on East or West German trade with CMEA states can be found in: GDR, *Statistical Pocketbook, 1989*, pp. 101-104; Bundesbank, *Statistische Beihefte zu den Monatsberichten der Deutschen Bundesbank, Reihe 3*, published monthly; and FRG, Bundesminister für Wirtschaft, *Der Deutsche Osthandel*, published periodically.

50. *Wall Street Journal*, May 30, 1990.

51. This compilation is drawn from Klaus Engelen, "Deutsche geben mehr also die Hälfte aller West-Kredite," *Handelsblatt*, December 10, 1990, p. 10.

52. *Handelsblatt*, April 17, 1991.

53. Deutsche Bank, *Special Eastern Europe*, 1990, p. 57.

54. OECD *Financial Market Trends*, February 1991, cited in *Financial Times*, February 7, 1991.

55. Rudolf Botzian, *Erfolgsaussichten einer deutsch-sowjetischen Zusammenarbeit auf dem Rohstoffgebiet* (Ebenhausen: Stiftung Wissenschaft und Politik, 1990).

56. Sachverständigenrat, *1990/91 Report*, Table 58. The Sachverständigenrat statistics do not include short-term capital movement or speculative movement but only investments of more than one year's duration; *Financial Times*, August 17-18, 1991.

57. "Die längerfristige Entwicklung der deutschen Zahlungsbilanz nach Regionen," *Monatsberichte der Deutschen Bundesbank*, January 1991, p. 22.

58. *Süddeutsche Zeitung*, April 23, 1991.

59. "Der Dienstleistungsverkehr der Bundesrepublik Deutschland mit dem Ausland," *Monatsberichte der Deutschen Bundesbank*, April 1990, pp. 13-16.

60. *Frankfurter Allgemeine Zeitung*, April 23, 1991.

61. *Business Week*, July 15, 1991, p. 56. The list was based on market value, a method that would normally favor Japanese companies because of their high price-earnings ratios.

62. *Die Zeit*, August 31, 1990, p. 12. It is undoubtedly to Germany's advantage to have firms listed by turnover than by capitalization, as the high Japanese real estate values do not count. German companies generally do better on performance than on valuation.

63. *Wirtschaftswoche*, June 22, 1990, p. 83.

64. Konrad Seitz, *Die Japanisch-Amerikanische Herausforderung* (Bonn: Aktuell, 1990).

65. *Ibid.*, pp. 283, 292, and 294.

66. Angelika Ernst and Hanns Günther Hilpert, Ifo Institut für Wirtschaftsforschung, "Gegenseitige Investitionen Deutschland/Europa/Japan im Vergleich zu anderen Industriestandorten nach regionaler und sektoraler Verteilung und nach Entscheidungsgründen," summarized in FRG, *Aktuelle Beiträge*, February 11, 1991. Citations are drawn from the summary.

67. Siegfried Böttcher, "Globalisierung, lokale Integration und Zusammenarbeit mit japanischen Partnern," Ifo Institute, summarized in *Aktuelle Beiträge*, No. 12/1991, May 14, 1991.

Nine

Germany in Europe: The European Community

If Germany's global role has been and remains beset with complications, its European role has to date seemed clear. West Germany concentrated its activities within the European Community (EC), in which it had considerable but not decisive influence. United Germany will be more influential. Nonetheless, in the light of changes in Eastern Europe and the Soviet Union, and in the light of the increasingly protectionist attitudes of some EC members, Germany may have to reflect more about which of its widening needs the Community can serve and which it cannot, and Germany may also have to reflect more on what kind of EC it needs in its new situation. Even if the EC remains the principal forum for German economic interests and activities, a united Germany may need to give the EC a less dominant role in some policies and plans.

West Germany and Western Europe were linked in an almost symbiotic relationship. Each depended on the other, as well as on their association. West Germany was the strongest economic center, especially in industrial production and monetary policy. It helped lead the way to integration and to prosperity. It also helped to keep the Community open toward the outside world, especially across the Atlantic.

After more than 40 years of West European integration, the drive toward further West European and perhaps all-European integration remains strong. It has even acquired a momentum of its own, although it may need to be seen in a new light because of the disintegration of the Soviet bastion in Eastern Europe. West European heads of government used their summits during 1989 and 1990 to reiterate their firm intention to complete the European Single Market plan by the end of 1992. In December 1990, they began two year-long meetings that widened their goals by including political union of the European Community as a specific objective and by promising to proceed quickly from the European Monetary System (EMS) to full European Monetary Union (EMU).

Although German economic and political interests have been most persistently reflected in the EC and the EMS, the West German government, like the German business and banking establishment, have long had separate and quite different attitudes toward the two institutions. Those attitudes, as well as the institutions themselves, will be explored in this and the next chapter, as will the future German role in each.

THE EUROPEAN COMMUNITY

The European Community and earlier or related institutions, such as the European Coal and Steel Community, the European Economic Community, and EURATOM, have always had a political as well as an economic purpose. They were, in fact, started with much more of a political than economic purpose, the containment of Germany and its integration into Europe. That political purpose remains important, and it conditions more German actions than many outsiders understand.

When Jean Monnet first conceived the European Coal and Steel Community (ECSC), and when French Foreign Minister Robert Schuman first proposed it, they wanted to avoid having Europe follow the same disastrous path that it had followed after World War I. They wanted the states of Europe to cooperate rather than to engage in the kind of ruinous commercial competition that had helped to bring on one after another economic disaster and political confrontation before World War I and during the 1920s.

Chancellor Konrad Adenauer shared those fears and objectives. As a Rhinelander, suspicious of Prussia's autocratism, militarism, and fascination for Russia, Adenauer believed that Germany's destiny lay with the democratic West and especially with Western Europe. He believed that Western Europe's liberal tradition would exercise a benign influence on German politics and that its prosperous people would offer a market for German goods.

France's ECSC proposal not only offered West German industry many links with other West Europeans, but it gave the new West German state a political legitimacy and a level of international recognition that the Weimar Republic had been denied until well into the 1920s. Few Germans now would have either time or reason to recall the intense emotion in Germany that greeted what was almost an act of redemption, but Schuman's offer probably did more to change the direction of the German nation—as well as of the German economy—than any other step taken in the postwar years. West Germany would not have achieved its economic growth as fast or as convincingly without its membership in the Community.

The EC became West Germany's economic home and vocation, while also offering it a sense of direction about the future. In the interminable wrangling about technical minutiae that often marks the negotiations of the European bureaucracy, few Germans or others stop to think about major purpose, but it is always there.

Chancellors after Adenauer gave the growing and changing Community different levels of priority. Ludwig Erhard gave it his personal attention even when he became Chancellor. Georg Kiesinger had to focus more of his efforts on inner-German issues and on relations with Moscow. So did his successor, Willy Brandt. But both remained as fully engaged in Western Europe as possible, and repeatedly made clear that the Federal Republic's *Ostpolitik* did not conflict with its Western links. Helmut Schmidt returned to greater concentration on the West, especially on relations with France. He saw in the Community and Western Europe an essential counterweight to both the United States and the Soviet Union.

Helmut Kohl has continued Schmidt's concentration on West European matters, especially because the EC has become ever more central to German interests and its laws and regulations have increasingly shaped German policy. He has on several occasions made special efforts to advance European structures to new levels of cooperation, especially concentrating on the drive to create an EC Single Market, EC-92. Kohl has also intervened on occasion to avoid potential conflicts between Germany's EC interests and its ties with America, although he hesitated about trying to bridge the argument over agricultural trade that broke out at the end of 1990. After German unification, he has widened the EC toward the East.

This has become increasingly important. If West Europeans were suspicious of Germany after World War II, many East Europeans remain even more so. They want German investments and German technology, but they are acutely sensitive about any German presence and even more about any suggestion of possible German domination. A European framework can help make the German presence palatable in Eastern Europe, just as German money and talent can make the European presence effective.

The Federal Republic has consistently pressed for closer integration of the Community. German public opinion has favored it as well. West German respondents, offered a choice in a 1987 survey between "European federation" or mere "intensification" of EC relations, chose "federation" by a two-to-one margin. Neither the French nor the Italian public favored federation by such a large margin, and the British public had a larger vote for "intensification."[1] The Federal Republic was among the five EC members that decided in the Schengen accords of June 1990 to permit the totally free movement of persons across their borders by 1992 as a step toward the elimination of all frontier controls by 1993. This step was controversial then because of the large numbers of migrants and refugees coming into Western Europe from east and south.[2] It has become even more controversial as refugee numbers grew during 1990 and gave every sign of continuing throughout the remainder of the decade. The German Federal Prosecutor's office warned that open borders throughout the Community could present real problems to law enforcement and migrant control,[3] but the German government nonetheless proceeded in conjunction with the other European states.

The Federal Republic has also been among the strongest European advocates for free trade. West German officials and political leaders have said that American fears about "Fortress Europe" were misplaced. Whereas some EC states—especially France and Italy—have long suggested (and separately imposed) limits on Japanese car imports, Germany joined them only reluctantly in 1991. It has imposed fewer restrictions on trade than most EC states.

West Germany, and especially West German industry, carved out an important niche for its exports within the Community. In the process, it made the Community an essential market for German goods and a important contributor to German prosperity. As one third of West German GNP went for export before unity, and one half of all exports went to countries of the Community, one can conclude that at least one of every six West German jobs was directly linked to the Community as a market. Many other jobs depend on imports from Community states or on the general prosperity that the Community has brought to its members.

This German role in the Community was reflected in West German trade statistics. Not only was 53 per cent of West German trade with other countries of the Community, but many West German industries relied on the Community for a major share of their total market—whether domestic and international. The following is the share of West German *production*—not only exports—that went to other EC countries.[4]

Category	EC Share of Production
Office Equipment	48 per cent
Chemical Goods:	24 "
Machinery:	24 "
Motor Vehicles:	23 "
Precision Machinery; Optics:	18 "
Electronics:	17 "
Textiles:	16 "
Iron and Steel:	14 "

The Community helped raise West German efficiency for the global market as a whole. A study of selected West German industrial production statistics showed that the development of common markets in Europe had important effects on the productivity and performance of German industry because of economies of scale and because of the competitive environment. Members of the Community also engaged increasingly in component trade or intra-industrial trade.[5] Jean Monnet had wanted the economies within the Community to become so scrambled that they could no longer be unscrambled, and that wish appears to have been amply fulfilled.

But if West European trade was vital for West Germany and remains vital for united Germany, West Germany was equally vital for the EC. It would be as difficult to establish any kind of successful European common market without Germany as without France. Even before German unification, there were more persons living in Germany—62 million—than in any other state in the EC. With unification, the figure came close to 80 million. West Germany alone already had the largest share of Community GNP, over 25 per cent. It had the largest amount of private consumption, over 1.2 trillion DM, in 1988, and the largest investment in other EC states, DM 56.7 billion.[6] West Germany regularly paid over 25 per cent of the EC budget, and united Germany will in due course pay more.

The Federal Republic was often termed the Community's "Paymaster," with its net contribution to the EC budget being over 4 billion Ecu in 1988.[7] Its share of EC imports was higher than any other EC member's. Each of those proportions can be expected to rise by the time the former GDR economy is fully integrated into the Community.

Even before German unity, five of the ten most competitive industrial/economic concentrations in the EC area were in West Germany (including West Berlin), and another four West German up-and-coming economic areas were expected to be among the most competitive in the future.[8] With East Germany added, German industrial areas could be expected to be even more important. The Community without German participation would represent a much less powerful force in global trade.

German unity will make Germany's role in the Community more important but also more difficult to handle. West Germany was at first called a *Musterknabe*—a model student—on European affairs, always careful to promote European interests without appearing to advance its own. Later, even after West Germany had gained stature and respect, German officials were usually more circumspect than others in espousing their national interests, at least in public. They much preferred to support positions advanced by other states (especially France) than to appear to be pushing an independent agenda. Germany's very size and power within Western Europe—as well as its history—imposed the obligation to act with restraint and modesty in the affairs of the Community. With unity, that obligation has become all the more important, and German capacity to act with understanding and tact will be consistently tested.

Although Germany needs the Community, it needs it less than many other members in pure economic terms. EC statistics showed that the EC share of imports and exports for the Federal Republic, while large, lagged behind most other EC states in 1987 (listed in descending order of export share):[9]

Share of EC in 1987 National Imports and Exports

State	Exports	Imports
Belgium/Luxembourg	72.3%	74.3%
Ireland	71.2%	73.5%
France	65.6%	60.4%
Portugal	63.4%	70.9%
Netherlands	61.5%	75.4%
Greece	60.9%	66.8%
Italy	56.5%	56.0%
Spain	54.9%	59.0%
West Germany	54.6%	52.7%
Denmark	53.5%	48.5%
Great Britain	51.2%	49.2%
EC Average	58.8%	58.7%

Of all Community members, including the most recent, only Denmark and Great Britain had a lower proportion of their imports and exports within the Community. Ironically, German unification will make the united Germany a more important player within the Community but may well reduce the proportion of its trade that is conducted within the Community. Germany may be more vital to the Community but—at least in some ways—the Community may be less vital to Germany.

Because of the close relationship between the German economy and that of the other Community countries, different ministries in Bonn could have different and even conflicting interests and policies toward items on the European agenda. Many ministries have their own direct links to the EC bureaucracy in Brussels, and German policy has from time to time spoken with several voices at different levels until the problems were brought to the attention of senior officials in Bonn and priorities were established. By the same token, West German ministries did not hesitate to use elements within the EC bureaucracy and even within other national bureaucracies to advance their own interests.[10]

It has been left to the two ministries with broad economic interests, the Ministry of Economics and the Ministry of Finance, as well as to the Foreign Office, to try to keep these separate issues in perspective and especially to prevent other ministries or the EC bureaucracy from imposing even more sector protection, regulation, or subsidies than already exist. The addition of East Germany, with its considerable agricultural interests and its generally inefficient production sector, could tip the balance toward higher protection within the EC, even if only on a "temporary" basis.

Management of the EC's Common Agricultural Policy (CAP) has illustrated some of the conflicts in intra-German interests. That system, by its virtually open-ended commitment to subsidize both production and exports, has become ever more expensive and now consumes more than half of the EC budget as well as tens of billions of dollars of national subsidies. The West German Agriculture Ministry has tried to use the EC mechanism to drive support prices higher and to keep out foreign farm products even more effectively. West Germany, in fact, had the highest average support price levels of any EC country as of the end of 1987.[11] The Finance Ministry, on the other hand, has wanted to reduce the CAP because of the burden it imposed on the EC budget and on the German contribution—burdens that became so onerous and controversial that the Community was forced to change the system that was being financed primarily by German taxpayers without, however, truly liberalizing agricultural trade.

The burden of EC agricultural policies on German and other Community consumers and taxpayers remains one of the most contentious issues with respect to the Community. Comparative figures show that agricultural subsidies in the United States represent 28 per cent of U.S. agricultural costs, with taxpayers covering 21 per cent (through government programs) and consumers 7 per cent (through higher prices); in the EC, subsidies represent 40 per cent of agricultural costs with 15 per cent being financed by the taxpayers and 25 per cent by consumers; in Japan, the corresponding figures are 69 per cent, with 17 per cent being financed by taxpayers and 52 per cent by consumers.[12]

Another problem area for the Community has been environmental policy, but in this area there was less disagreement within the West German government and more with other EC members. German industry, like industry everywhere, feared the costs that environmental controls would impose. But it could agree to European environmental regulation because it would prevent other Community industries from gaining a competitive advantage over German industries and because it became increasingly clear that pollution did not respect political boundaries. It remains a likely area for future conflict within the EC and for suspicion by environmentalists as well (see below).[13]

THE EUROPEAN INTERNAL MARKET, EC-92

As the West European economies have become more integrated, the remaining barriers to free trade became increasingly anachronistic. Although tariffs have been gradually reduced or eliminated, a number of other obstacles continued to exist, including technical regulations, limitations on services, the administrative burden of customs procedures, and bidding restrictions for government contracts. An EC Commission study estimated that eliminating these restrictions by establishing a truly competitive and integrated internal market would increase efficiencies and cut costs by at least 2.5 per cent, and perhaps by as much as 6.5 per cent, of the Community Gross Domestic Product.[14] The EC Commission argued that a truly integrated internal market would put downward pressure on costs and prices and create the potential for greater non-inflationary growth.[15]

To implement the changes necessary for a truly integrated internal market, the European Commission in 1985 submitted a White Paper to the European Council in which it listed a series of 225 steps that would need to be implemented. It also proposed a schedule under which those steps should be completed so that the internal market could be achieved by the end of 1992.[16]

The EC Council accepted these proposals, with West Germany strongly supporting the concept. West Germany was able to advance the process significantly during its presidency in the first half of 1988.[17]

There are many reasons to doubt that the Community will have become a fully integrated market by the end of 1992. A number of highly sensitive questions have not been solved as of this writing and may well not be solvable by the announced deadline. It has proven impossible so far to reach agreement on a common European tax system, especially one that combines the North European tradition of direct taxes with the different (and allegedly essential) system of indirect taxes that prevails in Southern Europe. There were indications in 1991 that the EC might give up the effort and instead try to equalize the tax burden in other ways.[18] The Community has also found national financial systems virtually impossible to coordinate, and it has had difficulty arriving at a common European corporate statute (in part because of German *Mitbestimmung*). Totally free movement of people may also prove illusory, especially because the removal of border posts would make it theoretically possible for any East European or North African to reach any state of the Community once he or she has crossed any Community border.

Even where there has seemed to be progress in Brussels, there have been problems elsewhere. In many instances, common regulations agreed upon in Brussels have not been translated into matching domestic laws and regulations, leaving one set of rules at the Community level and a contradictory set at the national level. The German Sachverständigenrat complained in 1990 that in a number of instances the same states that were arguing for a free internal market by 1992 were imposing domestic regulations that would negate the effects of the internal market.[19] It warned that the internal market would not be in place for quite some time after 1992, and that it might prove much less unified than now expected. The Presse- und Informationsamt der Bundesregierung in March 1991 released an estimate which warned that a lot of work remained to be done, that some states (like Italy and Greece) were proceeding very slowly, and that it would probably be necessary to have transition regimes in a number of areas.[20]

Not all Germans welcome the coming of the Single Market. Many fear that the guidelines for a common internal market will give so much power to the bureaucrats within the EC Commission that economic initiatives within the member states will be stifled. Many German businessmen dread the prospect of even more Brussels offices enforcing even more EC regulations. Some German states and communities have become disturbed by prospects that the Community will have such immense powers over economic life that the German federal system itself can be placed in jeopardy because the Community bureaucracy may have authority in areas that in Germany would normally be left to a *Land*. They fear that by the mid-1990s neither Germany as a whole nor its separate states will be in a position to exercise any control over their own economic affairs.

Despite the strong and consistent West German government support for the internal European market, attitudes in German business and economic circles remain mixed, depending on the size and interests of the affected firms:[21]

- Large German firms that have counted on export markets for years are well positioned for EC-92 and favor the internal market. They have efficient production facilities in Germany with established sales and agent links throughout Europe, or they have already sought out sites in other European countries with lower production costs, like Spain or Portugal.
- Mid-sized (*Mittelstand*) firms, which cannot relocate their main production sites or develop subsidiary sites abroad, have a markedly more cautious reaction. They would have to prepare for intensified competition throughout the Community area, including in Germany itself, but they might be in a less advantageous position than today.
- Smaller firms, especially those involved in trading, handicrafts, and services, have been even more deeply concerned about the competition that might come from other European countries with lower costs. In certain areas that rely on manual labor, no efficiencies can compensate for the disadvantage of having to pay higher wages.
- Firms in certain specialty areas long protected by procedural or regulatory arrangements, like finance and transportation, are afraid that standardized EC regulation and practice would undercut their privileged positions in the German market, and that other European firms, or American and Japanese companies, might be able to enter.

The West German government has sounded out German firms and institutes on a continuing basis to learn their attitudes and expectations, but it has not issued separate statements regarding the effect that an integrated European market might have on separate sectors of German industry. It reported in 1989 that only 10 per cent of German firms feared that the internal market would hurt their competitiveness, but that estimate appears optimistically low in the light of other reports.[22]

Just as firms of different sizes have reacted differently, so have firms in different industries. German producers of capital goods are the most optimistic, probably because they have already benefited substantially from the investment boom sparked by the prospects for EC-92 and because they expect to benefit further. German car manufacturers, tool-makers, chemical firms, and electronics firms regard EC-92 as an opportunity. On the other hand, German firms in telecommunications, banking, and insurance have seen the internal market largely as a threat. German transportation firms, especially truckers, have regarded EC-92 as a potential disaster, with cheaper foreign transportation firms being able to compete for German traffic even on German roads.[23]

Recognizing these potential difficulties and traditional German caution, the DIHT and the chambers of commerce have conducted extensive briefings, seminars, and conferences to alert German firms to the possibilities and the pitfalls of the European internal market. Senior government officials have assured German business that its interests would be respected.

EC-92 has also generated pressure for less restrictive German regulations because those regulations could handicap German firms in European competition. Firms that had long welcomed the very complex German system of laws and regulations, especially in the service sector, because the system kept out foreign competitors, have begun trying to ease the regulations. Their declared objective is "an even competition of rules," under which German firms will not be disadvantaged but will be obliged to conform only to those rules and regulations that apply across all of Europe rather than to be obliged to follow the stricter German regulations as well.

German trade unions have especially feared the EC internal market. They have warned that production would move to states and areas where wages are lowest and social benefits most limited. They have consistently warned of "social dumping," the temptation for manufacturers to look for those sites where social regulations are either the least stringent or are so negligently enforced that they can be substantially ignored. Despite the existence of strict EC standards governing worker rights and privileges, German trade unions fear that standards might not be uniformly applied. Germany, by applying the rules correctly, would maintain good working conditions. Other countries, by applying them less strictly, would attract investment and jobs.

German environmentalists also fear the worst. They fear that German manufacturers might shade their environmental commitment in order to keep their costs as low as possible against competitors who face fewer environmental problems in less thickly settled countries. They have also expressed concern that manufacturers will be tempted to locate production facilities abroad where environmental standards might be less rigorously enforced or where less severe population and land-usage pressures might make pollution less onerous. Given the burdensome costs of overcoming the lingering pollution problems of East Germany, many German environmentalists fear a period in which environmental standards will be more neglected than in the 1980s.[24]

THE *STANDORT* "QUESTION" AND EC-92

The prospect for further EC integration has given special urgency to the long-standing German concern about whether West Germany was an efficient and a competitive place to produce and a good place to invest (Chapters 5 and 8). Many industrial analysts expect the Single Market to unleash an investment boom in Europe, and the Germans do not want the boom to bypass Germany.

The EC-92 discussion raised the German buzz-words *Standort Bundesrepublik* and now *Standort Deutschland* to new levels of discussion and preoccupation.[25] The discussion for Europe revolved about all the familiar worries that have consistently beset German government, industry, labor, and agriculture: whether the many benefits and the many advantages that Germans had won for themselves by their efficiency and hard work would now be nullified by the readiness of other Europeans to accept a lower standard of living—and to work harder—than the Germans.

German investment in other European countries, which had been perceived as a relatively benign phenomenon because it helped finance the high German trade and current account surplus, began to be perceived as a threat to German workers and to German industrial modernization. As some U.S. states had drawn industry and jobs from others by creating a more attractive environment, now some EC states might draw investment from Germany.

The Germans have begun to perceive the competition for non-European investment as one of the principal forms of intra-Community competition. German economists have frequently stressed the familiar advantages of the well-trained German labor force and of the efficiency of German production methods, but the continuing evidence that productive investment was bypassing West Germany has left many Germans concerned. Many feared that West German and other investors would look particularly for EC states that were not in the European Exchange Rate Mechanism, to escape from the rising D-Mark and to keep their prices more competitive.

As the debate intensified even before unification, many commentators almost seemed to forget that West Germany had, in fact, been rather strong in European competition. Instead, they dwelled on the problems Germany would now face. A number of studies sounded the familiar alarms,[26] but others were more optimistic.[27] The German Ministry of Economics argued that even the high German labor costs actually represented a smaller portion of German production costs than the supposedly lower labor costs found in many other European countries.[28]

The BDI and the DIHT proposed a number of steps to improve the competitive position of German companies in the European Community. These included three particular steps to be taken in Germany, (1) lower tax rates, (2) a reduction in supplementary labor costs, and (3) greater flexibility in the application of regulations governing working hours.[29]

Germany's potential as a financial and investment center for the Community also drew a great deal of attention. Even though Berlin might be expected again to become an East-West financial center, many Germans believed that Frankfurt should serve as a commercial and financial center for the Western states of Europe and that it would be more acceptable than Berlin or another political capital as a site for the Bundesbank.

The Bundesbank and German officials indicated that they would make every effort to improve Germany's and Frankfurt's attractiveness as a financial center.[30] But they warned that they would not take steps that could jeopardize financial stability for the sake of competitiveness by loosening German regulations excessively. The German Institut für Kapitalmarktforschung expressed far more concern about Frankfurt's place as a future European financial center than the Bundesbank.[31] It warned that a more financially integrated Europe would tend toward a single financial capital and that London and Paris were not only better placed than Frankfurt but were also making much greater efforts to emerge as dominant financial centers. However, when Frankfurt tried to expand its own role in German capital markets it was sharply denounced by other German regional exchanges.

As 1990 and 1991 advanced, the European *Standort* debate shifted as the general *Standort* debate had shifted. Even if German and European unification did not materially lower an entrepreneur's cost of production in Germany, it did something more fundamental. It brought Germany back from the border of Western Europe to the center of a wider united Europe. It reconstituted a concept and a term, Central Europe, that had been forgotten in the international and especially the EC vocabulary. From the edge of one world Germany was moving to the center of a larger one. And a location on German soil at the core of Europe could have real advantages within the EC and elsewhere as well.

AN OPEN OR A CLOSED EUROPEAN COMMUNITY?

The greatest danger that many Germans perceive in EC-92, however, is the risk that the Community will become so internally focused that it will become too protectionist toward the outside world. The board of advisors to the West German Ministry of Economics warned in 1990 that such thinking, if not promptly countered, could jeopardize the Community's prosperity. The BDI and the DIHT have expressed similar concerns, warning that—despite the threats to some German firms from within the Community—the protectionist risk of the internal market had to be fought at every level to avoid driving Germany ever more into a limited European mold.[32] German industry, and especially the BDI, has consistently pointed out that Germany stood to lose far more than any other EC member if the global trading system collapsed due to the protectionist leanings within the Community.

This question came to a head at the end of 1990, as the European Community's long-standing dispute with the United States and with the Cairns Group of states about agricultural trade erupted, bringing about a potential collapse of the Uruguay Round of negotiations within the GATT. Although only a relatively minor portion of German GNP is agricultural, and much of that is produced by part-time farmers, Chancellor Kohl decided to support the EC agricultural policy, and especially to support France. He declined American proposals for major changes in EC agricultural policy. His decision provoked a storm of protest in Washington and many expressions of concern in Germany itself.

The BDI and other business groups again protested that the German government and the EC were risking world trade for the benefit of a small group of producers and for a system that annually cost the EC over $35 billion to finance and that the EC could no longer afford or justify. Ludolf von Wartenberg argued that the German government was not only forgetting the fact that the overwhelming majority of Germany's producers had an interest in an open global system, but it was also forgetting that the money that supported the agricultural subsidies was produced by the very industries that needed foreign trade.[33]

Kohl and other EC leaders tried to find ways out of the impasse, as did the U.S. government and other international trading states. Kohl kept assuring U.S. President Bush that he would not let the GATT talks collapse over agriculture. One reason for German concern was the growing conviction that the CAP would have to be revised dramatically not for the sake of the international trading system but because it had become prohibitively expensive as well as counterproductive; it was not solving Europe's agricultural problems but was making them increasingly unsolvable and adding billions of D-Marks to the German budget at a time when Germany could ill afford them. Proposals to change the CAP surfaced again, perhaps with better prospects than in the past. Although the Uruguay Round had been scheduled to end before the beginning of 1991, there were ample precedents for delays in trade and tariff negotiations. The Tokyo Round, when it had finally ended in 1979, had lasted about two years longer than originally scheduled. But the EC delegations for the GATT talks had consistently shown themselves to have inflexible instructions.

Kohl in late 1991 changed the German position and Bonn began urging greater EC flexibility on agricultural trade issues. This offered some hope that the Uruguay Round could be saved, but it was not yet certain whether the Germans were prepared to exert enough pressure to overcome the opposition. Although all sides expressed good will, it was clear that the forces of protectionism had grown more powerful everywhere and that the protectionist states of the EC were combining with the EC bureaucracy to set policy.

There was growing talk of three regional trade areas, the European Community, the Americas, and Asia, and perhaps of some collaboration between two of them against the third. There was also a growing inclination toward what was termed "managed trade," in which trade between states or groups of states would be subject to product or sector agreements—usually based on negotiated quotas. Some Europeans privately saw a chance to resurrect a pan-European market reaching from the Atlantic deep into Russia, and they saw this as the foundation for a new EC that could become the world's largest market and trading bloc.

These leanings toward trade regionalization and management in 1990 and 1991 weakened the commitment to the GATT system. The forces opposing free trade had strengthened, especially in Europe and the United States, and they reinforced each other. If the delays were too long, and the negotiations too cumbersome, separate solutions would become very attractive. Even if the Uruguay Round was concluded, it might prove to be the last of the great trade negotiating rounds.

Managed trade can represent a greater hazard to German exports than to those of other European states. For any such arrangement negotiated by the EC would establish quotas for each side, and Germany would almost certainly not obtain as large a share of any European quota as that which German exporters could obtain through their own competitive abilities. Moreover, no managed trade system would tolerate the kind of persistent surplus that West Germany had routinely achieved and that had become necessary to the functioning of the German economy, unless Germany was prepared to commit itself to make significant foreign investments to compensate for its trade surplus.

Whatever it may decide on this issue, however, the German government has continued to insist strongly that it will fulfill its commitment to complete European integration and toward the Single Market. Political considerations, especially Germany's relations with France, have an important influence on the policy. But if the policy becomes merely a step toward the creation of trading blocs, German interests will not be served.

JAPAN IN PORTAS

Germany cannot, however, take the European Community or even Europe as a whole for granted as a market while it turns its attention to German integration and to the East. The Community represents one of the largest and most prosperous markets in the world, and the prospects for the Single Market only enhance its attraction.

The main threat that many Germans and other Europeans fear comes from Japan. It represents the third element of the Japanese challenge to Germany and Europe, the first being Japanese technological superiority (Chapter 5) and the second being Japan's global operations (Chapter 8). During the 1970s and 1980s, when Japan was concentrating on the American market, it paid scant attention to Europe. Nonetheless, even then Germany had a trade deficit with Japan. But after 1989, as the United States sank into recession, Japan began concentrating more of its sales in Europe and especially in Germany.

Japan is increasing its efforts within the EC in two ways. First, by direct sales from Japan. Second, by investments in production facilities in Europe. Combinations of these threats are also appearing. The German government and German industrialists have increasingly been disturbed by what they see as Japanese targeting of European Community markets and about the effectiveness of Japanese competition in more and more important markets.[34] They have also watched in alarm as the Japanese trade and current accounts surplus with Europe ballooned in 1991.

With respect to investment, Japan increased its European productive operations as the EC Single Market approached. Japan began investing heavily in Western Europe as well as selling there. The decision of three Japanese automobile manufacturers to invest in production facilities in Great Britain drew a great deal of attention in Germany. Japanese cars have gained 15 per cent of the German car market, not as much as in some EFTA states or some smaller EC states, but far more than in Italy and France where Japanese market access has been limited.[35]

Given Germany's persistent difficulties in producing computers, the Germans also reacted with some alarm to the decision by the Fujitsu computer company to purchase a British firm in order to enter Europe. These steps could lead to serious competition for German firms. But they also provide competition for Germany as an investment site. German manufacturing and high technology jobs can decline significantly if *Spitzentechnologie* investment in the Community market goes to Britain or Spain, not to Germany, or if the main objective of foreign investment is to sell in Germany but not to produce there.

Germany is sensitive to Japanese competition. Japanese firms have long since captured the international market for precision optics, especially in cameras, that used to be virtually a German preserve. Now, Japan is advancing in the global market for a product long dominated by German manufacturers—that of luxury performance sedans. And Japanese computer firms are increasingly penetrating the European market.

Given the importance that Germans attach to machine tools, the single most important element of the German production mystique, they are also deeply concerned about the growing Japanese challenge in that area. Japanese production of machine tools rose from 6 to 19 per cent of world production from 1970 to 1988 while West German production fell from 24 to 20.5 per cent.[36] Japanese firms are better equipped to penetrate distant markets on a long-term basis, having greater financial resources than the German *Mittelstand* firms.[37]

More seriously, Japan has begun making inroads into the EC machine tool market itself, with Japan's share of that market rising from 2 per cent in 1960 to 10.5 per cent in 1980 and 18.7 per cent in 1989.[38] Most of the Japanese increase came at the expense of the United States, mainly because Japanese production of larger machine tools competes directly with American production. By accident or by design, Japan has not so far competed directly with German production, which is concentrated in smaller machine tools and in certain specialized markets. Nonetheless, the German share of the European machine tool market also declined slightly from 22.1 per cent to 20.5 per cent, and those sales were obviously lost to Japanese competition.

During German unification, machine tool production in the Western states of Germany will need to concentrate on markets in Eastern Germany and Eastern Europe. Japan will be in a position to penetrate even more German markets in the EC, markets that have in recent years bought three quarters of Germany's exported machine tools.

As Japanese investment and sales in the Community grew, one EC reaction was to negotiate an arrangement under which Japan would agree to limit the sales of its cars in Europe until 1999. But the limits it would impose applied more clearly to cars made in Japan than to Japanese cars made in Europe. Moreover, because the limitations were numerical, the Japanese automobile makers could undercut them by selling more expensive cars in Europe. The Europeans may have been less concerned about the details of the accord than about the often enunciated principle that they would not permit Japan to do to Europe what it had done to the United States. There were questions about whether such arrangements would be compatible with GATT or even with EC-92, but at least the French and the Italians were prepared to do what was necessary to keep out a wave of Japanese cars. From the German standpoint, however, the arrangement was far from ideal, for any agreement that would force the Japanese more into the high end of the car market would attack German sales more than others.[39]

The German government and German industry are also trying another tack, attempting to expand their sales in Asia in order to compete directly with the Japanese closer to Japan's home. Although Germany played only a small role in the industrialization of East Asia during the 1970s and 1980s,[40] German bankers and businessmen have increasingly been traveling to Asia to look into investments, joint ventures, or export possibilities. They made a strong effort during February and March 1991 at the "Technogerma" exposition in Seoul. This exposition represented one of the most important trade efforts that West Germany had ever held abroad. It was opened by President Richard von Weizsäcker and visited by a number of senior German industrialists and officials, who all made clear that they were not only interested in selling German products in Asia but in opening various cooperative ventures.

German companies, with government support, have also been attempting to enter the Japanese and Asian aerospace market, trying to sell the Airbus as well as smaller aircraft and helicopters.[41] Germany has begun to recognize that it could not count on keeping even with Japan if it permitted Japan to enter Europe and did not compete with Japan in Asian markets.

West Germany was always one of the principal proponents of an open European Community door to the outside world, even when some other states such as France and Italy were more disposed to seek protectionist solutions. And Germany remains the country that has the most to lose if the Community decides to establish itself as a closed trading bloc. The dilemma for united Germany, however, may be that it may need protection as much as France and Italy do while it is occupied with merging Eastern Germany. All this has contributed to Germany's hesitation about the Uruguay Round and about the direction of the global trading system.

THE GERMAN FUTURE IN A UNITED EUROPE

Germany must think not only about defending its market in the European Community. It must also reflect, and is clearly already reflecting, about whether it might have an even more important mission as a united state in a united Europe. This would imply not only the development of a more integrated European Community, but also closer ties between the EC, the European Free Trade Association (EFTA), the Central and East European members of the former CMEA, and even the new states breaking out of the Soviet Union as well as whatever might succeed the Soviet Union. That would open ties in all directions, and especially toward the East. The latter were long a German vocation, and could become that again. Former German Economics Minister Helmut Haussmann had once foreseen the prospect for an all-European market of 500 million, but adding the Baltics, Russia, and beyond, would bring in many more.[42]

Pan-European economic integration was long considered a futile prospect, and even a dream, because of Europe's division between East and West. Therefore, the EC stressed internal integration and cooperation with other West European states, especially with the EFTA members. Negotiations between the EC and the EFTA, intended to lead toward a "European Economic Space," had made sufficient progress by 1991 to warrant some expectation that an agreement could be reached during the early 1990s on a "space" that would not be as closely coordinated as the EC but in which there could be substantial cooperation, harmonization of laws and regulations, and considerable mutual trade. In conjunction with those talks, the EC would have preferred not to have EFTA members apply for EC membership, and it also made clear that it would not consider any membership applications from any EFTA states until the mid-1990s when the Single Market process would be well under way.[43] But some EFTA states are advancing their applications, and East European states ares showing an interest as well.

More intriguing, and potentially more important, might be an all-European economic area that would stretch literally from the Atlantic to the Urals or beyond. This idea, which has tempted many Germans since unification, has come up against the harsh reality that the gap between Eastern and Western Europe, in social and economic terms, was as great before the collapse of the Wall as it had been since the fall of Rome.

Despite this East-West disparity, many Germans hope that the EC, or at least a European economic zone, could be extended further eastward during the middle or latter 1990s. But more open trade with the East European states would also compel the Community to review its own structural policies. The products that the East Europeans can sell are mainly in two sectors, agriculture and basic industry. Both those sectors are already heavily subsidized in many Community states which are very reluctant to open their markets to Eastern European products. Other connections also raise problems. If Germany and the other highly developed states of Western Europe do decide to buy food, raw materials, and basic industrial goods from Eastern Europe, they would have to block similar imports not only from the United States and the Cairns Group but also from the southern states of the EC, from the Mediterranean, and from some of the former European colonies that still have privileged arrangements with the EC. They would also have to stop subsidizing their own producers.

There is, therefore, a basic choice to be made between a more widespread and a more integrated European Community. To date, EC members have preferred the more integrated EC because it seemed the only option and had a number of attractions as well. In the spring and summer of 1991, other opportunities opened, opportunities that were particularly attractive to Germany. German officials were saying privately that they hoped integration could be delayed or at least slowed until the Community could be widened.

In these discussions, as at the beginning of the EC, political considerations become important and perhaps dominant. So do broader questions as to whether the Community will be open or closed to non-member states, and whether it will be increasingly statist or not. The unification of Germany, the opening of Europe, and the structural problems of the EC all combine to raise major questions about the future of the EC.

These issues must be central to any German economic policy. Decisions cannot be postponed too long because the development of the Single Market and the constant furthering of EC laws and regulations will mean that by the middle of the 1990s many German economic decisions will be made in Brussels, not in Bonn, Frankfurt, or Berlin. A united Germany has to decide what kind of Europe it wants, and also how it wants that Europe to fit into the world. Some of those decisions may require a dramatic revision of EC attitudes. Germany has not so far shown that it is ready to lead that kind of revision, but German leadership would be essential for the success of any such process. The Germans thus have to voice their preferences.

The decisions are linked. With the EC representing the largest market in the world, the shape of Europe can decide the shape of global trade. A closed Europe means a closed world. An open Europe makes an open world possible, even if it does not guarantee it. A European decision for regional or managed trade will almost certainly mean a global structure of regional blocs and managed trade, especially if EC-92 is completed as now planned.

An opening of the EC to a pan-European system could generate major readjustments in all EC economies but could also open Europe as a whole to global trade.

The German decisions became more complicated in early 1991 when a new French Prime Minister, Edith Cresson, advocated an EC-wide industrial policy and denounced Japanese commercial practices as predatory while also insisting that there could be no concessions on agricultural trade. At the same time, France registered objections to private agreements between German and U.S. computer companies, as if all such matters had to kept within Europe.[44] France also expressed reservations about German wishes for a "more democratic content" in EC decisions through greater authority for the European Parliament.

Western Europe can offer Germany immense opportunities, but it can also deny them. Germany can be the major force in the European Community and on the European continent toward a more open EC in a more open world. But if Germany is obliged by other EC members or by the Community's regulatory structure and bureaucracy to agree to increasingly restrictive trading rules and to reduce its own global role or its opportunities to the East, German interests may not be served.

With Germany's powerful voice in the EC, Germany is in a position to influence and perhaps to determine EC decisions. As of late 1991, however, its preferences had not yet carried the day.

NOTES TO CHAPTER NINE

1. *The Federal Republic of Germany and the European Community: The Presidency and Beyond* (Bonn: Europa Union Verlag, 1987), p. 73.
2. The others are France and the Benelux states.
3. *Handelsblatt*, May 29, 1990.
4. Thiel, *Die Europäische Gemeinschaft*, fourth edition (Munich: Bayerische Landeszentrale für Politische Bildungsarbeit, 1989), p. 75.
5. Jürgen Müller, "Competitive Performance and Trade within the EEC: Generalizations from Several Case Studies with Specific Reference to the West German Economy," *Zeitschrift für die gesamte Staatswissenschaft*, September 1981, pp. 638-663.
6. Thiel, *loc. cit.*, pp. 67, 72.
7. *The Economist*, July 26, 1990, p. 40. An Ecu equals about 2 D-Marks.
8. Chang Woom Nam, Hans Russ, and Jochen Reuter, "The Competitiveness of EC Regions in the Nineties," P. Kremmel, ed., *The Single European*

Market in the Nineties, Ifo Studien zur Europäischen Wirtschaft, # 4 (Munich: Ifo Institut, 1990), p. 170.

9. Otto Mayer, Hans-Eckart Scharren, Hans-Jürgen Schmal, *Der Europäische Binnenmarkt* (Hamburg: HWWA Weltarchiv, 1989), p. 19.
10. A thorough discussion of the West German internal mechanics on EC affairs is presented in Simon Bulmer and William Paterson, *The Federal Republic of Germany and the European Community* (London: Allen & Unwin, 1987), pp. 25-107.
11. Commission of the European Communities, *European Economy: The Economics of 1992* (Brussels: European Commission, 1988), p. 79.
12. Thiel, *loc. cit.*, p. 84.
13. Bulmer and Paterson, *op. cit..*, pp. 244-246.
14. Commission of the European Communities, *loc. cit.*, pp. 17-19.
15. *Ibid.*
16. Commission of the European Communities, *Completing the Internal Market* (Brussels: European Commission, June 1985).
17. Hans-Dietrich Genscher, "Report on the German Presidency of the European Community," German Information Center, *Statements and Speeches*, June 17, 1988.
18. *Financial Times*, February 4, 1991.
19. Sachverständigenrat, *1990/1991 Report*, pp. 217-219.
20. FRG, *Aktuelle Beiträge*, No. 9, 1991, March 4, 1991.
21. Werner Weidenfeld, Forschungsgruppe Europa, Binnenmarkt '92: Perspektiven aus deutscher Sicht (Gütersloh: Verlag Bertelsmann Stiftung, 1989), pp. 94-95, 207-212.
22. "Bericht über den Einfluss der Vollendung des EG-Binnenmarktes auf die Branchen und Regionen in der Bundesrepublik Deutschland," FRG. *Aktuelle Beiträge*, January 25, 1989, p. 5.
23. Weidenfeld, *op. cit.*, pp. 207-208; Deutscher Industrie- und Handelstag, *Competitiveness and adaptation Strategies of German Companies in the Single European Market: Results of a Corporate Survey* (Bonn: DIHT, 1989), pp. 1-7; also published in FRG, *Aktuelle Beiträge*, No. 11/1989, January 25, 1989.
24. Weidenfeld, *op. cit.*, pp. 211-212.
25. An extensive discussion of this general problem is in Martin Bangemann, ed., *Produktions-standort Bundesrepublik Deutschland auf dem Prüfstand* (Herford: Busse-Seewald, 1988) and in other sources cited for the discussion of this topic in Chapter 5.
26. Hainz Dürr, "Der Produktionsstandort Bundesrepublik Deutschland aus der Sicht des Unternehmers," Bangemann, ed., *loc. cit.*, p. 68; Jörgen Hinze, "Voraussichtliche Auswirkungen des EG-Binnenmarktes für den Standort Bundesrepublik," HWWA study, pp. 57-76.
27. *The Economist*, June 23, 1990, p. 62.
28. *Wirtschaftswoche*, June 10, 1989, p. 29.

29. "Bericht über den Einfluss der Vollendung des EG-Binnenmarktes auf die Branchen und Regionen in der Bundesrepublik Deutschland, FRG, *Aktuelle Beiträge*, January 25, 1989, p. 6.

30. Johannes Wilhelm Gaddum, "Stärkung des Finanzplatzes Bundesrepublik im EG-Binnenmarkt," *Auszüge*, March 26, 1990; Karl Thomas, "Der Finanzplatz Frankfurt," *Auszüge*, February 19, 1990, pp. 3-4.

31. Institut für Kapitalmarktforschung, "Verliert der Finanzplatz Frankfurt den Wettlauf?" *Auszüge*, August 29, 1989, pp. 2-4.

32. Economics Ministry Board of Academic Advisors, *Challenges Facing the External Economic Policy of the European Community* (Bonn: Ministry of Economics, 1990).

33. Ludolf von Wartenberg, "Das vereinte Deutschland im internationalen Wettbewerb," speech made in Bonn, May 14, 1991, p. 23.

34. *Financial Times*, March 2, 1991.

35. *Frankfurter Allgemeine Zeitung*, April 26, 1991.

36. *Ibid.*, p. 2.

37. For a review of global machine tool production, with some insights on the potential Japanese threat to German exports, see "Maschinenbau - Nutzniesser des Investitionsbooms," *Deutsche Bank Bulletin*, December 1990, pp. 1-8.

38. *Ibid.* The 1989 figure is preliminary.

39. *Financial Times*, October 15, 1990; *Business Week*, May 13, 1991, pp. 57-58.

40. Thomas G. Parry, "The Role of Foreign Capital in the West Asian Industrialization, Growth and Development," Helen Hughes, ed., *Achieving Industrialization in East Asia* (Cambridge: Cambridge University Press, 1988), pp. 95-128.

41. *Handelsblatt*, February 6, 1991; *Süddeutsche Zeitung*, February 18 and 27, March 4 and 9, 1991.

42. *Süddeutsche Zeitung*, February 5, 1990.

43. This discussion of all-European economic cooperation is based largely on the following papers published during 1990 in Ebenhausen, Germany, under the auspices of the Stiftung Wissenschaft und Politik: Elke Thiel, *Wirtschafts- und Währungsintegration in der Europäischen Gemeinschaft und die Ordnung des Europäischen Wirtschaftsraumes;* Jürgen Nötzold, *Die Europäische Gemeinschaft, Ostmitteleuropa und die Sowjetunion;* _____, *Die Stellung Osteuropas im Europäischen Wirtschaftsraum;* Nötzold and Reinhardt Rummel, *Auf dem Wege zu einer Gesamteuropäischen Ordnung.*

44. *Financial Times*, May 23 and 30, 1991; *Frankfurter Allgemeine Zeitung*, July 22, 1991.

Ten

Germany and Europe: European Monetary Integration

West Germany was at the core of European monetary integration in the European Monetary System (EMS) even more than of commercial integration in the European Community. It helped to start the EMS and long provided the anchor of its principal operating element, the European Exchange Rate Mechanism (ERM). United Germany now exercises considerable, and sometimes even dominant, influence on the future evolution of European monetary affairs.

The EMS was much more difficult for Germany to propose or even to accept than the EC. Although West German business and government felt very much at home in the Common Market from the beginning, they had reasons to be much more anxious about monetary cooperation.

The two concepts are very different although they may be complementary, and they look especially different to the Germans. A common trading area within Europe helps Germany to do what it does best: to produce and to export. Although the Germans have also had to open their own borders to others, they have always been justifiably confident that they could meet such a challenge.

Money, however, is something else again, especially in Germany. West Germany's monetary policy was seen by many Germans as the guarantor of the Federal Republic's stability and prestige. Any West German political or economic debate assumed the solidity of the D-Mark as a national purpose. European monetary cooperation could only be acceptable in West Germany if it did not jeopardize either the D-Mark or the policy that had given the currency its success and had given West Germany its prosperity and domestic tranquility.

Many Germans feared that European international monetary cooperation would inevitably have a pernicious effect on Germany's own money by posing a risk to the independence of German financial and monetary policies. They believed, and not without reason, that many other states in Europe did not share Germany's belief in monetary stability as the principal objective of financial policy. They looked with particular suspicion at France and Italy.

The West German government and the Bundesbank tried, therefore, to make sure that no European monetary arrangement would interfere with Germany's freedom to choose its purposes and its policies. They consistently tried to construct arrangements that would give them a dominant influence over European policy or, if that was impossible, would enable them to pursue their traditional goals for themselves.

The West German government and the Bundesbank did not always agree about what constituted satisfactory arrangements, with the bank usually being more cautious than the government. Nonetheless, West Germany helped to establish the system and was among its main beneficiaries. Now, a united Germany must help decide how Europe should proceed toward the next phase of monetary integration.

THE BEGINNINGS OF EUROPEAN MONETARY COOPERATION

During the immediate postwar years, as indicated in Chapter 8, West German political and monetary authorities felt comfortable within the Bretton Woods fixed exchange rate system and within the dollar-based structure that then dominated the world's financial and monetary system. The D-Mark was undervalued, helping to promote Germany's exports and protecting its domestic producers, but not so undervalued that it generated inflation. The system offered a stable and relatively predictable environment, at least initially.

A number of proposals for European monetary cooperation were advanced and discussed as the European Coal and Steel Community came into being, as other plans for West European cooperation were considered, and as the Bretton Woods system began to crumble, but none came to fruition although they provided some of the intellectual foundations for later efforts.[1] It was only in March 1972, after the Smithsonian agreement, that the first arrangement for true coordination was put into place, the European narrow margins agreement which came to be known as the "snake." West Germany helped establish the system, which was a joint European float that tried to insure that European currencies would not fluctuate more against each other than against the dollar. It included the European Economic Community members as well as Great Britain and several smaller West European states. Even after the Smithsonian agreement broke down, the members of the snake continued their efforts to coordinate.

The D-Mark became the strongest currency in the snake. It remained at the top of the snake's trading range, in part because of West Germany's export surplus but especially because German domestic monetary policy inspired confidence that the D-Mark's value would be protected and might even rise against other currencies. Others soon learned that staying in the snake meant a commitment to emulate the policies of the Bundesbank or to suffer the exchange rate consequences of any divergence.

The snake could not remain intact as long as other countries were not prepared to make such a commitment. Great Britain and Italy soon withdrew their currencies, which had remained consistently at the bottom of the trading range. France withdrew in 1976. The Germans welcomed the departure of those currencies because the Bundesbank had often found it necessary to intervene in the foreign exchange markets to stabilize them. Some other European states, such as Norway and Sweden, also dropped out in 1977.[2]

By 1979, only West Germany, the Benelux states, Denmark, and Austria (indirectly) remained in the snake, which was being pejoratively termed the "worm." But the truncated snake did survive, in part because the smaller countries were prepared and to some extent obliged to follow the German lead and in part because, despite its imperfections, it offered a modicum of stability. The experience also, however, left some deep questions as to whether such states as Germany and France could coexist successfully in a monetary arrangement.

As the 1970s drew near an end, there were debates about monetary policy in almost all European countries. Whatever the imperfections of the snake, it was clear to many states that any port in a storm might be better than none. The oil shocks confronted Western states with pressures that could paradoxically be both recessionary and inflationary. Some governments, such as the American, chose to counteract the recessionary pressures. Others, such as the West German, chose to counteract the inflationary threats. The members of the snake as well as other European states increasingly found the German approach more congenial than the American.

The main debate in Germany, as in several other large European countries, was between those who came to be known as the "monetarists" and those who came to be known as the "economists."[3] The "monetarists" believed that introducing fixed exchange rates would force countries to pursue similar policies and that this would make frequent interventions less necessary and perhaps even unnecessary after some time. The "economists" argued that common economic policies had to precede fixed exchange rates because the exchange rate system would break down otherwise. They thought a common currency should cap a structure of common policy, not help to build it.

Most West German economists as well as government and Bundesbank officials belonged solidly in the "economist" camp.[4] They did not want to join in any European monetary collaboration until European states had agreed to coordinate economic policies. The experience with the snake, and the costly and frequent interventions that it had required before it finally broke down, only hardened their attitudes. Even those Germans who favored D-Mark revaluation, as Karl Schiller did, wanted it to take place on German terms.

The Bundesbank insisted that its mandate to protect the D-Mark extended to the currency's external as well as internal value. The Bundesbank's Direktorium questioned the readiness of the other major European countries to follow its policies, and it would not accept the inflationary risks of having constantly to intervene. Bank officials and private German bankers derided the *Europäische Währungsgemeinschaft* as the *Europäische Inflationsgemeinschaft*.

It was against this deeply skeptical background that Chancellor Helmut Schmidt decided to take Germany's policy on European monetary integration into his own hands after Roy Jenkins, then President of the EC Commission, in October 1977 proposed a new framework for European monetary cooperation. During the next 12 months, Schmidt and French President Valéry Giscard d'Estaing worked closely with Jenkins and with each other to devise an acceptable system. Because of the Bundesbank's and the Economics Ministry's opposition, Schmidt conducted the initial phase of the negotiations through his economic assistant, Horst Schulmann, keeping them from the Bundesbank and the bureaucracy.

Schmidt and Giscard decided to establish EMS largely because they feared that the global economic order might well collapse if nothing was done to reinforce European collaboration. They were profoundly disturbed by Washington's policies, especially by the American decision in the late 1970s to let the dollar fall. Schmidt was encouraged to find that France, which had left the snake, was now prepared to take another look at European monetary cooperation and even to recognize some merit in German policies. He hoped for what he termed a "European zone of stability" in an unstable world.

When Schmidt and Giscard presented their proposal at the European summit in Copenhagen in April 1978, they found broad support or at least interest from virtually all participants except British Prime Minister Jim Callaghan. Even Italy was prepared to rejoin a European currency system, although it wanted special arrangements to give the lira a wider band. The Europeans hoped that the EMS would succeed where the snake had failed.

The EMS also established a European currency named the Ecu. The name represented the acronym for European Currency Unit and was also, perhaps not coincidentally, the name given to French gold and silver coins in the late Middle Ages. It was designated to represent a basket of currencies from the countries of the European Monetary System, to be used initially for certain clearing and credit transactions and ultimately to become a common currency for Europe.[5] The widespread use of the Ecu as a transactions currency was expected to save $25 billion annually in exchange transaction expenses, and its advocates also expressed the hope that economic growth would be boosted by as much as 5 per cent because investors would no longer be discouraged by the risks of exchange-rate fluctuations.

When the EMS and its companion, the ERM, were formally agreed in December 1978 and established on March 25, 1979, Schmidt's role committed him to their success.[6] And this was no idle commitment, for the EMS and the ERM were to include the two major states—France and Italy—that had left the original snake and that the Bundesbank regarded as dangerously inclined toward inflation.[7] Because of the possibly temporary character of the EMS/ERM structure, it did not become part of the formal EC Treaty of Rome but was provided for in a separate agreement.

Thus the Germans engaged into Europe in an area that was of the utmost sensitivity to them. They did not do so without some reservations. But they saw no alternative to the EMS/ERM, and they hoped that they and others in it could find a safe haven in a world economic environment increasingly dominated by what they regarded as irresponsibility and even recklessness.

West Germany's decision to join was far more than a financial decision. It was most profoundly political. Even if the EMS was not formally part of the Treaty of Rome, it supplemented the European Community because it represented a step toward the creation of a more united Europe and of a much stronger Europe, a Europe that could perhaps shelter its members no matter what might happen outside. As sovereign nations, they retained their independence of action. But they had a structure that they could use to cooperate if they wished. For two pragmatists like Schmidt and Giscard, and for the highly skeptical Zentralbankrat of the Bundesbank, it represented a remarkable leap of faith as well as a token of their despair at what was happening across the Atlantic.

EMS PERFORMANCE AND THE GERMAN ROLE

The EMS and especially the ERM did succeed in making Western Europe something of a "zone of stability." After a difficult beginning, marked by frequent currency realignments during the early and middle 1980s, and even by a time of D-Mark instability because of the second oil shock and a negative German current account balance, the exchange rates of the ERM currencies have been much more stable toward each other than toward the dollar and the yen. In that sense, the ERM has constituted the joint float that some of its proponents had envisaged. The divergences between the ERM currencies declined consistently between 1979 and 1989, whereas the divergences between the ERM currencies and the dollar continued.[8]

Equally important, the ERM may well also have had the effect of reducing inflation, one of its most important objectives, and it certainly contributed to inflation's decline. Average annual inflation rates in the ERM states fell from 12 per cent to 3 per cent between 1980 and 1988.[9] The ERM achieved this essentially by imposing the discipline of the Bundesbank on the other states and central banks. This amounted to a cold shower for several ERM countries, especially at the beginning. But the Bundesbank did relax its rigorous discipline on occasion to make it easier for others to remain in the system. It permitted the growth in German money supply to exceed its targets during the mid-1980s to help ERM states.

Some major currencies, such as the franc, stabilized earlier than others, such as the lira, in part because of a more determined early French commitment to the ERM and in part because of high Italian budget deficits. Whatever the pace of adjustment, however, there were no defections as there had been during the snake. In fact, other currencies—such as the Spanish peseta—joined the ERM. The BDI proclaimed a "European Stability Zone," showing how certain European currencies had remained stable against each other even as the dollar had fluctuated widely during the early and mid-1980s, and also illustrating how the price deflators for consumer goods in ERM countries had converged during the 1980s.[10]

Greater price stability in Western Europe could not be credited exclusively to the EMS and the ERM. Inflation rates declined globally during the 1980s as a gradual process of disinflation set in after the second oil shock. But political leaders and economists could argue convincingly that the ERM had played a role in that process. They could also recognize that there were certain advantages to be gained from joining West Germany in a commitment to price and currency stability, and they could even note—perhaps with some surprise—that the Germans appeared to have gone out of their way to help others work with them to a common purpose.

The Bundesbank's evaluation of the EMS in 1989 recognized these achievements and particularly cited the ERM as an example of successful cooperation at a time of "turbulence evident in the dollar rates."[11] It asserted that the ERM had stood the test of time and that the other countries in the ERM had imported stability from the Federal Republic.

Nonetheless, the Bundesbank questioned whether the ERM should be used to keep exchange rates constant when competitive forces argued for devaluation. It complained that the Federal Republic was generating almost three quarters of its foreign exchange surplus within the EMS area although only half of its trade was with EMS countries. It warned that such surpluses pointed to competitive differences that could not and should not be offset only by capital flows, as later adjustments would be more painful. It also warned repeatedly that constant D-Mark interventions in currency markets in order to support delinquent ERM currencies could finally undermine the stability of the D-Mark itself.

Other evaluations of the ERM had a similarly positive tone but warned that the last word might not yet have been spoken. Appraisals published by the International Monetary Fund and the *Financial Times*, while observing that the ERM countries were not the only states to benefit from declining inflation and interest rates during most of the 1980s, nonetheless concluded that the improvements shown by the ERM economies, and the correlation between them, had gone beyond pure coincidence and had been more visible than in a control group.[12]

Jacques de Larosière, the governor of the Banque de France, went further in his praise for the ERM.[13] He stated that the inflation rate in non-ERM OECD states had declined less than in the ERM states, and that this convergent performance was directly attributable to increased economic policy coordination and to "the discipline of the exchange rate mechanism."

However one might choose to allot credit for the success of the EMS and of the ERM, it represented a theoretical setback for the Bundesbank even as it represented a practical triumph. For it showed that the "monetarist" school might well have been correct, and that a stable exchange rate mechanism, accompanied by a commitment to hold to the agreed rates, could compel states and their central banks to pursue congruent policies as long as they were determined to stay within a system. It suggested also that the exchange rate mechanism might act as a catalyst in facilitating policy coordination because it gave states an additional reason to coordinate and could be said to provide a reproach of sorts if they failed to coordinate.

While the "monetarists" and the "economists" might extend their debate, the ERM experience had achieved one significant and even revolutionary breakthrough. It had convincingly demonstrated the benefits of coordination, thus opening the door to further proposals for European monetary cooperation.

GERMANY IN THE ERM DURING THE 1980S

The German anchor role was central to the success of the EMS and the ERM. It has often been said that the ERM represents a "D-Mark zone" within the European Community, with Austria and perhaps Switzerland added from outside the EC. The D-Mark has been the lead currency, the principal intervention currency, the principal reserve currency, and the psychological as well as the practical anchor. Karl-Otto Pöhl could report by January 1990 that, of the one fifth of all global currency reserves held in D-Marks, many were held in EMS central banks and treasuries as a sign of mutual commitment and confidence.[14]

During the ten years of the ERM, the revaluation of the D-Mark against other ERM currencies had been 38 per cent (including 58 per cent against the Italian lira and 45 per cent against the French franc), but most of the revaluation had taken place at the beginning and the practice had declined sharply during the last five years.[15] At the end of the decade, it could be said that the ERM had been a considerable success for all the states involved. But it had mainly been a success for West Germany, demonstrating the benefits for others of associating themselves with Germany's economic philosophy.

The size of the German economy relative to other ERM economies probably made little difference. Neither did the volume of its international trade, although West Germany led the ERM in both categories. The United States had enjoyed similar relative standing vis-à-vis the remainder of the world at the beginning of the 1970s, but the Bretton Woods system still collapsed when others (especially Germany) were not prepared either to emulate the policies of the United States or to draw the consequences. ERM worked because other states were prepared to accept German doctrine and the discipline that it required.

Moreover, Germany was at several key points more ready to help the system to succeed than the United States had been, although the Bundesbank periodically muttered during the decade about the special burdens that the ERM placed on it and on the D-Mark.[16] The German government may well have been contemplating that Germany might be obliged to play a long-term leadership role in Europe and that this was a good time to show that it was ready to do so.

Actually, the performance of the D-Mark and of the Bundesbank were not quite as stable throughout the ERM period as their high standing might suggest. From the beginning of 1980 until February of 1981 the D-Mark was weak against the dollar and against most ERM currencies because of the second oil shock and because the Federal Republic was suffering the reaction to its reflation policies of the late 1970s.[17] The D-Mark then remained weak against the dollar but strong within the ERM until 1985. It later strengthened against the dollar but stabilized within the ERM, essentially compelling the ERM countries to take the same ride that it was taking.

Nor was German performance always the subject of unalloyed admiration in Europe. Several ERM states had heated discussions between 1986 and 1988 about whether or not the Bundesbank's determination to preserve the value of its currency might not be exporting deflation as well as, or instead of, stability. The alleged "deflationary bias" of German policy became a subject of speculation throughout Europe and the United States until the German economy itself began to resume its growth rate toward the end of 1988.[18] The term "Eurosclerosis," which had surfaced periodically throughout the 1970s and 1980s, again found favor among Western and especially among American economists.

The ERM also offered Germany some very real commercial advantages. It helped to make possible the persistent West German trade surplus within the European Community during the latter 1980s, when European currency stability was in full force. Such a surplus could not have been maintained under traditional circumstances, as it could probably not have been indefinitely compensated by financial and investment flows and would sooner or later have brought about either revaluation by Germany or devaluations by those Community countries most subject to the imbalance. Either would at some point have made German products less competitive. Moreover, as the Bundesbank itself suggested, the D-Mark was somewhat undervalued, as its real (i.e., price-adjusted) external value actually fell against most EMS currencies in the ten years after 1979.[19] But the other states still measured their currencies against the German currency and wished to be tied to it, despite the commercial disadvantages.

Germany's partners may, therefore, have paid a price in large trade deficits and in some slowdown. By the end of the 1980s, both the French and the Italian economies were turning down even as West Germany's was taking off. France and Italy also found their trade deficits doubling during the last half of the decade,[20] and France was not yet fully competitive in Europe and the world despite the strong dose of stability.[21] But both France and Italy, as well as other ERM states, appeared to have decided that the long-term benefits of stability would reverse the negative trends.

If Jacques Rueff had been correct in asserting that "L'Europe se fera par la monnaie ou ne se fera pas," then the West German government, the Bundesbank, and the D-Mark had helped show the way toward a united Europe with the success of the EMS and the ERM. The 1980s ended and the 1990s began with intense European discussion about the possibilities of a wider ERM and about the prospects for true European monetary union under a common currency.

FROM EMS TO EMU

The members of the European Community decided even before the end of the 1980s to explore further monetary cooperation as the Community advanced toward the single internal market. In June 1988, at the European Council meeting in Hanover, they established a commission chaired by the President of the European Commission, Jacques Delors, to study and propose "concrete stages leading toward economic and monetary union." Delors's report, submitted on April 17, 1989, envisaged a transition in three stages toward a European Monetary Union (EMU) with a single common currency:[22]

- The first stage, to be entered on July 1, 1990, was to expand the ERM to include all Community members, most notably Great Britain, to permit free capital flows, and to take other measures that would further coordinate economic and monetary policies.
- The second stage, for which no date was then proposed, was to create a European system of central banks, leading to a single central bank, and an exchange rate mechanism under which European currencies would be permitted to float within very narrow bands smaller than those of the then current ERM. The Community was also to be empowered to set basic economic targets for its members on even such sensitive subjects as the size and financing of budget deficits.
- The third and last stage was to provide for the creation of a single currency managed by a European Central Bank and for even greater Community powers to direct the policies of member governments in order to achieve common financial policies.

The Delors report balanced and combined the conflicting theses advanced by the "monetarists" and the "economists." It placed a high premium on the expanded ERM in the first stage. It provided for the free movement of capital as part of that first stage because capital movement combined with the ERM would compel nations to coordinate their economic policies whether or not they had agreed to do so. But it also envisaged structures for policy coordination even in that first stage and it actually envisaged a European role in guiding national economic policies as part of the second stage. By then, the combination of the ERM and some centralized target setting would exercise the kind of control that both the "economists" and the "monetarists" had sought, and the European governments would be in an increasingly tight lock-step. The final stage, a common currency, could not be far behind, and might have no more than symbolic meaning if the other pieces had already fallen into place.

Even as the discussion about the shape and objectives of European Monetary Union proceeded, steps toward that union were advancing. In June 1989, at Madrid, the European Council endorsed the recommendations for EMU, including the date of July 1, 1990, as the date for beginning the first stage. Eight EC members eliminated all capital controls by that date, and four others (Greece, Ireland, Portugal, and Spain) were given different grace periods until the end of 1992 to do the same. In June 1990, at Dublin, the European Council agreed that a conference of EC member states would meet in December 1990 to discuss the EC treaty amendments that would be necessary to complete economic and monetary union.

The purpose of the 1990 conference was to arrange to have necessary amendments ratified by national parliaments before the end of 1992, at the time that the Single Market was to enter into operation. It was also intended to make certain that the EMS, ERM, and EMU processes, which had been managed on the basis of intergovernmental agreements and consultations separate from the formal legal structures of the EC's Treaty of Rome, would become integrated into those structures. The EMU and the EC with its single market would, in effect, become a single entity.

The European banks joined the governments in moving toward a common European currency, but did so in a manner calculated to reinforce their own roles and their own independence from those governments. A crucial step was taken in December 1989, when the European Community central bankers met in Basel, Switzerland, and agreed to the demands that Pöhl and other Germans advanced, especially with respect to the independence of central bankers against government influence. They took a number of steps that would, in Pöhl's words, make the committee of central bankers "a kind of forerunner for the future European central banking system" and an embryo from which the future central bank of Europe might grow.[23]

Pöhl cited four points on which the bankers had agreed:

- Their main objective was to fight inflation.
- They would organize themselves to "strengthen the position of the committee as a partner of the Council of Ministers in Brussels," a sign that the bankers intended to play a central role in the move toward EMU.
- The committee was the forerunner of the European central banking system.
- The research staff of the Bank for International Settlements (BIS) in Basel would coordinate monetary targets "with the objective of price stability as a policy objective of all member central banks."

The bankers met several times during 1990 and 1991 to continue to assert their views and to organize themselves for further action.[24] They showed ever greater determination to shape the process of European monetary integration and especially to make certain that governments did not have final control over decisions that bankers believed they were better qualified to make. Pöhl almost certainly urged them in that direction. These meetings, as well as a study commissioned by the Association for the Monetary Union of Europe,[25] showed not only the momentum that was arising behind EMU but also the degree to which the concept that money should be a real store of value as well as a medium of exchange was becoming widely recognized.

The EMU process continued apace. The EC Foreign Ministers met in Ireland in May 1990. And on July 1, 1990, stage one of the EMU formally began. In September 1990, in a major shift of policy, Great Britain finally joined the ERM with a 6 per cent band. This was a significant addition to the ERM, although it was taken as reluctantly as many earlier British steps toward Europe had been taken. Great Britain also offered a separate proposal for a "hard Ecu," under which the Ecu would become another currency trading in Europe for certain purposes and would be exchanged for existing currencies but pegged to the strongest of those currencies. It was to be available for public use and to settle debts, but it would theoretically not add to the money in circulation because it would be issued in exchange for other currencies.

THE GERMAN DISCUSSION OF EMU FROM 1989 TO 1990

After the Delors Plan was announced, the German government and the Bundesbank reacted cautiously although Pöhl had helped to draft the report. Having been pleased with the achievements of the ERM, the Germans were prepared to examine an arrangement that would go further toward monetary union. But they were not ready to agree to anything that would upset what they regarded as the foundations of their own prosperity.

German reactions to the Delors Report came from many sources, but mainly from the Bundesbank. Bank officials formed a chorus to list the conditions under which Germany would adhere to EMU. Pöhl himself used virtually every possible opportunity to clarify the bank's views about EMU and the European central bank. Pöhl maintained that the Bundesbank was in no hurry to see any kind of European monetary integration or common currency unless it was the right kind.[26]

The Bundesbank was highly skeptical toward the Ecu. Leonhard Gleske, the member of the Direktorium responsible for international matters, warned already in 1989 that the Ecu as then conceived could not match the vital role that the D-Mark had played in making the ERM work effectively. He said that the Ecu represented a useful accounting unit but he warned that it could not serve as a reserve currency, intervention currency, or store of value, as the D-Mark had. He also warned that national currencies should not and could not be replaced by an international currency that did not have the same characteristics as a successful national currency.[27]

The Bundesbank nonetheless recognized the value of having a European Monetary Union and an artificial currency, the Ecu, for certain purposes. Klaus Köhler, a member of the bank's Direktorium, recalled that both the dollar and the pound sterling had suffered on balance from their roles as the principal currencies of the Bretton Woods system and its predecessors. The current account deficits that were needed to provide global liquidity could not be sustained without a loss of confidence and finally a collapse of the fixed exchange rate system. Köhler said that this was why the Bundesbank had supported the Ecu for certain purposes despite some reservations. Nonetheless, he warned, the Ecu was far from ready to perform as a key currency, and the D-Mark was finding itself increasingly obliged to serve at the center of the EMS and the prospective EMU. He warned that the Bundesbank did not want to perform this role, insisting that it would be more desirable to "share the burden," but that the D-Mark could not be replaced until an adequate substitute was available.[28]

The Bundesbank did, however, outline the conditions under which it might be prepared to support European Monetary Union and a European currency. They contained no surprises:[29]

- The European currency must be as strong and stable as the D-Mark.
- It must be issued by an independent issuing bank, impervious to instructions or pressures from governments or from European institutions.
- The bank must not be subject to drawn-out consultations before it can make decisions, especially in circumstances like the 1982 debt crisis or the 1987 Crash, when a central bank must be able to act fast and flexibly.
- The bank must be able to follow long-term strategies and policies, as money flows require time to work through a financial system.
- Any system that relies on "coordination" between governments and central banks would be "half-baked" and must be avoided, for banks must be independent.
- There can be no limitations on the European central bank's authority to protect the stability and value of a currency.
- If all European states and institutions were to exercise "self-discipline," fewer formal rules might be needed.

It would be misleading to believe that German conditions about EMU and about a possible European currency represented only the attitude of the Bundesbank. The Advisory Council of the German Economics Ministry issued a report that fully matched the Bundesbank in content and in tone. The 30-member body, which had several times met to discuss the possibilities for a European currency system, said that it could see a number of advantages to a common European currency but it warned that such a currency could prove disastrous if it became an instrument or an object for manipulation.[30]

As 1990 advanced, the Bundesbank became ever more deeply concerned about the risk that EMU might not emerge as it wished.[31] Even as the bank went through the motions of negotiating with other banks about EMU and of watching the government conduct its own policy, it was becoming increasingly disturbed at the prospect at having to stabilize closer European monetary integration at a time when its resources were fully committed toward East Germany and Eastern Europe.

On September 19, 1990, the Bundesbank took the unusual step of issuing a lengthy official statement clearly intended to set forth its views on EMU in the most formal possible manner. The statement also asserted that the problems posed by German monetary union had to be completely under control before further European integration could be contemplated.[32]

Returning to the old arguments of the "economists," the Bundesbank said that "economic union" must be the basis for monetary union, adding that "sufficient and durable convergence among member states" had to precede EMU. Before EMU could proceed, the Single Market had to be implemented, fiscal border controls had to be eliminated, and inflation had to be "very largely stamped out." The Bundesbank emphasized the importance of a bank board with "durably guaranteed independence," listing the conditions needed for that independence. It proposed a central bank structure much like that of the Bundesbank itself, adding that the bank system would have to give priority to monetary stability. No bank or nation should be able to follow independent policies.

The most striking part of the Bundesbank document, however, was the warning that it issued to the German government. It stated that the conditions listed in its statement represented "unconditional, not negotiable, requirements." It stated that the German delegation would have to represent these views at an upcoming government conference with no compromises. To underline its warning, it asserted that the risks which EMU posed for monetary stability applied especially to Germany. Finance Minister Waigel issued a brief statement supporting the bank's position.

An even more negative statement on EMU came from Helmut Schlesinger, who was to become president of the bank in August 1991. Speaking in London in September 1990, he listed not only the usual Bundesbank reservations about European Monetary Union, but he added another. Speaking "personally," he said that he questioned whether Europe could manage a common currency until it had created what he termed the "relevant political structures." To the "monetarists" and the "economists," he added what appeared to be a third group, perhaps to be termed the "politicists," who also wanted even certain political preconditions fulfilled before Germany would agree to monetary union.[33]

The Bundesbank continued the steady drumbeat of its concerns and reservations about EMU throughout the remainder of the year. Speeches by one member of the Zentralbankrat after another concentrated on the dangers of EMU. Almost half of every copy of the Bundesbank publication, *Auszüge*, carried statements pointing out the dangers of EMU and underlining the necessary preconditions. The Finance Ministry, while less voluble, also remained cautious.

The Bundesbank was not, however, carrying the day within Germany itself. The Foreign Office, especially Foreign Minister Genscher, continued a quiet prodding toward EMU, in part because of Genscher's own belief that the time for closer European integration had come and in part because of consistent pressure from France and perhaps other European states. Chancellor Kohl shared Genscher's commitment to European integration but also listened carefully to Pöhl. The result was a policy that increasingly confused the listeners to the German dialogue, especially as it was interwoven with moves toward German unity that undoubtedly took priority in the minds of German politicians and officials.

Other voices joined the debate. Both the BDI and the Sachverständigenrat supported the Bundesbank. On the other hand, a major West German weekly, *Die Zeit*, attacked what it termed the "Mischief of DM-Nationalism" and warned that behind the Bundesbank's tirades against EMU proposals one could begin to hear a *Kommandoton* (command tone) that gave no credit to Germany. It reminded its listeners of Thomas Mann's famous saying that he would rather have "a European Germany" than "a German Europe."[34]

THE EUROPEAN SUMMITS AT THE END OF 1990

Despite the coincidence of European Monetary Union and German monetary union, and the potential for conflict, progress toward EMU continued during the remainder of 1990. The EC Commission released a report, optimistically entitled *One Market, One Money*, which positively assessed the probable impact of EMU on the European and world economies. It specifically recommended an early transition to the second stage, an early establishment of the new European central bank, which it termed the "Eurofed," and the designation of the Ecu as the single EC currency. The report raised some eyebrows in Bonn and Frankfurt, as it appeared to put European governments and central banks—and especially the German—under pressure, but no immediate German action followed.

The next step in the EMU process took place at a special EC summit in Rome in October 1990. At that summit, Chancellor Helmut Kohl and the other European leaders (except Margaret Thatcher) agreed that the second phase of EMU was to enter into force on January 1, 1994. This date was not as early as the mid-1993 date originally proposed by Delors and supported by Genscher, but it also represented a setback for the Bundesbank which wanted no date to be set.

In the same vein, the Rome summit agreed that, within three years after the beginning of the second phase, the EC Commission and the monetary institutions would report on the functioning of that phase and on the progress made toward what it termed "real convergence," so as to prepare a decision regarding passage to the third phase—which was to occur "within a reasonable time."

The agreement set the date of 1994 for the establishment of the Eurofed. The Eurofed would thus begin to play some role in the management of the ERM and EMS during stage two of the EMU process. It would presumably help to coordinate the policies of the European national central banks—including the Bundesbank(!)—and would prepare itself for the day when it was to take over full responsibility for European monetary policy and for managing the Ecu as the single European currency.

The Eurofed was to be modeled after the Bundesbank and the U.S. Federal Reserve, with more of the characteristics of the Bundesbank, but its precise organization, powers, and responsibilities were yet to be negotiated and determined. Even before stage two and Eurofed, however, the intensity of monetary coordination was to accelerate through the establishment of a Committee of Central Bank Governors that was to become the principal body to discuss EC/EMS monetary policies as well as external monetary relations, as with the U.S. dollar and the U.S. Federal Reserve Bank. It was also understood that economic coordination had to progress from what Delors termed "an academic exercise" to something more concrete and more effective.[35]

Shortly after the Rome summit, Mrs. Thatcher fell and was succeeded by John Major as Prime Minister. While that change would probably not put an end to Britain's reservations about European monetary integration, it meant that London's reservations would be uttered less categorically and would perhaps be held less tenaciously. Great Britain would presumably be more flexible, and that meant a greater probability that EMU might come to pass. That might have been good news for Kohl and Genscher, but not for the Bundesbank.

Even more dramatically, at the European Council summit in Rome on December 14-15, 1990, the heads of government agreed to transform themselves into two Inter-Governmental Conferences (IGC's) to negotiate terms for European economic and monetary union on the one hand and for European political union on the other. These two IGC's, reminiscent of the IGC that had convened in 1985 and had produced the Single European Act, promised to lead the Community to new levels of integration. Although Delors used the summit to complain about recalcitrant states, and specifically included Germany among those states, the atmosphere in Rome was positive and promising. EMU was on track, speeding ahead, and the combination of moves toward political and monetary union showed that the leaders of Western Europe were dead serious about establishing a truly united European economy.

THE BUNDESBANK CALLS A HALT

Within weeks of the beginning of 1991, however, the Bundesbank made clear that it had heard enough, and that it would have the final say on EMU even if its views had not fully prevailed on some other issues. The first step taken by the bank was to raise the discount rate by half a point on January 31, 1991. It made the move without apparent consultation with its major ERM partners, disturbing both the French and Italians who nonetheless decided not to devalue but to follow suit. The second step was to propose its own draft for the Eurofed, a draft that fully complied with the bank's views of the Eurofed and that also postponed its creation until the *end* of stage two of EMU.

The Bundesbank did not stop there but added additional conditions, stating that EMU members had to have their fiscal deficits under control (a slap at Rome and at Bonn) and had to signal their interest in the process by making their central banks independent *before* EMU began (a slap at Paris and London). The bank also argued that it might be desirable to reach EMU in geographic as well as substantive stages, with the first countries included to be only those whose governments and central banks were truly ready (a slap at almost all major and some minor European states).[36]

To reinforce the bank's views, Pöhl on March 19 made an allegedly offhand remark in which he termed German monetary unification a "disaster," prompting an immediate fall in the D-Mark. Pöhl's purpose was not primarily to denounce German monetary integration, which was a done deal on which his views were well known and had not been as ignored as totally as he and other Bundesbank principals later suggested, but to warn that European monetary integration would fail if it were to proceed before the right conditions had been fully created.

Members of the German government followed divergent paths. Chancellor Kohl, in a joint statement with Britain's Prime Minister John Major on February 11, supported the British plan to go slow on EMU, and specifically not to create the Eurofed until the end of stage two. The following month, however, Foreign Minister Genscher issued a joint statement with French Foreign Minister Roland Dumas in which he committed the German government to creating the Eurofed at the beginning of stage two.[37]

German financial officials and bankers were plainly getting worried. The burdens of German unification were proving to be far greater than many

Germans had expected. United Germany was being called upon to finance or to help finance virtually every international venture, from the U.S. military campaign in the Gulf to the reconstruction of Eastern Europe, the Soviet Union, and perhaps the new Russian republics, and nobody could be certain what might come next.

Cyclical influences were equally confused and confusing. The United States was lowering interest rates to ease out of a recession. It was, as usual, pressing Germany to do the same. German imports were rising and exports declining for the first time since the mid-1980s. France and Italy, also in recession, were increasingly reluctant to follow more Bundesbank rate increases and France even lowered its rates. The Spanish government, committed to matching Germany's stability policy, came under increasingly sharp fire at home. Those states could not afford a weaker dollar as Germany could, for more of their exports competed on a price basis.

An outsider could be pardoned for wondering if the Bundesbank had become so deeply concerned about the risks of EMU in an unstable and even risky environment that it was prepared even to weaken the EMS and the ERM to delay or perhaps scuttle progress toward EMU. Whatever its purpose, the bank was conducting its business in the shrillest tone that it had used since the oil shocks and the monetary crises of the 1970s.

The bank was also getting results. At a meeting of Finance Ministers and central bankers in May 1991, the idea of a "two-speed Europe" was presented and discussed, opening up the possibility that Germany and the Bundesbank would have to cooperate in the early phases of EMU only with those states that would present no undue stability problems, like the Benelux states and (perhaps) France. There were also reports that the date for the Eurofed had been set back for two years, to 1996, at German request. By the end of the meeting, the Bundesbank had again shown that it, and it alone, would have the final word on Eurofed and EMU and that it would set the timetable. Anybody who disagreed was welcome to stay out.

In case any doubts remained about the attitude of Hans Tietmeyer, whom Kohl had put on the Direktorium and who was to succeed Schlesinger in 1993, Tietmeyer in April 1991 made it obvious that he also was in no hurry about EMU.[38] He strongly advocated the "two-speed Europe," saying that a number of states in the EC (he cited Great Britain, Italy, and Greece) did not yet fit into the *Stabilitätsblock* and that a common monetary system could not overcome excessive policy divergences. He made it clear that the Bundesbank would simply not join any EMU that included states and central banks it regarded as unqualified. He also denounced Delors for setting target dates as a way (in Delors's alleged words) "of testing Germany's commitment." He warned that nobody could force the Bundesbank to act against its best judgment and its basic mandate and obligations, and he stated that convergence had to precede monetary union.

As if to make sure that nobody would miss his point, Tietmeyer pronounced the solemn rule that "a stable currency is more important than a united currency."

GERMAN POLICY AND THE FUTURE

The sharp debate about EMU during 1991 forced the German government, the Bundesbank, and all those involved in the German economy to look again at the entire process of European monetary integration, and to look at it with fresh eyes because of what had happened in Germany and Europe during 1990 and was to happen in 1991.

Chancellor Kohl feels strongly that Europe—*united* Europe—represents Germany's future. He wants to work with French President Mitterrand to move toward Europe as fast as possible, if necessary at the price of going against some of the Bundesbank's views. Kohl, like earlier German Chancellors, perceives a virtue in West European integration as an object in itself. He is not prepared to sacrifice German prosperity or stability to that objective, but he believes that European integration will in itself contribute to prosperity—as it always has to date.

Moreover, although Kohl is one of the most pro-American Chancellors in the history of the Federal Republic, he questions whether Germany's economic future should be entrusted primarily to an association with the United States. Other Germans share his feelings. Even those who are most fundamentally pro-American believe that Europe cannot depend on the unpredictable and self-serving U.S. economic and monetary policy that they all too often perceive.

The Chancellor also wants to show that German unity and German *Ostpolitik* will not diminish Germany's commitment to the process of West European integration. Although uncertainty about whether Europe should be the *Klein-Europa* of the European Community or the *Gross-Europa* from the Atlantic to the Urals may open new questions for the Bundesbank and for others, Kohl has not wanted to hesitate because any delay will arouse suspicion about Germany's deeper objectives. Genscher shares that belief.

Just as the government may feel more ready to advance, the Bundesbank feels more reluctant. It fears that the government may want to make a political agreement that might tie the bank's hands, and it is determined to make that impossible. It wants to have all uncertainties eliminated in advance, and it has become especially troubled to see those uncertainties not disappear but instead multiply. More than ever, the Bundesbank seems to want not an Ecu, but an E-Mark, a currency that would be like the D-Mark in all but name, and one that it can control throughout the potentially troubled times ahead.

The Bundesbank can take some satisfaction in the evolution of the EMU debate. Its repeated insistence on the type of European central bank that it wants, and on the policy that the bank should pursue, has already shifted the agenda and even the consensus of the discussion in the Bundesbank's favor and has put those who oppose its ideas on the defensive. Whereas any European monetary arrangement, and especially a European bank, once appeared very likely to have resembled the French or the British model under considerable government influence, the discussion has shifted toward a bank charter and toward bank policies that much more closely resemble Germany's.

Even if European Monetary Union does not come to pass as originally scheduled, the Bundesbank will have achieved an important purpose in rallying support and understanding in all European states for bank policies oriented more toward monetary than political goals, and that particularly stress stability. The ERM has also convinced many European businessmen and economists that the German model has its merits, although the recessions that developed in France and Italy in 1989 and 1990 raised questions about the suitability of Bundesbank policies for every nation in Europe.

The Bundesbank has not, however, taken any pleasure in winning the argument about EMU. Instead, in 1991, the bank saw capital shortages and budget deficits everywhere. It feared that political leaders everywhere were not taking monetary policy seriously enough, but were leading the continent into arrangements that were at best unsound and at worst dangerous. The bank may also have begun to suspect that France, disturbed at some of the Bundesbank's actions in early 1991, was supporting the Ecu as a way of diminishing the importance and the leadership role of the D-Mark, and that other European states—especially England—were increasingly turning to the Ecu not out of a devotion to Europe but as a way to avoid taking the responsibility for serious monetary policy. In this situation, only the Bundesbank remained as the true guardian at the gate.[39]

British membership in the ERM, and the prospects for British membership in the EMU, have undoubtedly given the Bundesbank special pause. The British pound represents a different order of magnitude as an international currency from the lira, the peseta, and even the franc. The pound is a true international currency, one that is held in reserve accounts by global central bankers, in slightly greater proportions by developing than developed states and also in some of the petroleum-exporting states where Great Britain long had an influence.

If there is any speculation against the pound, it can represent a major burden on the currencies that need to intervene against it. Those who want to speculate against the franc or the lira, or central bankers who might want to sell those currencies prior to a possible devaluation, do not normally own enough of them to mount a major attack or to precipitate a collapse. They have to borrow them or use currency reserves intended for normal transactions, and they would find it expensive to hold speculative or hedge positions for very long. But the pound is held by central banks or others in much larger quantities. It is the currency of a major financial center, the City of London. A German commitment to support the pound could be not only costly but futile, and the Bundesbank could not regard the prospect with equanimity. In some ways, the Bundesbank could be pleased not to have had Great Britain in the ERM during the 1980s.

The gravest problem, however, remains in the continuing risk of global disequilibrium as the international system is subject to powerful and diverse strains of inflation, recession, and possible deflation, and as new obligations appear almost daily with the collapse of the Soviet system. The Bundesbank has had a recipe against inflation but has not traditionally done well against recession. Nor has it had to finance major aid programs. Other West European states and central banks might not be as prepared to accept German wisdom in a turbulent environment full of contradictory pressures as they had been in an environment where the main and perhaps only danger was inflation. The economic forces of the 1990s could pose problems for the ERM, the EMU, and German influence as well.

This issue can become a problem even in Germany. The German formula, which rejects demand stimulation and places a high stress on savings, investment, and the supply of quality products, may not work as well for Germany once it becomes the rule and not the exception. German exports may do best when other countries do not behave as Germany does. Although exports to the EC boomed during the latter 1980s, they were weakening toward the end of the decade as growth slowed in other states. Whatever one may conclude, one could safely say that a much closer look might have to be taken at all the consequences and implications of the ERM before a full-scale move to EMU should be made.

One must thus also ask whether Germany may not only export deflation but also import it. A state that is as dependent on exports as Germany cannot over the long run permit itself to pursue policies that weaken the economies of its foreign markets, for it will lose exports. This was one of the reasons why German exports fell during 1990 and 1991, although demand from Eastern Germany took up the slack. German monetary theorists would refuse to countenance such a theory, for they believe that they export not deflation but stability and that stability will promote growth. But it appeared in 1990 and 1991 that it might well be necessary to explore that possible consequence of the ERM as well before advancing to EMU, for the sake of united Germany as well as for the sake of united Europe. On all these problems, the doubts aroused in Germany and elsewhere became ever more pronounced as the moment of truth neared. And if the government might not be ready yet to make decisions about the EC, the Bundesbank was very ready to make decisions and demands about the EMU.

As the debate advanced, one fact became ever more central to the future of EMU and even to European monetary cooperation at the EMS/ERM level: The move toward West European monetary integration threatens to stall in Germany, where it was once initiated. It will not be possible to advance integration until the Bundesbank believes that it can master all the many problems that it sees ahead. And the first price that Germany and Europe may pay for their hard-won unification is a delay in the monetary integration that Western Europe had so carefully planned for many years.

NOTES TO CHAPTER TEN

1. For a discussion of these earlier plans, as well as broader discussion of EMS, see Rolf H. Haase, Werner Weidenfeld, and Reinhold Biskup, *The European Central Bank: Perspectives for a Further Development of the European Monetary System* (Gütersloh: Bertelsmann Foundation, 1990), pp. 39-44.
2. Helmut Steinel, "Europäische Währungspolitik," *Wirtschaftspolitik* (Bonn: Bundeszentrale für politische Bildung, 1990), p. 441.
3. Kaufmann, "The Deutsche Mark between the Dollar and the European Monetary System," *Kredit und Kapital*, April 1985, p. 32.
4. Germany's fundamental views toward the European Monetary System are in Kaufmann, *Germany's International Monetary Policy and the European Monetary System* (New York: Brooklyn College Press, 1985), pp. 12-111.
5. The D-Mark component of the Ecu and its exchange rate with the Ecu can vary. They are currently at about 30 per cent and DM 2 per Ecu, respectively. For their history, see Haase et al., *op. cit.*, p. 210.
6. For Schmidt's own recollections of his decision, and especially of his cooperation with Giscard d'Estaing, see *Die Zeit*, August 31, 1990.
7. A considerable source of confusion is the frequent use of the terms EMS and ERM as if they were the same thing. They are not. The EMS, the European Monetary System, includes all members of the European Com-

munity and gives all their currencies a share in the value of the Ecu. The ERM is the structure under which a certain number of states establish firm rates of exchange between their currencies. It has not included all members of the EMS (for example, it did not include Great Britain and the British pound until 1990), but it has consistently included the D-Mark. Some states that are not in the EC or the EMS, like Austria, also tie their currencies to the ERM through their link with the D-Mark.

8. Steinel, *loc. cit.*, p. 445.

9. *Ibid.*

10. Graphs showing the decline in currency fluctuations, in inflation, in the deflators, and in long- as well as short-term interest rates of the ERM countries, as well as the growth in their external current accounts, are in Manuel Guitian, Massimo Russo, and Giuseppe Tullio, *Policy Coordination in the European Monetary System* (Washington: International Monetary Fund, 1988), Occasional Paper No. 61, pp. 29-33; OECD material is in OECD, *OECD Economic Outlook 46* (Paris: OECD, 1989), p. 38; BDI chart is in BDI, *Wirtschafts-und-Währungsunion* (Köln: BDI, 1989), pp. 16 and 28.

11. "Exchange Rate Movements within the European Monetary System," *Monthly Report of the Deutsche Bundesbank*, November 1989, pp. 28-36.

12. Horst Ungerer, Owen Evans, Thomas Mayer, and Philip Young, *The European Monetary System: Recent Developments* (Washington: IMF, December 1986); John Plender, "Recycling West Germany's excess savings," *Financial Times*, July 5, 1989.

13. Jacques de Larosière, speech on February 26, 1990, printed in *Auszüge*, March 19, 1990, pp. 1-5.

14. *Auszüge*, January 16, 1990, p. 2; for further records of the D-Mark role, including the volume of interventions in the ERM, see Guitian, Russo, and Tullio, *op. cit.*, pp. 50-56.

15. *Monthly Report of the Deutsche Bundesbank*, November 1989, p.31; The precise shifts between the value of the D-Mark and other principal currencies, including several ERM currencies, since 1972, are published periodically in *Auszüge* under the title *Entwicklung des Aussenwertes der D-Mark*. Those figures reflect an increase in the D-Mark's value against all other currencies except the Swiss franc and the Japanese yen, and an increase of 23.6 per cent vis-à-vis the Ecu between the end of 1978 and the end of 1989.

16. A discussion of the complications that the EMS/ERM has presented for its members, including West Germany, can be found in Francesco Giavazzi, Stefano Micossi, and Marcus Miller, eds., *The European Monetary System*, the record of a conference held under the sponsorship of the Centro Interuniversitario di Studi Teoretici per la Politica Economica (STEP) and the Center for Economic Policy Research (CEPR), in October 1987 (Cambridge: Cambridge University Press, 1988). See especially pp. 5-20.

17. Kaufmann, *loc. cit.*, p. 43.

18. Thiel, "West European Economic and Monetary Integration and the Atlantic Relationship," Paper presented at the Woodrow Wilson Center for International Scholars, Washington, August 17, 1989, pp. 8-9.
19. Bundesbank, *loc. cit.*, pp. 32-33.
20. Tommaso Padoa-Schioppa, *Financial and Monetary Integration in Europe: 1990, 1992 and Beyond* (New York: Group of Thirty, 1990), pp. 18-19.
21. Christian Deubner, *Die Konkurrenzfähigkeit der französischen Industrie und die deutsche Europapolitik* (Ebenhausen: Stiftung Wissenschaft und Politik, 1991), pp. 5-8.
22. A summary brief and comment on the Delors report is in *The Economist*, April 22, 1989.
23. *The Independent*, London, December 13, 1989, quoted in Deutsche Bundesbank, *Auszüge*, December 14, 1989, pp. 1-2.
24. For further information on the meetings and on the rules governing cooperation among the central bankers, see *Monthly Report of the Deutsche Bundesbank*, July 1990, pp. 34-37, and *Auszüge*, April 3, 1990, pp. 10-11.
25. *The Economist*, May 19, 1990, pp. 87-88.
26. Pöhl speech, December 29, 1989, reported in *Auszüge*, January 2, 1990, pp. 1-2.
27. Leonhard Gleske speech, November 27, 1989, reprinted in *Auszüge*, December 4, 1989, pp. 1-4.
28. Claus Köhler, "The Single Market in Financial and Professional Services," *Auszüge*, March 30, 1990, p. 2.
29. Samples of Bundesbank views are in two speeches by Pöhl, December 11, 1989, and January 16, 1990, reprinted in *Auszüge*, December 12, 1989, pp. 1-5, and January 16, 1990, pp. 1-6.
30. The report of the Advisory Council is reprinted by the West German Ministry of Economics as *Europäische Währungsordnung: Gutachten des Wissenschaftlichen Beirats beim Bundesministerium für Wirtschaft*, Studien-Reihe 61 (Bonn: Federal Ministry for Economics, 1989).
31. *The Financial Times*, October 16, 1990.
32. The text of the Bundesbank statement and the accompanying press and other commentary are carried in *Auszüge*, September 25, 1990, pp. 1-9, and in *Monthly Report of the Deutsche Bundesbank*, October 1990, pp. 40-44.
33. Speech presented at the IDEA 1990 Conference, London, September 27, 1990, reprinted in *Auszüge*, October 1, 1990, pp. 1-5.
34. These positions were expressed respectively in the Sachverständigenrat's *1990/91 Report*, pp 430-437; BDI, *Wirtschafts- und Währungsunion* (Köln: BDI, 1989), pp. 32-33; *Financial Times*, November 16, 1990; *Die Zeit*, October 19, 1990.
35. Jacques Delors, "A new Frontier takes Shape," *Europe*, December 1990, pp. 25-26.
36. *The Economist*, March 9, 1991, pp. 43-45; *Financial Times*, February 27, 1991.
37. *Financial Times*, February 12 and March 23/24, 1991.

38. Text of speech in *Auszüge*. April 17, 1991, pp. 1-7.
39. For a statement of these arguments, see Lothar Müller, "'Hard-ECU' - Sackgasse zur Europäischen Wirtschafts- und Währungsunion," *Europa-Archiv*, April 25, 1991, pp. 247-254.

Eleven

The Crossroads

Any person who might have taken a look at the West German economy in the summer of 1989 would have almost certainly concluded that things were proceeding well. The economy had broken out of a long downtrend in growth and was advancing on a sound foundation, even if its growth was excessively export-dependent. It was being integrated gradually and successfully with those of other West European states. It had structural weaknesses, but those were not unique and they were obviously not paralyzing. Its continuing success in its traditional and chosen fields compensated for whatever problems might exist.

The West German economy functioned effectively, if in a manner that would not have pleased all economic theorists. It was having a modest boom. Its central bank was running much of Europe. The policies of the *Wende* were boosting the private sector, reducing state encumbrances, and encouraging investment. The West Germans were prosperous, secure, and at peace with themselves as with others, the first Germans in the twentieth century who could make that statement.

That same observer would have concluded that West Germany with its declining and aging population and its enduring inefficiencies was slowly but surely easing into a kind of *rentier* mold, in which its capital exports would over time enable it to produce a great deal abroad while many of its people lived comfortably on the earnings. The observer would have seen a land that had rediscovered and even expanded its traditional place in the global division of labor and was generally satisfied with that place and with the comfortably prosperity that it produced.

The observer would also have noted that Germans were pleased to let others be in the forefront of the decision process about the global and even the European economy, at least as long as the Germans could insulate themselves when they felt it necessary, could choose their own policies when they wanted, and were not prevented from having the kind of economy they preferred. They would also have seen Germany participating actively and even centrally in some important but carefully prepared changes that were being made in Western Europe, such as the Single Market. They might have seen a threat from Japan or from elsewhere, but no overwhelming danger.

At the turn of the decade, however, everything changed, both for the better and the worse. In 1989, the Wall collapsed. In 1990, Germany was united and much of historical Europe reappeared, to the joy of those in the East even more than of those in the West. Then, in 1991, the menacing Soviet imperium broke apart, opening countless opportunities (as well as posing some risks) even as it struggled to find a new shape acceptable to most of its members. Its final shape could not be determined for a long time, being probably subject to evolution through several stages, but it could offer a real opening for German talent, influence, and capital.

The changes between 1989 and 1991 created a new situation for Germany in two important ways. First, they blocked, at least temporarily, the prospects for a continuation of the incrementalist path on which the West Germans had long and successfully set their course. Second, they put Germany into a situation in which it could again shape the course of Europe and of history. But the instrument with which it would have to act would be economic, not military or political.

Suddenly and unexpectedly, Germans are faced with such far-reaching and complex choices that it can be truly said that they are at a crossroads. For the Germans, or at least the West Germans, were not only accustomed to the earlier situation but even content with it. But they must now decide where to go next, and even where to lead.

German economic decisions, like political decisions, cannot be made on the same basis as before. In a geoeconomic world, German economic policy will shape Germany's, Russia's, and Europe's political as well as economic future. And the policies that slowly nurtured West Germany and Western Europe until 1989 cannot continue.

As the Preface indicated, West Germany rose to economic influence largely because of its domestic economic policies, policies that promoted solid growth, exports, and a strong D-Mark. Those policies shaped not only Germany's domestic prosperity, but also its place in Europe and the world.

The German economy had not been oriented toward the prospect of unification or toward a widening of Europe. It had been on a West European course. With German and European unity, the conditions under which West Germans had won their prosperity shifted, as Europe changed irretrievably.

One reason why Germany was often termed indecisive during late 1990 and much of 1991 was that the Germans literally did not know what might be best. They had not anticipated any of the decisions with which they were faced, and they had not even imagined the new world although it resembled older Europe in many important ways.

Now, under new and radically different political and economic circumstances, the German government and the Bundesbank must make decisions that will determine the new shape of Germany, of Europe, and of the global economy and polity.

There are three specific areas in which Germany must make crucial decisions: German unification, European unification, and Germany's place in the global division of labor.

With respect to German unification, the long-term prospects are overwhelmingly positive. Over time, unification can and will strengthen Germany's economic position considerably. Germany's location in the center of Europe offers a powerful multiplier. While unification adds only slightly to the Gross National Product, at least at first, it adds immeasurably to Germany's capacity to function again as the center of continental Europe for production, assembly, trade, communications, and services. Unity can revitalize the German economy. Germany can become far more influential and, if it chooses to return Eastern Germany to its historical vocation as a center for high technology, far more productive and globally competitive.

The central dilemma of German unification, however, is how to get from the present to the future without mortgaging that future. More specifically, how to get there without expanding social and subsidy programs to the point where they not only reverse the benefits of the *Wende* but where they risk returning Germany to the very conditions that brought on the *Wende*.

If the Treuhandanstalt and the German government decide to take the slow route, to absorb and finance the inefficient enterprises of Eastern Germany, and to subsidize workers in place at fundamentally unjustifiable jobs, the costs of the transformation and the perpetuation of the Eastern norms of planning and coordination may not only delay reform in the Eastern portions of Germany but may upset the delicate balance on which the West German synthesis itself has rested. West Germany would have incorporated the East, but in the process would itself have been transformed and compromised.

That process has, however, some important advantages from the standpoint of the German government. It would help to keep a number of people at their places in Eastern Germany. It might even give some East German industries a chance to reform themselves and to become competitive. And it would keep the situation in Eastern Germany relatively stable, enabling the government to concentrate on other problems.

Beyond German unification, but intimately linked with it, lies the second question, the unification of historical Europe. So does the question of the future of the Soviet Union and of Eastern Europe as well as of the European Community.

Before German unification, and before the opening to the East, Germany's role and policy in Western Europe, the European Community, and the European Monetary System, was clear. The combination worked, to the advantage of Germans and others. West European institutions functioned effectively if ever more bureaucratically. They provided an ample framework for West German activities and interests.

Since unification, and since the opening to the East, the Community looks different. So do other West European institutions and arrangements. They may not primarily offer opportunities but impose limits. What once was an attractive arena may appear to become costly and perhaps confining.

Germany has already begun reviewing its commitment to the monetary side of European integration. European Monetary Union will be postponed or limited to those states where it had to all intents and purposes already existed.

The German commitment toward the European Single Market is still firm but may also come under review. The Single Market will probably have be postponed beyond 1992, for reasons more closely related to West European problems than to continental unification. Too many questions have arisen, not only in Germany but elsewhere, to proceed as planned. But the delay may be crucial and perhaps fatal.

As the Single Market process advances, it may increasingly run against the new realities of a uniting pan-Europe. A tightly integrated European Community might make it impossible for East European states, especially those who are least developed, to associate themselves. But such an association might be attractive for Germany, for political as well as economic reasons.

Germany has to make a decision, for it is German economic and political interests to the East that may be most directly affected by what happens in and to the Community. Traditionally, Germany sent industrial products, advisors and investment funds to its Eastern neighbors in exchange for raw materials, agricultural products, and seasonal as well as migrant labor. The division of Germany shifted some of those patterns. But there may be sound economic reasons for historical links to re-assert themselves, and their relationship to EC ties and commitments has to be carefully examined. Moreover, if the EC does not act, others, such as the Japanese and the Americans, may move.

Fundamental decisions have to be made about the direction of the Community itself and about how the further integration of the Community can be coordinated with the creation of a wider Europe. The Soviet Union and the East European states cannot hope to export food and other things to Germany without changes in Community rules. Nor can they hope to export basic level industrial goods as long as Western Europe subsidizes its own. This will put a limit on trade with those states. The GATT problem also remains, even as the world changes.

Germany must help decide whether the Community will remain open, and to whom, whether it will close itself off, and from whom, or whether it will opt for managed trade, and with whom. The German attitude in EC councils will be crucial. Several other European states may be ready to curtail imports and to insulate the Community and greater Europe, including Eastern Europe and perhaps even the Soviet Union, as a whole. They are only waiting for German support. The temptation must be very real, for an expanded and sealed Community could create an economic zone that would run from Lisbon to Vladivostok.

For Germany, as perhaps for other European states, a reinforced and expanded European trading and financial environment could appear promising. Such a Europe would contain a market of perhaps 600-700 million persons, considerable productive capacity, and perhaps over time a stable currency system under the management of the Bundesbank. It might be largely self-sufficient. But it would risk destroying the GATT system and would also risk converting Europe into a high-cost, low-technology backwater. It would also demand considerable German resources to make it a reality. It would pose an irreconcilable conflict between Germany's European and global vocations.

The German government, German industry, and the Bundesbank must also decide, in conjunction with the future of the EC and of Europe, how they want to shape or influence the global system. The American-built system, based on the GATT, the IMF, the summits, and so on, may not survive, especially if there is a major global downturn. The American government is no longer in a position to decide and to structure a new system unilaterally, if indeed it ever was. The German view will be more important than ever.

The third and perhaps most difficult area for German decision is about Germany's place in the global division of labor and thus about the policies it will pursue at home.

The dominant West German philosophy, demonstrably successful, has been a cautious monetarism with an underlying conservative bias, mixed with decreasing doses of Schumpeterianism and a steady mercantilist drive. Such a policy cannot thrive if every other state is also pursuing it, whether in Europe or in the world as a whole, and it also cannot thrive in a global system that does not have free trade or a prosperity independent of German policy. German economists and central bankers may find that they need to reflect on the kinds of growth they want not only for themselves but for others as well.

It may also no longer be possible for Germany to continue the kinds of structural policies that have grown up over time if it loses its competitive position in a world roaring ahead into new areas of production and services. But it will prove immensely difficult to make choices on structural policies at a time when Germany must finance unification and the opening to the East as well as maintain its stability in the case of a global downturn. This issue surfaced during the 1991 budget debate but was not really solved or even addressed.

All these questions must be seen as one. The decision to conduct a certain type of policy for German unification can influence and perhaps determine what is possible in European and global policy. A heavily subsidized united German economy cannot compete indefinitely in an open environment any more than a heavily subsidized West German one can. It can only compete in Europe if Europe is prepared to shelter it. And the Europe that is ideally suited to shelter a subsidized Germany may not be the one that can best serve German purposes internationally, either in Eastern Europe or across the world at large. Finally, the type of global environment that Germany prefers may in turn determine the kind of policy Germany can or even must conduct toward Europe, toward unification, and at home.

Germany has finally made the breakout that it has long sought. With one of the world's strongest currencies and perhaps the most stable economy, Germany has become the center of attraction and even the center of decision for a vast and populous area whose borders are still undefined but are potentially very wide. It still needs friends, but it now meets them on a more equal and independent basis. And it now has the power, the authority, and perhaps even the obligation to decide on its future direction and on the future direction of the world as a whole.

After years and even decades of carefully guided and thoughtfully weighed policies, the government and the Bundesbank are truly in a situation where they can, more than ever before, shape the world in which the German people will live. What they need to decide is how they wish to shape it, what philosophy they will follow, the leeway they will give to others, and the priorities that they will set.

The one thing they cannot choose is to abstain, because the choices will be made for them either by others, by events, or by inertia.

The choices are far from easy. Germany wants to advance and to consolidate a united Western Europe, in which it and others have thrived. But it also wants a united Europe that goes well into the East, and it does not want to choose Europe over the global trading system. Germany also wants a united European currency, but wants to delay its introduction until the Bundesbank can be certain that the problems caused by German unification have been overcome. It also wants European monetary union to be supported by a political mechanism that will avoid making the currency bear the full strain of conflicting national policies.

Germans are acutely conscious that the choices they make will have implications not only for economic but also for political and strategic stability. They are also beginning to see that immediate political and economic objectives may be in conflict. For example, they recognize that their credits to the Soviet Union and Eastern Europe have for the first time put their currency at risk for a political objective, and they have to find a way to advance their political objective and also keep the currency safe.

Germans must insist firmly on the maintenance of conditions that made their own prosperity and that of others possible, but they cannot insist too forcefully without creating political problems that can undo much of what they and others have achieved.

Most of all, the Germans must recognize that the choices that they make for themselves will also shape the world as a whole.

One can only hope that Germany will make choices that will succeed as brilliantly as the other choices it has made since its currency and regulatory reform in 1948, and that those choices will in turn sustain and advance global, continental, and German prosperity.

The French writer and philosopher Raymond Aron is said to have observed, as he walked through the rubble of postwar Berlin, that this could have been Germany's century. In a sense, of course, it was. But it was not a century that reflected Germany's best instincts or interests. Instead, it was a century dominated by worldwide as well as German confusion about where Germany was to fit into the global order.

If Germany, Europe, and the world were calm over the past 40 years, it was because the question had been answered. Now it is posed again . And, as always, the answer will be portentous for all. It will help to shape the remainder of this century and perhaps the next as much as past German decisions have shaped this one.

INDEX